In Wartime

In Wartime

Stories from Ukraine

TIM JUDAH

ALLEN LANE
an imprint of
PENGUIN BOOKS

ALLEN LANE

UK | USA | Canada | Ireland | Australia
India | New Zealand | South Africa

Allen Lane is part of the Penguin Random House group of companies
whose addresses can be found at global.Penguinrandomhouse.com.

First published 2015

001

Copyright © Tim Judah, 2015

The moral right of the author has been asserted

Set in 12/14.75 pt Dante MT Std
Typeset by Jouve (UK), Milton Keynes
Printed in Great Britain by Clays Ltd, St Ives plc

The author and publisher are grateful to the following for permission to reproduce material:
Roderick Heather, *The Iron Tsar: The Life and Times of John Hughes* (Authors Essentials, 2010);
Vlad Mykhnenko, Dmytro Myedvyedyev and Larysa Kuzmenko, *Urban Shrinkage in Donetsk and Makiivka, the
Dontesk Conurbation, Ukraine* (SHRINK SMART @ EU FP7 Socio-economic Sciences and Humanities
Research. (March 2010)); Vassily Grossman, *Everything Flows* (Vintage Books, 2011)

A CIP catalogue record for this book is available from the British Library

ISBN: 978–0–241–19882–7

www.greenpenguin.co.uk

Contents

Contents

Contents

List of Illustrations

Front cover: A destroyed Ukrainian medical evacuation vehicle whose wheels have been looted. It was on the road between Ilovaysk and Novokaterinivka and was destroyed during the Ukrainian flight from Ilovaysk. September 2014. The words come from a piece I wrote for the *New York Review of Books*.

Autumn 2015

Separatist-controlled areas

Roads

| 0 | 50 | 100 | 150 miles |

| 0 | 50 | 100 | 150 | 200 | 250 km |

RUSSIA

Desna R.

Kharkiv

Poltava

LUGANSK OBLAST

Dnieper R.

Sloviansk

DONBAS

Dnipropetrovsk

Lugansk

Savur-Mogila

DONETSK OBLAST

Donetsk

ryvyi-Rih

Ilovaysk

Don R.

Zaporizhia

Mariupol

Rostov-on-Don

herson

Askania-Nova

Sea of Azov

N

CRIMEA
(annexed to
Russia 2014)

W   E

S

ack Sea

Introduction

Dying for Ukraine

This is what I saw: the bloated corpse of a man, hanging folded over the high power cables in the eastern village of Novokaterinivka. He had been part of the Ukrainian retreat from Ilovaysk at the end of August 2014. When a rebel or Russian missile hit his armoured vehicle and the ammunition inside it exploded, the top of it peeled off like the lid of a sardine tin. His body was flung into the air and then caught on the wire. In the wreckage there were the charred remains of another young soldier and, by the blasted top of the vehicle, lying on the road, the blackened torso of a third man.

His arm was held over his head. The body on the wire, which had completely escaped the flames, looked waxy and somehow unreal, swelling and gleaming slightly in the late summer sun. His trousers had come off, dangling from his feet, his shirt and jacket hung down over his head. It was a symbol of defeat – or of victory, depending on which side of the war you were on.

I tried to find his name, but failed. Quite possibly the dead soldier and I came close again a few months later in Lviv. Maybe he was buried here, almost 1,300 kilometres to the west, close to the Polish border in the grand Lychakiv cemetery. Much of the history of Lviv and western Ukraine is here. Literally. In November, the leaves are mouldering in the damp and you can stroll past bronze men with bushily confident nineteenth-century moustaches and weeping, lichen-stained angels. Every tomb tells a story, but even more than that, every memorial, or at least the more recent ones, is still fighting the history wars for those who fell for their cause. Over here are the men of the Austro-Hungarian army who died fighting the Russians in the First World War. Up here are the Poles who died fighting the Ukrainians when it was over, and next to them are their Ukrainian enemies. Here are the people murdered by the Soviets in 1941. Here are the Soviets who died fighting the Nazis. Here is the monument to the local Ukrainian SS division. Here are the other Ukrainians who fought with the Nazis, against them, against the Poles again and then against the Soviets.

And now the new sections for a new generation: here are the heroes of Lviv who were killed fighting the regime of president Viktor Yanukovych during the Maidan revolution of 2014. And here, beginning a few months later, are eighteen graves piled high with wreaths and draped with yellow and sky blue Ukrainian flags. In the framed photos on top of the graves you can see how young were some of these men who died in the war in the east, or maybe some looked so young because the last proper portrait of them was taken when they graduated from school?

Olha Vaskalo was fussing around the grave of her son Roman, who was twenty-five, as though he was in hospital and not six feet below her. He had joined up in May 2014 and was killed in July. He had been in Lugansk. He was injured in the leg with shrapnel from a Grad missile. 'Was it worth it?' I asked. She looked confused, uncertain what to say. Then she replied: 'The children are dying for nothing.' He had a two-year-old son and worked on the railways. An old lady called Nadya, who had been listening, joined in. 'Only *our* boys are fighting,' she said, meaning boys from Lviv and the west of the country. 'The rest are sitting around drinking vodka. As always!' It is untrue. But it is true that across Ukraine everyone believes that *they* are suffering more, contributing more and doing more while everyone else is doing nothing.

A few graves away was Ruslana Holets. 'They had nothing to defend themselves with,' she said quietly. 'They were just left there.' She talked to her son on Monday evening and he died on Tuesday. 'They were surrounded and our army abandoned them. There were mines all around them. He said "all's fine, we have food", but it was not true.' It was drizzling, grey and cold. This is what many believe, that there was treachery, or that the top brass does not care what happens to its men on the ground. It is easier to believe this than that your son might have died simply due to incompetence or a lack of coordination in a military bled dry by more than two decades of corruption and theft of its resources.

On the other side of the line, in Donetsk, one of the two main rebel-held cities, is Vladimir Antyufeyev, a 63-year-old Russian, who led a unit of Soviet special operations troops in the dying days of Soviet Latvia. For many years he was wanted by the Latvians for his role in an attack on their Ministry of Interior in 1991 in which five died. By his own account he escaped two hours before the Latvian 'fascists' came to arrest him in 1991. Then he was sent to Moldova, or more precisely Transnistria. On the left bank of the Dniester river, anti-Moldovan activists declared its secession from Moldova in 1991 and then, with Russian military help, this was consolidated in a brief war against Moldovan 'fascists' in 1992. Here Antyufeyev adopted the pseudonym of Major-General Vadim Shevtsov and set up and ran the breakaway statelet's fearsome little

KGB for twenty years. This oversees the territory's smuggling empire, its main source of cash apart from its subsidies from Moscow. In 2012 he was ousted and charged with abuse of power and corruption. He also helped in security operations in Abkhazia and South Ossetia, the breakaway regions of Georgia controlled by Russia. In 2014, in the wake of the Maidan revolution, he went to Crimea to prepare for it to be snapped off from Ukraine. Now he was going from strength to strength. In July he was setting up the security services of the Donetsk People's Republic, or DNR to use its Russian acronym, which had just declared independence from Ukraine's 'fascists'. He sat in a large conference room in the city's central, Soviet-era regional administration building which the rebels had taken over. He was balding with a tidy grey, close-cropped goatee beard. He wore a neat white shirt and a black suit and black tie. Nearby, cradling a Kalashnikov, sat a podgy old man who looked as if he must have had trouble puffing all the way up to the eleventh floor of this building, because the lifts were not working. Also present, a younger, more serious-looking guard with an ever so fashionable, just slightly cocked Cossack-style black hat.

Antyufeyev – he had returned to his old self having shed his Major-General Shevtsov personality – spoke with the assurance of a man who *knew* that at long, long last he was back on the right side of history. He was back, after years in exile in dull, provincial Transnistria, war-wrecked Abkhazia and South Ossetia, which is little more than a village connected to Russia by a tunnel. At *last* Russia was back and he had magically, for no one knew how, become a 'deputy prime minister' of the DNR and was, at least for a few months until he vanished into obscurity again, at the centre of things, where he should always have been. The tone was smug. Ukraine had squandered its chances. It was not disintegrating he said, as opposed to, well, 'disassembling'.

Ukraine was like 'a kit' he explained, made artificially at Russia's will and in accordance with Russia's geopolitical interests. Ukraine existed only within its borders, which he was now at the forefront of redrawing, thanks to Russia. Now, America and the European

Union had intervened and so it was time for Russia to take back what was 'primordial' Russian territory from this 'artificial' Ukrainian state from which others, such as Poland, Hungary and Romania, would also sooner or later be reclaiming chunks. And for that matter, he added, Ukraine's recent leaders were not really Ukrainians at all, but people from the west of the country who were 'by their genetics, Poles, Hungarians and Romanians, pursuing interests opposed to the interests of Ukrainians'.

Maybe Antyufeyev believed what he said about genetics. But does it matter? What matters is what the majority of Russians and Ukrainians believe about what is happening and why. And here is a depressing thought: in 1991 at the beginning of the Yugoslav wars foreigners were at a loss to explain how millions of people appeared to have become crazed, to have turned on their neighbours, and simply suspended their critical faculties. Milos Vasic, the great Serbian journalist, used to explain it like this: if the entire mainstream US media were taken over by the Ku Klux Klan, it would not take long before Americans too would be crazed. People had TV sets for heads, he said. Almost a quarter of a century later, the internet and every other means of modern communication not only have not made things better but rather, have made them worse. Now there are even more ways to spread poison, lies and conspiracy theories.

Despite being such a big country, Ukraine, for most of us who live in the western part of the continent, is, or was, somewhere not very important. *Is Odessa in Russia? It is on the Black Sea, yes, but my geography is a bit hazy there. They had that revolution a few years ago, led by that woman with the braids, didn't they? What happened to her?* How quickly those days have vanished. For too long Ukraine, the second largest country in Europe after Russia, was one of the continent's most under-reported places. For most of the last century, what little reporting in the foreign press there was, was done in the main by foreign correspondents living in Moscow, who inevitably absorbed some of the imperial and then former imperial capital's patronizing attitudes. Now, with revolution and war, the interest of editors has inevitably been awakened, but most outlets still do not give journalists the space to make people and places really come alive.

The aim of this book is not to record a blow-by-blow account of events that led to the Maidan revolution of 2014, the annexation of Crimea or the war that has followed. Others have written that. Others will also write books which will answer who exactly gave the orders to shoot people on the Maidan during the revolution, the circumstances of the shooting down of Malaysia Airlines flight MH17 over rebel territory and how some forty-two anti-Maidan-cum-pro-Russians died in a fire in the Trade Unions House in Odessa in May 2014. This is not a history of Ukraine either but I do write about what happened in Lviv and the west of Ukraine in the Second World War and look at the history of Donetsk because these two stories are key to understanding what is happening now. Each section of the book is a story in itself. Together they should give an impression of what Ukraine feels like, now, in wartime.

What I thought was that between journalism and academic books there was not much which explained Ukraine, that made it a vibrant place full of people who have something to say and to tell us. Wherever I went I found, as in few other places I have been, just how happy ordinary people were to talk. Then I understood that this was because no one ever asks them what they think. Often, when they started to talk, you could hardly stop them. If we listen to people we can understand why they think what they do, and act the way they do. In Ukraine (and not just in Ukraine of course, but across much of the post-communist world), people have been taken for granted for so long, as voters, or taxpayers or bribe payers, that when finally the rotten ship of state springs leaks and begins to list, everyone is shocked. But they should not have been. It was just that no one, especially in the West, was asking what was happening below deck. This book is about what I saw, what people told me and also those parts of history, which we need to know in order to understand what is happening in Ukraine today.

Just Angry

The war began in the wake of the Maidan revolution. Russian propaganda holds, and quite possibly Russian leaders really do believe, that it was all a cleverly orchestrated Western coup. What they cannot see is that it was nothing of the sort. In reality there was no mystery. People were just angry. When President Yanukovych, after Ukraine's years of work on preparing two key agreements which would begin the process of European integration, announced, on 21 November 2014, that the deals were off, he unwittingly lit the blue touch paper of revolt. For those who supported the revolution, and in the end hundreds of thousands came to demonstrate their support, it was hardly because they believed that the strictures of gradually implementing a dull-sounding Deep and Comprehensive Free Trade Area agreement with the EU was going to quickly change their lives but it was something more fundamental, primal even. In a country rich enough to provide its inhabitants with very decent lives, the EU deals were seen as some sort of lifebuoy to grab on to. By linking their fate to the West, many thought that the gradual implementation of the agreements would create the thing that had been missing in their lives – a state of law. It may yet happen, as the agreements were indeed signed after the revolution, but it will be a long haul. Even if membership of the EU is not, at least for now, on the agenda, the agreements do foresee many of the same reforms gone through by all of the other former communist countries which have joined. They commit Ukraine to a process which is supposed to, and if the experience of the other former communist countries is anything to go by, would to a good degree transform and modernize its institutions. In that sense the Maidan revolution was a collective plea: 'Save us from these people!' And likewise, while it was natural for many in the west and centre to look westwards for a saviour, it was also natural for many in the east to look to Russia, because of their historic, ethnic, language, family and business ties. I am generalizing of course because the picture was not black and white – but it was not so complicated either. To a Westerner Ukraine seems very familiar on the surface, but, while obviously Western countries have all sorts of political, economic and social problems, on balance, and with the exception of countries such as Greece, which never went through the type of transformative process now required by the EU, they tend to pale in terms of what these problems mean for the individual Ukrainian.

It is not right to compare Ukraine to Britain or Germany, or even the tiny Baltic states, but a serious point of departure is to be made with Poland, a country whose population size, at 38.5 million is in the same ballpark as Ukraine's. In 1990 the GDP per capita of both countries was similar, as were life expectancy rates. Just before the war began, Poland's GDP per capita was more than three times greater than that of Ukraine and Poles could expect to live almost six years longer than Ukrainians. Likewise Russia's GDP per capita, which started at more or less the same place, was some three and half times greater before the war, and while its life expectancy rate was virtually identical to Ukraine's it had increased more than its neighbour's since 1990. Ukraine was and is not a poor country, but the experience of Poland, and even that of the Baltic states rather than oil and gas rich Russia, suggested to what extent Ukrainians had been short-changed by their leaders since independence and explained why they no longer wanted to continue hearing about their country's potential rather than actually seeing and experiencing it.

Next Year in Donetsk

When wars begin there is a strange period when ordinary, pre-war life continues before the new rhythm of wartime begins. It is also the period of disbelief and delusion, euphoria or shock. At the beginning of the First World War millions across Europe enthusiastically cheered their men marching off to fight, having no inkling of the catastrophes that lay before them. In 1939, in the West, after war was declared and before the Germans began their advance, we had the 'phoney war'. In our times, in Bosnia in 1991, as war raged in neighbouring Croatia, many assumed that it would not spread because, as everyone *knew* and *said* just how bad it would be, no one believed that anyone would be *so stupid* as to actually start it. When it did start in 1992, the first months were chaotic. No one knew who was firing at whom and from where. Then things settled down: frontlines became clear and for three years people got killed, cities and towns were besieged and hundreds of thousands fled or were ethnically cleansed, but the front did not move much until the very end. All of this was in my mind as the war began in Ukraine. All too often I saw similarities with the Balkan wars, all of which I had reported on. A period of the surreal preceded the new reality. You could see this both in Kiev and Donetsk where, even if people talked of war, it was clear that they did not believe it was really coming.

In early April 2014, in the centre of Kiev, on the Maidan and

Khreshchatyk, the city's central boulevard, and on the road leading up to parliament you could see the remnants of revolution. There were makeshift shrines and candles for the 130 who died during the revolution, many of whom had been cut down by snipers. A year later no one had been brought to justice for this crime, which was widely assumed to have been ordered by Yanukovych or someone close to him. The failure to find the guilty, bad enough in itself, nourished conspiracy theories, namely that the pro-Maidan protesters had killed their own people in order to blame Yanukovych and hasten his downfall. There was no memorial for the eighteen Berkut riot and other policemen, many who came from units brought in from Crimea and the east, who had died fighting the protesters – deaths which were not forgotten or forgiven in the places they had come from, a fact which did much to engender bitterness.

Around the Maidan there was a tent encampment. Perhaps a thousand people remained here. They had collection boxes for their different groups. People dressed as bears, Micky Mouse or zebras ambled about hoping that you would want to pay to have your photo taken with them. There was a large catapult which looked as if it had been taken from the set of a film about the siege of Troy. The stage from where people had spoken remained, though now it sported a large advert for the newly formed military National Guard. It also had a large crucifix propped up in front of it. There were pictures of Stepan Bandera, the controversial and divisive Ukrainian nationalist leader of the Second World War, and Vladimir Putin, Russia's president, who had been given a Hitler moustache and hairstyle. Those who remained here said they wanted to stay until the presidential elections on 25 May. Many just seemed lost. They included men and women from outside Kiev to whom the revolution had given a sense of purpose for the first time in their lives; now they were staving off a return to humdrum lives back home. Between the Maidan and parliament, all sorts of militias in different uniforms marched up and down, but to what purpose was not clear. Outside parliament I asked Andreii Irodenko what he and his men were doing and might they not serve Ukraine better in the east, and he replied: 'If we left this spot provocations would start here.' He said that provocateurs could be agents of the FSB, Russia's secret service, and other supporters of Russia.

While the threat of losing complete control of the east loomed, all sorts of people and groups demonstrated outside the building of the Verkhovna Rada, Ukraine's parliament. Some were demanding a lustration of judges and some were protesting about legislation concerning duties on imported cars. At the door of parliament Myroslava Krupa, who had made herself a cloak of cigarette boxes, was protesting because she had not received compensation for damage to her health caused, she said, by poor conditions at an American tobacco company she had worked for in Lviv. Strange groups roamed around and roads were blocked. Suddenly a black car driven by a glamorous woman frustrated at not being able to get to where she wanted, veered off down a path in the park only to be stopped and surrounded by an angry crowd. One man was dressed as the Grim Reaper, with a black cloak, mask and scythe on which he had written: 'Putin, I am coming for you.' No one in Kiev quite seemed to grasp what

was happening in the east, which was surprising since Crimea had already been lost more than a month before.

Many were alarmed and disappointed. They had braved the bullets and the cold for a root and branch change for Ukraine, but now the leading candidates for president were Yulia Tymoshenko, the oligarch and former prime minister who had been jailed by Yanukovych, and Petro Poroshenko, a billionaire who had earlier been a minister under Yanukovych.

Middle-class Natalyia Yaroshevych, aged forty-eight, who sells cosmetics for the American company Amway, said she had liked what she had seen at the beginning on the Maidan, but later felt that 'political games were being played' there by Russia, the EU and the US. As we sat in a café at Ocean Plaza, a Kiev shopping mall featuring a giant fish tank with sharks, the French supermarket Auchan, Gap, Marks and Spencer and many of the other big Western chain stores, she said she was 'anxious but not fearful' of war but what concerned her and many of her friends even more was the cost of living. Her husband, an engineer, had his own small company installing and maintaining industrial gas meters. Orders had plummeted because of the crisis and he was worried about the family's income because like many, not only in Ukraine but other parts of the former communist world, they had taken out a mortgage denominated in a foreign currency. Few understood the implications of these when they borrowed. When the Yaroshevych family took out their mortgage, just before the financial crisis of 2008, the exchange rate for $1 stood at 5.5 hryvnia. Before the Maidan revolution started it was 8 hryvnia. Now it was 11 hryvnia. For ordinary people, whatever was happening in the east, bills still had to be paid and the risk of losing your home to the bank was a more immediate and existential threat to them than the idea of losing Donetsk in a war which might or might not come to Kiev. (A year later, $1 was 22 hryvnia, but the Yaroshevych family had been able to solve their problem. Natalyia's husband sold his office and paid off the home mortgage.)

On 6 April 2014 armed men seized the regional administration building in Donetsk. Then they began to fortify it with sandbags and tyres and a few thousand came to show their support. For many outside the building there was a sort of carnival atmosphere. Road-blocks manned by armed men went up. At one, near the town of Sloviansk, which would briefly be a rebel stronghold, a man said that what was happening here was going to be 'just like Crimea'. In other words, he thought that without a shot being fired, Russia would swiftly annex the Donbass, the name of this eastern region. Nearby, at another checkpoint manned by rebels, who mostly seemed to be locals, they lined up rows of Molotov cocktails a stone's throw from a roadside shop selling serried ranks of garden gnomes.

On 11 April there were just a couple of hundred milling around in front of the regional administration building. The building flew Russian flags, Soviet flags and those of the new Donetsk People's Republic, which had been proclaimed on 7 April. In a city of 900,000 people there did not seem to be much popular support for the rebels, but there was also a climate of fear. Who knew what the future would hold? Still, those that were here were neither frightened nor shy about expressing their opinions. Yulia Yefanova, aged twenty-four, who was posing for pictures in front of a mock Russian frontier post which had been erected there, said she wanted the Donbass to unite with Russia because the ties were close and much of her family was there. Crowding around, people began to shout their opinions. 'It is impossible to be friends with Europe and with Russia,' said one man, 'they are like cat and dog.' Another said: 'If Russia was here, she would put everything in order. She would fight corruption.' People shouted that the hard-working people of the Donbass subsidized lazy people in the centre and west of Ukraine. Then, repeating the line pushed by Russia's media, the people began shouting about Kiev's 'fascist junta'. Said one woman: 'Only Russia can save us from a power which is not democratic!'

Three days later I was invited to the Seder, the Passover dinner, of the local Jewish community. As a guest from abroad I was asked to say a few words. I described the roadblocks I had seen outside the city and said that it looked to me like war was coming. Much of what I had seen was eerily similar to the beginnings of the Balkan wars. No one seemed to believe me. No one believed that their world was about to come crashing down. They clapped politely when I said that while the traditional Passover saying of 'Next year in Jerusalem!' was fine, 'Next year in Donetsk!' would be good too. Few who were present would be. Likewise, on the barricades no one really believed there would be fighting – because they thought Russian troops would soon come pouring over the border to finish off what they thought they were starting. Those who were euphoric and took snaps in front of the mock Russian frontier post had no inkling of what was coming. They thought of bigger Russian salaries and pensions and not of their tiny walk-on roles in starting a war that nobody expected or wanted.

This strange atmosphere lasted for a few weeks more. On 9 May, the countries of the former Soviet Union celebrate Victory Day, the day when the dead of the Second World War are remembered and elderly men and women, dressed in their uniforms and bedecked with medals, are honoured. In then rebel-held Sloviansk the ceremonies began in front of the Lenin statue in the town square. Old men and one woman stood in a line in front of it while rebel leaders, who had seized power here on the same day as in Donetsk, stepped forward to make speeches to about a thousand people. Given that the Ukrainian forces had by now surrounded the town, what was most surprising was the sheer emptiness of what was being said. Pavel Gubarev, then an important rebel leader, who had just been released in a prisoner exchange with the Ukrainians, said: 'Fascism! It is coming for us again!' Then he talked of Novorossiya, the would-be new state he and his friends wanted to create from the south and east of the Ukraine they wanted to destroy, and finally he began proclaiming 'Eternal glory!', his voice rising and falling in dramatic cadences, referring to the fallen of the Second World War. As though at a religious service, or as if they were taking part in a mystical experience, the crowd, which was mostly but not entirely elderly, began to respond in unison:

'Glory!'

'Glory!'

'Glory!'

Then Gubarev said: 'Glory to the heroes and victors of the Russian Spring!' by which he meant the anti-Ukrainian revolt in the east.

The crowd responded:

'Glory!'

'Glory!'

'Glory!'

At this point came a distraction. Five armoured cars captured by the rebels drove down one side of the square and appeared on the other side, but they could not do a victory lap around it, because the roads were blocked by concrete and other barricades. With militia-men sitting on top they drove up as far as Irina, the ice cream vendor, and then clumsily, in a cloud of exhaust fumes, had to back up to get out again. The sales girls from the local Eva, a cosmetics supermarket chain, and others ran out to cheer on their men, kiss them and give them cigarettes.

Thus the victories in 1945 and 2014 ran seamlessly into one another. At the same time Russian television, which many people had on in the background at home or in shops, was showing live footage of the huge military parade in Moscow, and later in the day of Vladimir Putin celebrating in newly annexed Crimea.

Now everyone moved off in a procession towards the war memorial. Victims of this new conflict, said one man in a speech, when we got there, 'would be lifted to the heavens on the wings of angels'. Then, flags were dipped for a brief silence. They were the DNR flag, Russian flags, communist flags and variations of old Russian imperial and tsarist flags. Then I spotted one I had never seen before. It was white with a big blue snowflake in the middle. Thinking this might be the flag of a new and significant political movement I shoved through the crowd to get to the man who was holding it. He told me that it was the flag of 'Fridgers of the World' and that from Siberia to the Baltics 'they are supporting us'. It took me some time to understand who the 'Fridgers' were. They are people in the refrigeration business across the former Soviet Union who have an online forum to discuss issues relating to fridges and their maintenance.

Stepping away from children and old ladies weeping as they laid flowers at the eternal flame, I ran into sprightly Anatoliy, aged eighty-six, who was walking home, his chest decorated with medals, including one of Stalin. He had been too young to take part in the Second World War he told me, but had seen action in 1956 in, as he called it, 'the war with Hungary'. He described the anti-communist revolt there as one having been organized 'by the remains of the pro-fascists' and thus it had been absolutely right to intervene. When I asked him about the current conflict he talked of 'fascism' just like everyone else. 'We want a free Ukraine,' he said, 'but the *Banderovtsi*' – the term once given to followers of Stepan Bandera and now used to insult the post-Maidan leadership and their supporters – 'want to take control over the whole of Ukraine. We just want justice.' Josip Vissarionovich, he said, referring to Stalin, would never have let the country get in such a mess. He had had a writing table, a couple of chairs and a pipe. But 'these presidents now surround themselves with gold. They have golden toilets and golden chairs.' He was talking about Ukraine's leaders in general but I was surprised by his reaction when I asked him about Putin, whom many in the DNR and other pro-Russians in Ukraine see as a saviour. In terms of gold, he said, 'our presidents pale into insignificance next to him'.

Anatoliy's face was smudged with lipstick. As a veteran he had been given flowers by children and kisses by women. I said I hoped I could be like him at his age and he said: 'Your wife would kick your arse!' before briskly setting off home. Except for certain specific places where there had been fighting, the war still seemed remote and unreal to most people. When it began in earnest and as it dragged on, old people would suffer the most.

I. MEMORY WARS

Weaponizing History

Just because something is a cliché does not mean that it is not true. In his book *1984* George Orwell famously wrote: 'He who controls the past controls the future. He who controls the present controls the past.' The war in Ukraine is not about history, but without using or, to employ the fashionable term, 'weaponizing' history, the conflict simply could not be fought. There is nothing unique about this. In our times, in Europe, history was deployed as the advance guard and recruiting sergeant in the run-up to the Yugoslav wars, and exactly the same has happened again in Ukraine. In this way people are mobilized believing horrendously garbled versions of history. On the Russian and rebel side, fear is instilled by summoning up the ghosts of the past and simply ignoring inconvenient historical truths. On the Ukrainian side, the ugliest parts of history are ignored, as though they never happened, thus giving the enemy more propaganda ammunition to fire.

In this conflict the words 'info-war' or 'information war' have replaced the word 'propaganda'. In one way that is fitting because fighting the info-war is more complicated than disseminating old-fashioned propaganda. The battlefields include Facebook, Twitter, vKontakte (the Russian equivalent of Facebook) and YouTube. On news and other websites tens of thousands of people 'comment' on articles in such a way as to make them feel as though they are doing something useful. They are, as a boy who was about to start military training in Kharkiv told me, 'sofa warriors'. But some it seems are mercenaries too. According to numerous reliable reports, the Russian authorities contract firms to employ people to 'comment' and spread, among other things, the central line of Russian propaganda, which is that the Ukrainian government, after the Maidan revolution, is nothing but Nazism reincarnated.

What is odd is how much rubbish people believe, disregarding what they must know from their own experiences or those of their families. What has happened on the Russian side of the info-war especially, bears close resemblance to the experience of Serbs in the early 1990s. Then, most of their media painted all Croats as Ustashas, after their wartime fascist movement, and Bosnian Muslims as Jihadis. While of course, just as there were indeed then some admirers of the Ustashas, and some Jihadis too, just as there are admirers of Ukraine's wartime fascists now, the big lie is to give them a significance they didn't and don't have. As in the Balkans, the same is happening again: in Russia all of the mainstream media is following the modern party line. As the rebels seized control of eastern regions of Ukraine in April 2014, they moved quickly to take over local TV buildings and transmission facilities, turning off Ukrainian channels and tuning in to Russian ones. On the other side of the line, Russian channels were switched off and removed from cable packages. However, in the age of satellite TV and the internet, it is not possible to deprive everyone of *all* information bar that which you want them to see, but it is nevertheless remarkable how people so often accept what they are told. In this story, or 'narrative' to use the technical term, history is something of a foundation and bedrock and this is why rewriting history is as important as writing the news. What you believe today depends on what you believe about the past. In that sense it is important for the 'political technologists', to use the pithy and apt term popular in post-Soviet countries, who might be understood by Westerners as turbo-spin doctors, to fashion a past which suits the future they are trying to create.

When Vladimir Putin, Russia's triumphant president, spoke on 18 March 2014 to his parliament, the Duma, and other Russian leaders and announced the annexation of Crimea following its referendum, which took place with no free debate and was rammed through under the watchful eye of armed men and Russian soldiers, he repeated the line that maybe even he believes, but certainly many Russians and those in rebel-held territory believe. There had been a *coup d'état* in Kiev against the lawfully elected government of President Yanukovych executed by 'nationalists, neo-Nazis, Russophobes and anti-Semites'. Some of these there were, just as there are plenty of the same on the Russian and rebel side, but to tar the whole revolution in this way made sense only to people who actually wanted to believe it. For supporters from Western countries and other foreign admirers of Putin and the rebels, it also provided what seemed like a noble 'anti-fascist' cause to belong to, rather than subscribing to an invented and racist interpretation of events in which all Ukrainians were fascists and the Russians or the rebels were heroic liberators. 'We can all clearly see the intentions of these ideological heirs of [Stepan] Bandera,' said Putin, 'Hitler's accomplice during the Second World War.'

In Kiev I talked with Professor Grigory Perpelytsia, a former Soviet naval man, who now teaches at the Foreign Ministry's

Diplomatic Academy. We walked down the hill from the academy and ducked into a dark restaurant serving hearty old-fashioned Ukrainian cuisine, meaning mostly large portions of meat. Putin, he said, wanted Russian troops to be welcomed with 'flowers and songs' – as they were by many in Crimea, though anyone who did not feel this way was hardly likely to be on the streets. In order to achieve this, he said, Putin had launched an info-war against 'Ukrainian fascists' and *Banderovtsi*. Many were receptive to this kind of message, he explained, especially older people in Russia and to a certain extent in Ukraine, because many still retained a Soviet mentality, 'want to go back to the USSR' and perceived Russia to be its inheritor. To burnish this image Russia exploited the victory of the Second World War and the symbols of the USSR, which disoriented people and confused them. In Ukraine, all this served to consolidate divisions which already existed. One of the great failings of the modern Ukrainian state is that it has never been able to create an all-encompassing post-Soviet narrative of modern Ukrainian history that was broadly accepted by most, if not all. The modern Ukrainian state has no common soundtrack of history, which for Britain for example includes Churchill telling Britons they would fight on the beaches and in the hills, or de Gaulle telling the French that they had lost a battle but not the war. Reality might have been more complex but nevertheless there are no serious challenges to these modern narratives, even in France where there was plenty of collaboration. In Ukraine's case, however, the story is different and, as the conflict has shown, two baleful figures loom over it, those of Bandera and Stalin. Understanding this is essential to understanding Ukraine today.

2.

Thumbelina in Donetsk

In April 2014, as the war began, Ekaterina Mihaylova, aged thirty-five, ran the press office of the newly proclaimed Donetsk People's Republic. She told me that she used to be a journalist. Her office was in the regional administration building in Donetsk, which had been seized by a motley collection of protesters and activists and surrounded by Maidan-style walls of old tyres. There were posters of the European Union flag crossed out in red and reproduction Second World War Soviet posters urging people to watch what they said in case of spies. One picture showed an angry Putin spanking a naughty child Obama who was laid across his lap. A large misspelled sign in English pasted to a low wall decorated with mining helmets said: 'NO FASHISM'. Someone had photocopied a photo of Red Army troops being welcomed into Donetsk in 1943, stuck it on the wall and written 'Liberation of Donetsk' on the A4 sheet of paper. Why was there so much Soviet iconography?

As we talked Mihaylova echoed Putin's famous speech to the Duma in April 2005 saying that the collapse of the USSR was a geopolitical catastrophe. 'It is not just Putin who thinks that,' she said, 'and many people believe that one of the results of that was an artificial border between Ukraine and Russia.' Both points are debatable. Many borders are artificial and that is exactly why the post-Soviet republics decided not to challenge them. If one border could be legally and militarily contested, and not just relatively minor ones as in the Caucasus, then all could be challenged. Now that they have been – in Crimea formally, and in the east of Ukraine quite possibly, depending on the outcome of the war and whether Russia finally decides to annex these areas too – this is a threat

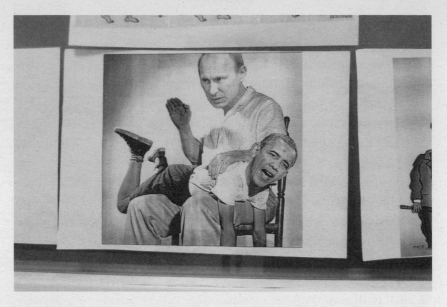

across the post-Soviet space including of course Russia. It is note-worthy that in his April 2005 speech Putin underlined that one of the most disastrous consequences of the collapse of the USSR was that 'for the Russian nation, it became a genuine drama. Tens of millions of our co-citizens and compatriots found themselves out-side Russian territory.' And it is precisely this that Putin has begun to correct.

Russians outside Russia, however, was not the topic of the moment. Mihaylova was warming to another theme. Ukrainians should be grateful to Stalin, she declared, because he had fashioned the Ukrainian Soviet republic out of diverse bits of territory and this was now the state they had. Historically this region, known as the Donbass, had belonged to Russia, but Lenin had given it to Soviet Ukraine in the aftermath of the Russian Revolution and civil war when the region, or rather communists here, had declared this to be the Donetsk–Krivoy Rog Soviet Republic. It was a short-lived affair, extinguished as the Red Army defeated its enemies, includ-ing the also short-lived German-supported Ukrainian state, which the Donetsk–Krivoy Rog republic had resisted. Now, she said, it was a ridiculous irony that Ukrainians were destroying statues of Lenin when they should be grateful to him.

Although in 2015 the DNR declared itself to be the legal successor of the 1918 republic, few people there actually knew much about it, as it was a taboo topic in Soviet times. This was of course because it had fought against incorporation into Ukraine. Today's black, blue and red DNR flag is based on its flag of 1918, though then it was soon dropped for a red banner. What is more revealing for us though are Mihaylova's views on Stalin which, shocking though they may be to us in the West, are widespread in Russia and among many Russians. I was baffled, I said, that she could expect Ukrainians to be grateful to Stalin, when he was responsible for the famine of 1932–3 in which some 3.3 million are estimated to have died. (The figure is that of Timothy Snyder, the Yale historian of the region and the period, but many put it far higher.) 'The legend of the *Holodomor*,' she said using the name given to it by Ukrainians and which means 'hunger-extermination', was created in Canada by fascist Ukrainian exiles. Yes, some had died, but to argue that Stalin had deployed it as weapon against Ukrainians was a 'fairy tale'. Russians had died too. There is a legitimate debate about this issue and to what extent Stalin used the famine to eliminate and break the will of the Ukrainian peasantry – because they were Ukrainian – but the tone of the conversation suggested something else. Stalin was a great man and the death of millions was a minor detail which should not sully the big picture. So, when it came to the Gulag, to which millions of Ukrainians were sent, not to mention Russians and other Soviet citizens of course, she argued that 'that story is like Snow White, or . . .' and at this point Ludmila, who was translating for me, stumbled, looking something up on her iPhone translator. 'Thumbelina? Do you know what that is?' Yes, said Mihaylova, there was an organization and there were prisons, but it was nothing more serious than this. Stalin took this country, one in which people used 'wooden ploughs and left it with nuclear weapons and he was no more evil or tough than Roosevelt or

Churchill at the time'. Stalin has a 'bad image in the West' but he was 'good for us'.

Listening in was Viktor Priss, a 28-year-old IT systems administrator, who worked in the office. In a previous job he had worked for the confectionary company of Petro Poroshenko, the man who would a few weeks later be elected as Ukraine's next president. Viktor is the type of man much in demand by Western IT companies, either to work for them in Ukraine or abroad. He was only a small child when the USSR expired. He did not think that the Gulag was a fairy tale. Stalin's problem was that 'it was very difficult to hold the country together with such an ideology and some people disagreed, so it was necessary to re-educate them'. Stalin was a product of his time and 'time creates its leaders'. In that sense, he argued, he had been a product of the will of the people to create a dictator. The Soviets created a signal that 'we were in danger', and as a result had sent a message, which was interpreted by the people as meaning 'we are ready to help you' and hence Stalin 'was a dictator by the will of the people'. Viktor was not sure if the same applied to Hitler given that he was after all elected, unlike Stalin. As for Putin, while there were no social conditions for him to become a new Stalin, he could certainly become the type of leader ready to respond to the will of the people. And presumably, for those who think like Viktor, that is what he is already doing.

For a foreigner it is hard to fathom such logic and quasi-mystical thinking about leaders and especially Stalin, responsible for so many millions of dead. But, in this context, what is important to understand is that, if people think that Stalin made the world tremble and that everything has gone to hell in a handcart since the end of the Soviet Union, then, with such a black and white view of history, for them restoring him to greatness makes sense. If this is what you believe, then Stalin cynically doing business with the devil, or in this case Hitler, by drawing a line from the Baltic to the Black Sea and destroying other countries, as was done in the Molotov–Ribbentrop pact of 1939, is fine. And what does Putin think of this? In 2009 he said that the pact had been 'immoral' but in 2014 he revised his opinion and claimed it had been to avoid fighting, and what was wrong with that?

When, to the shock of the world, Hitler and Stalin agreed to carve up eastern Europe, Stalin sparked off the Second World War. In the period from 1939 to 1941, the Soviet Union was allied to Nazi Germany and supplied it with the raw materials it used to make war on the Western allies. After Hitler attacked the Soviet Union everything changed of course, but officially the Soviet account could only say that the war had begun in 1941. Understanding this is central to understanding Ukraine today. The story of the great sacrifices of the Soviet people in the Second World War and the struggle against Nazism has been detached from the years 1939 to 1941, which saw the conquest and annexation of Lithuania, Estonia, Latvia and eastern Poland; from Romania, Bessarabia and northern Bukovina were annexed. When the Red Army met the Nazis in Poland, there were cordial meetings of military commanders and soldiers and an agreement to crush any Polish resistance. The NKVD, who were interior ministry security men and troops, and part of which was the progenitor of the KGB – now the FSB in Russia and the SBU in Ukraine – went into action. Tens of thousands were deported from the conquered Baltic states, Bessarabia and northern Bukovina, and hundreds of thousands of Poles were sent to the Gulag. Thousands of Polish officers were murdered, most infamously in the Katyn Massacre of 1940.

Today, what you think of this past, how you relate to it, determines what you think about the future of Ukraine. And what you think of the past is quite likely to be bound up with the history of your own family and where you live. This is true for the Donbass, a mining region, just as it is for anywhere else. People came from all over the Soviet Union to work and settle in this flat land pockmarked by pyramids and hills of slag and scruffy little mining and industrial towns. Donetsk was a working-class mining town. For many of its inhabitants then, Ukraine, which had been part of imperial Russia, was not a land where they had roots. With the demise of the Soviet Union it was harder for many of these people,

almost all of whom spoke Russian as their first language, to identify or to *love* Ukraine as their own country. It was just where they
ended up when Soviet republican borders became international
frontiers.

When I left the regional administration building I got a taxi and
asked the driver if he would like Donetsk to remain in Ukraine or
become part of Russia as Crimea had done. He said: 'I don't care. I
just want to get paid.'

In post-Soviet Ukraine, working-class professions were not val-
ued as they had been, at least nominally, before. All Ukraine (and
Russia) fell to predators and sharp operators who knew how to
make money, to steal and to get rich. But, while many in the east
remained wedded to their Soviet heritage and hence its interpretation of history, the west of Ukraine did not. And the twain have
not met. History did not start the war. It is just that history has
been used to shape the present by politicians.

3.

'Our history is different!'

Every time there has been an election you can see the regional divides on maps, with the east and south voting heavily for more pro-Russian parties and the west and centre for more pro-European ones. If you drew a map of memorials you would find something similar. In much of the west and centre of Ukraine, though by no means everywhere, statues of Lenin, especially prominent ones, have gone. During the Maidan revolution, and even afterwards, many remaining ones were toppled because they were regarded not merely as memorials to the man and to communism, but as symbols held dear by those who see Russia as their lodestar and not just the past but the country's future too. In the west, and in particular in Galicia, the largest former Austro-Hungarian part of Ukraine, annexed by the USSR in 1939 and retaken again in 1944, Soviet memorials decay while more and more are built to honour the Ukrainian Insurgent Army, the UPA, of Stepan Bandera. Travel in the Carpathian region though, which was the tip of Czechoslovakia until amputated in 1939, and they vanish, because, as Vasyl Khoma who runs a hotel in Rakhiv on the Romanian border and who had been its deputy mayor, told me sternly 'Our history is different!'

And so it is – sometimes even happily so. In this part of the country one of the most popular attractions and tourist draws is at the nearby village of Dilove. If someone had invented its story, few would have believed it. It is a monument erected in 1887 by the Austro-Hungarian Military Geographical Institute which the locals claim marks their discovery of the centre of Europe. They believe this thanks to an incorrect Soviet-era translation of the original Latin inscription that in fact makes no such claim. But at least the site, which attracts visitors on the basis of actually being the centre of Europe and gives work to people in the café and those selling souvenirs and trinkets, is perhaps the most harmless of misconceptions commemorated in stone in Ukraine.

Far away, in Ukraine's east, tourists once came to the monument of Savur-Mogila, an hour and a half's drive from Donetsk. This was also the site of an annual pilgrimage to commemorate the crucial battle fought here in 1943 in which thousands of Red Army soldiers died. Now the ruins of this vast Soviet memorial are a tragic sight. The place was fought over then because it was virtually the only hill in otherwise flat eastern Ukraine. In 2014 it was even more important than before. Now it is 10 kilometres, as the crow flies, from the Russian border, so whoever controls the hill, controls the corridor to the border and the road along it.

At the bottom of a ceremonial-style walkway and steps to the top are Second World War tanks, artillery pieces and lorries. Now in the hands of DNR forces, one of the tanks has 'To Kiev' painted on it. Among the surrounding burned pines are the remains of a destroyed Ukrainian armoured vehicle. On either side of the walkway are the heavily shrapnel-pockmarked giant steel sculptured heads of tank drivers, soldiers and classic Soviet tableaux of fighting men. Before this war the main part of the monument was a huge 36 metre-high obelisk, which dominated the surrounding landscape. By the time DNR forces finally captured the monument on 26 August the obelisk had collapsed. Now, ragged Soviet-era flags fly there as a group of DNR soldiers camp by the giant stump and a remaining steel boot, all that's left of a once huge triumphal statue. It is boring being stuck here so the soldiers play target practice and know how to laugh. Journalists are not supposed to take pictures showing their faces so one obliges. Surrounded by the rubble he dons a Shrek mask.

Between Soviet triumphalism and a giant Stepan Bandera statue in Lviv, however, perhaps the most interesting and even poignant place to consider how Ukraine remembers is in Kiev itself, which after all is halfway between Savur-Mogila and Lviv. During the

Second World War Kiev, now a big city of 2.8 million inhabitants, was so badly destroyed that much of it is Soviet, and now increasingly post-Soviet. But churches destroyed under communism have been rebuilt or restored, including the Pecherska Lavra monastery complex, founded in 1051. From its walls you can look down on the mighty Dnieper river below that flows through the city. You can also see the 102-metre-high Soviet Motherland memorial of a woman, sword drawn. Nearby is a memorial complex with walls of giant bronze soldiers and workers on which children climb and play. Next to that is the military museum and captured rebel tanks and vehicles identifying them as having been supplied by Russia. On the other side of the monastery stands an obelisk and eternal flame commemorating the wartime defence of the city. It is a tradition, observed to this day, for couples about to wed to come and lay flowers here. Right next to that is a monument designed to look like a candle, sitting atop the city's *Holodomor* memorial, commemorating the dead not just of the 1932–3 famine but of the far less well known ones of 1921–2 and 1946–7.

Compared to Yad Vashem, the Holocaust memorial in Jerusalem, and the Tsitsernakaberd museum and memorial to the victims of the Armenian genocide of 1915 in Yerevan, Kiev's memorial is tiny. There is a reason for that. It reflects the place the *Holodomor* has in Ukraine's national consciousness. Obviously the famine, which was caused during the period of forced collectivization, when peasants were compelled to give up their land and join collective farms – a policy enforced in such a way that millions died unnecessarily – was not going to be commemorated in Soviet times. Now, making the *Holodomor* a seminal event in modern Ukrainian history has to depend on who is in power. In the early post-independence years the issue was discussed and among other things memorial postage stamps were issued, but, as everyone in power was a former communist, this was not a subject to be played up too much. It was a question of calibrating the political usefulness of the *Holodomor* versus any potential harm it could cause by association.

With the inauguration as president of Viktor Yuschenko in 2005 after the Orange Revolution of the year before, the position of the *Holodomor* in Ukrainian life and politics changed significantly. Yuschenko took a far more explicitly nationalistic stance on history than his predecessors had done and the *Holodomor* memorial is one of the products of his otherwise disastrous time as president. It was his quarrelling with Yulia Tymoshenko, the other hero of the Orange Revolution and his prime minister, which opened the door for the return to office of Viktor Yanukovych, who, thanks to the revolution, had failed in his bid to cheat his way to winning and holding the presidency.

With the return of Yanukovych, first as prime minister in 2007 and then as president in 2010, the *Holodomor* began to fall back again in terms of public remembrance. Because of this political shift and because this was a taboo topic in Soviet times, the *Holodomor* has not entered into the DNA or soul of Ukrainian politics, or worldview, as the Holocaust and the Armenian genocide have in Israel and Armenia. Besides, there is another element here which is different from the other two genocides. The Holocaust was an act committed by the Nazis and their collaborators against the Jews and, more randomly, Roma. Likewise, in 1915 Armenians were killed by the Ottoman Turks or Kurds led by them. The point is that it was something done by *others* against *us*. In Ukraine, as indeed in Cambodia during the Khmer Rouge genocide of 1975–9, it was not something quite so clearly done by *others*. The lack of a major memorial in Kiev until 2008 can thus stand in stark contrast to what happened in Armenia. As communists had no role in the genocide, *they* could sponsor the building of its 44-metre black stele and memorial, which opened in 1967. In Ukraine, however, communists were the perpetrators and many of them were Ukrainians. Among the security men who prevented peasants leaving their starving villages could have been people to whom those about to die were actually related. There is another element which acts as a break, to a certain extent at least, in discussing the *Holodomor*. That is the issue of cannibalism, which some of those crazed with hunger resorted to. It is not exactly a forbidden topic, but it is one that any Ukrainian would understandably feel uncomfortable discussing.

At the memorial schoolchildren are led underground to see the exhibits. You can look at books incorporating death registers in which, incredibly, many but not by any means all who died had their ends recorded by Soviet bureaucrats. The victim's ethnic nationality was also noted and you can see that it was not just Ukrainians who died, but Russians, Germans, Bulgarians, Jews and so on. At the centre of the circular underground memorial chamber is a glass and black stone shrine holding grain, representing, says Oleksandra Monetova, the young guide who showed me around, the souls of those who died. She dipped her hand in the grain and then let it slip through her fingers. I told her I thought it was odd that this monument is next to the Soviet memorials, since those who died in the famine were victims of Stalin and communism. She told me that many people from the west of Ukraine, where there was no famine because it was then part of Poland, say that this is indeed a contradiction. Then she added, like a person who

had reflected on this and had no nationalist agenda to pursue or persuade me of, 'to us from the east and the centre it is not. My great-grandfather fought in the war and people in my family also suffered in the famine . . . People did not join the Soviet army because they loved the Soviet Union, but because they had to.'

4.
'How can this be?'

One of the greatest Soviet writers was Vasily Grossman. He was born in 1905 in Berdychiv, then one of the main centres of Jewish life in Ukraine, and died in Moscow in 1964. Grossman is rightly best known for *Life and Fate*, his extraordinary novel of Stalingrad. Far less well known is *Everything Flows*, a book on which he was still working when he died. Because it was never finished it is a patchy affair, but his chapter on collectivization and the famine is simply unparalleled, and worth recording here for its power to explain something about the period, the *Holodomor* and its legacy.

Based on what Grossman knew, his character Anna Sergeyevna recounts her experience in a Ukrainian village where she was working as a bookkeeper in the *kolkhoz*, or collective farm. First, she explained, had come the period of 'dekulakization' when the richer peasants, known as *kulaks*, were dispossessed, arrested and deported. Quotas of the numbers to be arrested were drawn up and names selected by the village Soviet, whose members could be bribed, and because there were 'scores to be settled because of a woman, or because of some other past grievance . . . Often it was the poorest peasants who were listed as kulaks, while the richer peasants managed to buy themselves off.' Worse however, but relevant today in an era where the power of propaganda is as strong as ever, is the description of what happened to people as the campaign took hold. 'The activists were just villagers like anyone else, they were people everyone knew, but they all seemed to lose their minds. They seemed dazed, crazed, as if they had fallen under a spell.' People convinced themselves, she says, that *kulaks* were evil and should be shunned. As they ceased to be equal human beings, it was but a short step to seeing them dead, which was of course the aim of Soviet propaganda then and Russian wartime propaganda now by which Ukrainians are dehumanized as 'fascists'.

The anti-*kulak* campaign Anna recounts was at its height in February and March of 1930 as thousands were packed on trains and sent eastwards, but it often left chaos in its wake. The amount of land cultivated fell, as did production, but 'everyone kept reporting that, without the kulaks, our village life had immediately started to blossom'. Lies about how much was being produced went up the chain of command because 'everyone wanted Stalin to rejoice in the belief that a happy life had begun . . .' Orders came back down that the village was to produce a grain quota 'it couldn't have fulfilled in ten years', and if the village could not produce the grain then people were 'idlers, parasites, kulaks who had not yet been liquidated! The kulaks had been deported, but their spirit endured.' The deportation of the *kulaks*, some 300,000 by the end of the campaign in Ukraine, out of 1.7 million deported in the entire Soviet

Union, was obviously not the only cause of the fall in production but whatever the reasons 'the authorities searched for that grain as if they were searching for bombs and machine guns. They stabbed the earth with bayonets and ramrods; they smashed floors and dug underneath them; they dug up vegetable gardens.' Later Anna asks: 'Who confiscated the grain?' and answers her own question. It was overwhelmingly locals, not people sent from Moscow. It was local communist officials, local policemen and men from the secret police and occasionally soldiers.

By winter the village was starving but people were not dying yet. Party officials said that villagers should not 'have lazed about'. People were desperate. There was no help from the state or party and the grain was being exported for cash, which was being used for industrialization. The descriptions of the full-blown famine that now set in are harrowing. Grossman's Anna explains how people, who were prevented from going to the railway station, would beg by the track of the Kiev–Odessa express hoping that someone would throw them a scrap of bread. This was something Grossman witnessed himself. Meanwhile, some managed to escape to towns where, with no permission to be there or coupons for bread, they died on the streets. Anna recounts in horrific detail how villagers lay in their homes barely breathing, incapable of moving. 'The whole village died. First it was the children, then it was old people, then it was the middle-aged.' At first graves were dug for the dead but then they were just left where they had died. Eventually those who worked for the local administration were taken to the nearby town.

After this settlers from less fertile Oryol, in Russia, were brought to repopulate the village. First the men had to clear the corpses with pitchforks and then the women were brought to clean and whitewash the walls. Whatever they did could not get rid of the smell of the dead though, so they left to return to Oryol, but in many other places demography was changed like this, a legacy with which Ukraine lives today. At the end of the chapter Anna remembers the life of the village: 'There had been love. Wives leaving husbands, and daughters getting married. People had drunken fights, and they had had friends and family to stay.' The children had gone to school, she recalls, people had sung songs and when the mobile cinema came they had gone to see a film.

> And nothing remains of all that. Where can that life have gone?
> And that suffering, that terrible suffering? Can there really be noth-
> ing left? Is it really true that no one will be held to account for it all?
> That it will all just be forgotten without a trace?
>   Grass has grown over it.
>   How can this be? – I ask you.

The scale of the catastrophe was unparalleled, but Kiev's *Holodomor* museum apart, the reticence about dealing with this part of history is nowhere better symbolized than in the city's large national history museum, which devotes one single cabinet to the famine. An explanation on the wall in slightly shaky English reduces the deaths of millions to one sentence.

> Industrialization brought up Ukraine to a new level of devel-
> opment. For a decade (1929–1938) hundreds of plants, factories,
> tens of power stations and mines had been constructed.

> In 1929, the Bolshevik power had begun a mass collectiviza-
> tion of agriculture which was carried with forcible methods
> by a dispossession of kulaks and eviction of peasant families to
> the north and to Siberia. In 1932–1933, Ukraine went through
> the scourge of famine (Holodomor), which was artificially
> organized by the Soviet totalitarian regime and resulted in
> the deaths of millions of people.

> The aims of cultural revolution were literacy campaign, devel-
> opment of national education, science, culture. In 1923 the
> policy of an Ukrainianization was brought in.

When I asked Olesia Stasiuk, the 34-year-old director of the

Holodomor museum, about Ukraine's patchy memory of the famine, she told me the story of her mother. When she had begun researching the *Holodomor* her mother found out from her own mother that more than ten people in the family had died. Olesia's mother had known nothing about it and when she asked her mother why she had never told her she said, 'because it was a taboo subject and to protect you'. If she had mentioned the subject at school, then her parents, who worked in a *kolkhoz* in the Vinnitsa region, could easily have lost their jobs. The legacy of this Soviet-era denial is that it makes it easy now to persuade those who want to rehabilitate Stalin, who want to forget the reality of his regime, that, yes, while there were tough times as the USSR industrialized, it is not a subject really worth spending more than a sentence or two on.

5.

Pickling and Planting to Victory

Karapyshi is heartland Ukraine. The village is ninety minutes' drive due south from Kiev. Everyone here speaks Ukrainian and feels Ukrainian and there is not a scintilla of doubt about who is right and who is wrong in this conflict. Galya Malchik, aged seventy, who wears a red headscarf and knitted waistcoat, told me that a local man with a lorry asked people for help for soldiers on the front. He gathered jars of pickles, potatoes and *salo*, which is traditional Ukrainian salted pork fat. Galya wanted to help, but by the time she got there, he had already filled his lorry and left. So, she said, 'I gave money when they were buying underwear for soldiers.' During the Maidan revolution period many, especially young people and teachers, went at weekends to join the protesters and, said Galya, 'our neighbour collected food to send to the Maidan'.

Valentina Trotsenko teaches Ukrainian at the local school and is also the curator of the village museum. When I asked her what people would do if the conflict continued, she replied, 'Well, as people say: "We will pickle and plant more."' Referring to the devaluation of the hryvnia since the beginning of the Maidan revolution, she said stoically: 'Half my salary has gone. I go to the supermarket and realize that I can get only a couple of kilos of sugar and cereal for porridge now, so I will have to grow the rest. But I don't consider it a catastrophe. It is just life, and how it teaches us to save.'

As the crow flies Karapyshi lies midway between Donetsk, proud of its Soviet heritage, and Lviv with its Galician, Austro-Hungarian and Ukrainian nationalist one. What makes Karapyshi quintessentially Ukrainian is that historically Ukrainians were villagers, while

Russians and Russian-speakers, Jews and others tended to be the townspeople. It is a generalization of course, but basically true. Karapyshi sits in the middle of Ukraine, forty minutes' drive from the mighty Dnieper river which physically divides the country, flowing from the north and out into the Black Sea. But more than that, it also sits squarely at the centre of Ukraine's modern history and experience. Its stories echo those of thousands of other villages and small towns.

Most of Karapyshi's museum is frozen in aspic, remaining just as it was in the late Soviet period, with the last major addition being an exhibition celebrating those who had fought in Afghanistan. It has a bust of Taras Shevchenko (1814–61), who is considered one of Ukraine's two national poets along with Ivan Franko (1856–1916). Next to Shevchenko are objects of ethnographic interest such as an old village loom, earthenware jugs and so on. The only concession to the post-Soviet period are sheets with the names of villagers deported to the Gulag during the era of collectivization in the 1930s. They have been printed on A4 paper and stuck over a stylized mural of Lenin leading a group of armed men and one woman to victory.

No one knows the origin of the name Karapyshi for sure, said Valentina, but there are two theories. One is that it means 'black earth' – *kara* means black in Turkish and Turkic languages such as Tatar. Another theory is that it means 'black small bread'. Village lore holds that the ancestors of the people of Karapyshi offered this to marauding Mongols in the thirteenth century in the hope that they would just pass by and not burn and pillage the village. In more modern times the village was part of the estate of a Polish noble family. As elsewhere in the Russian empire the serfs here were freed in 1861. A census of 1896 records that there were 6,326 peasants and 173 others. Many, but not all of the others, were Jews who had a synagogue. There were nineteen mills, thirteen shops, one hotel, two taverns and a well-developed market. Today, said mayor Sergiy Rudenko, as we walked around the museum, there are 3,100 inhabitants in the village, though in the 1960s there were up to 8,000.

Many began to move away after that, either to Kiev or even just to nearby Mironovka, where there was more work because it was the regional centre.

During the period of collectivization, 300 people deemed *kurkuls*, which is the Ukrainian word for *kulaks*, were arrested and deported. The war memorial records 485 confirmed dead during the Second World War, though more went missing or just never came back and their fate is unknown. In the cemetery there is a tall black crucifix which, said Sergiy, as we stood before it at dusk, marked the place where many who died in the *Holodomor* of 1932–3 were buried in a mass grave. The inscription at the base says 'Eternal Glory to those who Died', but it does not record how they died, why they died or how many died. Sergiy is unclear why this should be. Moreover there is no consensus about the number. Valentina believes it was around 2,400 but others think it was far fewer than this. There are no lists of names of those who died.

In a small village everyone has long memories of other people's history. Nadya Shermet, aged sixty-three, is the sister of Galya Malchik. She lives in Kiev and works in the office managing property belonging to the municipality. She is about to retire and intends to return to the village. The sisters think perhaps only 400 died here in the *Holodomor*, while their brother Sergiy Makarov told me he thought it was fewer than thirty. I find it hard to understand how the numbers can vary so enormously in such a small place. Surely in a village like this, everyone would know exactly who had died, even if the reason why had been a taboo topic for so long. According to Nadya, Valentina's father was a *kurkul* while theirs was a tractor driver in the *kolkhoz* or collective farm. Because he was an employee he got paid in food and had no land to be forced out of; in this way, the family was fed in hungry times. Valentina, however, has the inherited psychology of the *kurkul,* she said, which is to say that of 'someone who has had something taken away from them', which would explain why they were 'angry' and might exaggerate what all would nevertheless agree were communist crimes. Galya concurred and remembered that after the war Valentina's family got rich again because her father became the chief accountant in the *kolkhoz*. Hence his daughters had 'silk dresses and we had cotton ones and were envious'. Still, they had it better than others. Their mother made them bread and little *pyrizhky* pies to take to school, but those whose fathers had not come back from the war did not have anything, so they shared what they had with them.

As in all Ukrainian villages the population is predominantly elderly. Galya said 'there are almost no children in the village'. When she was young 'there were four or five children in every house and now there are only pensioners sitting in their homes'. Just as Nadya is intending to retire here, others have already done so after a lifetime working in Kiev. Between the village and the city there are strong links because many of those who work in the cities, and those who migrated there as Ukraine industrialized after the war, maintained their links with their home villages. Typically their children would spend their summers in the village. They would have fun if they were lucky, but dig, weed and water if they were not.

Today the pensions of many who live here are supplemented by

income from land. Like everywhere else those who worked in the *kolkhoz* got parcels of land when it was broken up after the dissolution of the Soviet Union. Either, like Galya, they are too old to farm the land, or they don't have the money to do so. So it is rented to a company which then groups as much of it together as possible, in effect farming much of the same land as the *kolkhoz* had. The person who owns the land usually gets a portion of the income of the crop sold but can take some of the crop too. Even if a villager wanted to farm their land it might be virtually impossible. For example Galya's 2.75 hectares is surrounded by plots belonging to others so she could not even get to it, let alone drive a tractor to it, without crossing their land. 'It is just part of one big field.'

The law does not allow people to sell this land but you can pass it on when you die. Galya herself inherited her plot from her sister. In some parts of the country big companies run the farms but in others the companies tend to be smaller. Here, said the sisters, most of what makes money is controlled by one local politician and his wife, who have built themselves a fancy home and drive a fancy car. Galya described the wife as a 'famously cruel bitch'. They were the real power here, rather than Sergiy the mayor. There are a few shops in town and when someone not connected to the Karapyshi power couple tried to open one he was told in no uncertain terms that the next day it had better 'no longer be here'. I asked the sisters why they and others put up with this, and Galya shrugged and said: 'Ukrainian villagers are very obedient.' It was rare for them to rise up against authority. Nadya pointed to an ambiguity. Both of them had been members of the Communist Party, and had mixed feelings about this past. For sure communism brought suffering but now people suffered in a different way and, since they were used to a life of not complaining, 'they' (meaning those with power) could get away with giving them just 'a piece of freedom'.

During the Second World War the Germans passed through the village but there was no fighting here. Before the Soviets evacuated they took most of the cattle and other animals. The rest were taken by the Germans who nonetheless did not give the *kolkhoz* land back to the locals. A few joined the German-recruited Ukrainian police and then fled at the end of the war. I asked them how they felt about this period and Nadya said: 'we were patriotic Soviets', although she added that there was not much alternative on offer here at the time. But this memory does not mean they confuse a former patriotism with an admiration for Vladimir Putin and his Russia, which wants to claim the sole mantle of the glory of the Soviet Union's role in the crushing of the Nazis, while forgetting the *Holodomor*, the Nazi–Soviet pact, Stalin's purges and so on. Nadya said of Russians, 'we were brother nations' and Galya added, 'until last year when things changed with the annexation of Crimea'. But whatever has happened they think that Putin is the problem, not Russians with whom good relations can be restored. Putin does not come in for as much bile as I had expected. More is reserved for people closer to home. Nadya told me that army officers she knows complain of unclear chains of command and illogical decision-making which her friends say is impossible to explain. But their deepest scorn is reserved for Britain and the US. They expected them to give weapons to the Ukrainian army so it can better fight the Russians, because until now all they had given the country, said Nadya, was the equivalent of feeding 'a fly to a dog' – in other words, nothing.

6.

Chernobyl: End and Beginning

'The nuclear meltdown at Chernobyl,' wrote Mikhail Gorbachev, the last Soviet leader, in 2006, 'even more than my launch of *perestroika,* was perhaps the real cause of the collapse of the Soviet Union five years later. Indeed, the Chernobyl catastrophe was an historic turning point: there was the era before the disaster, and there is the very different era that has followed.'

Gorbachev, who had been in power just over a year when the catastrophe happened, may overstate the case but there is little doubt that it was one of those pivotal moments in history when it was nudged in a particular direction that it might not have taken otherwise. The explosion happened at 1.23 in the morning of 26 April 1986. At first there was confusion as to what had occurred and how serious the situation was. It was only at 14.00 on 27 April that people in the town of Pripyat, three kilometres away, where most of the plant workers and their families lived, were evacuated. They were told it would be for three days, but it was for ever.

The news first emerged abroad on 28 April when routine testing on the shoes of a worker returning from the toilet at a nuclear plant in Sweden, 1,100 kilometres away, detected abnormal levels of radiation. During the day it was determined that this had come from the Soviet Union and that night the Soviet authorities admitted that something had happened at Chernobyl. Gorbachev argues that there was no deliberate attempt to cover up what had happened, which was then and is still widely believed. He claims that the authorities themselves did not understand the gravity of the situation. Then, he argues, the disaster, 'more than anything else, opened the possibility of much greater freedom of expression, to the point that the system as we knew it, could no longer continue'. Ordinary people lost what faith they had in the system and a direct line can be drawn from here to the demise of the Soviet Union. Ukrainians, for example, now understood that the plant was not under their control but run from Moscow. Hence it made sense for many people, as the USSR began to unravel, to think that the authorities in Kiev should be in control of what was going on in Ukraine.

To this day no one knows how many people were afflicted by cancers and other illnesses that they would not have got otherwise. More than 500,000 participated in the clean-up operation and it continues to this day. An exclusion zone was imposed covering some 2,600 square kilometres. There is an inner core around the plant and the second, wider, surrounding belt. This includes the town of Chernobyl itself, home to a few thousand who now maintain the defunct plant or work on building the new 'sarcophagus' to encase the reactor that exploded.

Chernobyl is 120 kilometres north of Kiev. It is in wooded, marshy land close to the border with Belarus, where even more ground was contaminated than in Ukraine itself, because of the way the radiation fell. For Ukrainians, although Chernobyl is, for sure, part of their history, there is no real feeling of the momentousness of what happened. Throughout the country there are monuments commemorating those who died, just as there are to those who fell during the Soviet intervention in Afghanistan, but 'Chernobyl' as an event does not loom over the country as do, for example, the events of the Second World War. The reason for this is that what happened here is not an issue which can be fought over zealously and ideologically. It feels almost as though Ukrainians have given the Chernobyl part of their history a collective shrug.

That is a pity. The exclusion zone is one of the most extraordinary places in Europe. You need permission to enter it or you have to be on a tour, which has got it for you. Entering the zone is like entering another country: you have to show your passport. You also have to be checked off against the list of names of those who have permission to enter for the day.

To the side of the road are abandoned villages, gradually being engulfed by nature. A very few elderly locals have returned. At first the authorities used to turf them out but eventually gave up and allowed them to stay. Research shows that, on average, they live longer than those who were evacuated and never came back, perhaps because they are happy to be pottering about in their own homes, weeding their own vegetable gardens, even though the fruit and vegetables they grow can be contaminated. Indeed, while some of the area is still contaminated, it is only in patches, and much of the zone is now no more radioactive than anywhere else. Chernobyl town feels empty as it has so few inhabitants, and it is an unexceptional place. Most of those who live here are authorized to do so because their work is somehow connected to the continuing clean-up. The town is actually 15 kilometres from the plant but when the nuclear station was begun in 1972, it was felt demeaning to call it by the name of Kopachi, a nearby village, and since Chernobyl was the name of the wider district, this is how it got its name.

The area is part of the Polesia region which stretches from Poland across southern Belarus and northern Ukraine into Russia. Chernobyl's recorded history goes back to the Middle Ages when it was a little town, trading on the banks of the Pripyat river. In 1897 almost 60 per cent of its population was Jewish and it was the home of a Hassidic dynasty. Today the followers of this branch of Hassidism come on pilgrimages to the restored tombs of their *tzadiks*, or righteous ones. On 9 May everyone who once lived here can return to meet old friends and visit their family graves. The explosion altered not just the history of the world in general, but in the most profound way that of the 200,000 or so people in Ukraine who lived here and who lost their homes. Others lost their homes in Belarus and some even in Russia too.

Arriving at the plant you see the cranes surrounding two unfinished reactors, just as they were on the day they stopped work. They stand next to the lake-like cooling pond. Throw bread into the water and soon it is gone, gulped by giant catfish, the size of a man. They are not mutants but simply grow this big because fishing is prohibited as the water is contaminated. Sometimes people still fish though. The plant itself is unremarkable. It looks like what it was – a nuclear power plant. The block that blew up is encased in concrete but it is deteriorating and the concrete is beginning to crack. So, a huge hangar-like structure is being constructed next to it, a vast, arched affair on rails. When it is completed it will be rolled over the old reactor and then work will begin underneath this new sarcophagus to dismantle the old one underneath and dispose of the radioactive material still entombed inside it. It is due to be finished in 2017 and will have cost some €2 billion. According to the European Bank for Reconstruction and Development, which is coordinating the funds for the shelter from the EU and forty-two other countries, it would be big enough to cover St Paul's Cathedral in London or Notre Dame in Paris.

Three kilometres away is Pripyat. Unlike the town of Chernobyl no one is allowed to live here. Even if you have seen pictures or film of this abandoned town, which once housed 49,000 people, nothing can prepare you for the reality. Trees and undergrowth are slowly taking over this utterly silent place. Wide roads have become narrow as earth encroaches. As Pripyat was a new town, founded in 1970, it was all blocks of flats and large municipal buildings. In the school, books and toys and everything else you might find there lie scattered on the floor or on the shelves where they were left. It is extraordinary that in buildings with smashed windows open to the elements, everything has not rotted or simply been blown away. In the kindergarten in Kopachi, one of only two buildings not to have been bulldozed here after the explosion, a letter on the floor reads:

Application

I request that you admit my child Kostuchenko Maryna Mykolay-ivna, born 28.08.1982 to kindergarten from 01.03.1984.

The letter paper is decorated with a little print of a statue of a lady wearing a flowing gown. Nearby are metal bunk beds for the children's naps and an official portrait of Konstantin Chernenko, the virtually forgotten, grizzled old Soviet leader who led the Soviet Union from February 1984 until his death thirteen months later. In the centre of Pripyat, by the decaying dodgem cars, is a Ferris wheel which was due to be officially inaugurated a few days after the disaster. Today fans of the video game S.T.A.L.K.E.R., in which you can fight human mutants in Pripyat, make pilgrimages here and the uninitiated, thinking they are about to have their photo taken underneath it, are doused with rainwater as the lowest carousel is swung above their heads.

Across the street you can climb to the roof of a sixteen-storey building and see a city slowly disappearing amid a sea of trees, almost like a lost Inca city in the jungle. You can wander in flats and see the beds and furniture people left behind on the day they were evacuated. Everywhere there are piles of pipes and electrical fittings. Some of the metal has been taken out legally, but much has been cut out by looters who then for some reason abandoned their hauls. Some of this is due to corruption. When exclusion zone

bosses change, some looters may lose their protection, which is then bestowed on others.

From the top of the blocks you can see the plant and the colossal Duga-3 military radar. It is a complex structure divided into two separate vast metal grids which look like some extraordinary art installation. Together they stretch 750 metres from end to end, one part is 146 metres high and the second is 90 metres. This was a Soviet 'over-the-horizon' system designed to give early warning against incoming intercontinental ballistic missiles. It was one of two; the second was in eastern Siberia. Because it transmitted a strange tapping sound that interfered on certain radio frequencies which could be heard in the West, it was dubbed the 'Russian woodpecker'.

Today the massive structure stands on sandy ground surrounded by trees. As it was a super-secret military object even people in Pripyat did not know what it was, although from top-floor flats they could see its wall of steel pipes, cones and wires. They dubbed it the 'modern macaroni factory'. Maps made out that the site was an abandoned camp of the Communist Party's Pioneer youth organization or, alternatively, the KGB let slip that it was some sort of experiment in housing technology.

You can climb to the top, or as high as you dare, and hear the strange rushing noise the wind makes as it blows through the antennas. From a distance it sounds like the din of traffic. In the abandoned military buildings around it lie the remains of ancient pieces of electrical equipment and walls decorated with murals of a fantasy future in which cosmonauts are building a circular space station that recalls the one from Stanley Kubrick's film *2001: A Space Odyssey*, made in 1968. Now the radar is slated to be dismantled and sold for scrap. It would be a tragedy if that happened. Like everything else in the zone, it is a historical monument to what feels here like a vanished civilization, a kind of Ukrainian Pompeii. That is worth more than its scrap metal value.

II. WESTERN APPROACHES

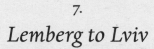

7.

Lemberg to Lviv

One of the best places to think about Ukraine's past and its relationship with the present is Lviv. Its centre is a fabulous collection of gothic, renaissance, baroque and classic nineteenth-century Austro-Hungarian styles, the buildings increasingly restored to their previous glory. It takes no imagination to see how this city was once part of the same cultural space which stretched from here to Zagreb, Croatia's capital, which in some respects it resembles.

It would not be true to say that Lviv's history was more traumatic than that of many other places in Ukraine. Lviv, however, is different in the sense that historically it was an important and cosmopolitan city which, until it became part of the Soviet Union, was connected, both as part of the Austro-Hungarian empire and then as part of Poland, with the main currents of European life. Today, some of its history weighs very heavily on Ukraine, because of what really happened, what people believe happened, what people are told happened and what is forgotten.

Elsewhere I have not enumerated the different names of each place in every language but with Lviv I will, because some readers may recognize it by one of its other names. The name means 'city of lions' and the lion is the city's symbol. Lviv is what this city of a million people is called in Ukrainian. In Russian it is L'vov, in Polish Lwow, in German Lemberg and in Yiddish either Lemberg or Lemberik. During the Austro-Hungarian period, which lasted from 1772 to 1918, the city, the heart of eastern Galicia, was officially known by its German name. From 1918 to 1939 it was the third biggest city in Poland. Then it was taken by the Soviets, followed by the Nazis, and the Soviets returned in 1944. Like Thessaloniki in Greece and Vilnius in Lithuania, it is one of those European cities whose population today is so different from what it used to be that few people who live here nowadays can say that their families lived here before 1945.

In 1931 about half the population of the city was Polish, roughly a third was Jewish and 15.9 per cent was Ukrainian. In the previous decades those proportions had fluctuated, but not very dramatically. In eastern Galicia though, the ethnic make of towns was not the same as in the countryside and region in general. Here some 60 per cent of the population was Ukrainian, and only a quarter Polish. Jews made up most, but not all, of the rest. After the war, virtually all of the Jews had been wiped out and then, in the period to 1947, the vast majority of the Poles were 'repatriated' to Poland because Lviv and eastern Galicia had become Soviet again. The word 'repatriation' was Orwellian, of course, because these Poles were being sent to places they had not come from. Fear was a big motivating factor: many of those who had survived the war and arrests and deportations during the first Soviet occupation did not want to risk staying in the USSR. In the villages many left because they were afraid of attacks by the nationalist partisans of the Ukrainian Insurgent Army (UPA) and there were also tales of NKVD, ministry of interior troops, pretending to be UPA fighters to intimidate people in order to prompt them to go.

According to the historian Timothy Snyder, some 780,000 Poles were sent to Poland from what was now Soviet Ukraine. Including Belarus and Lithuania, the official number sent was 1,517,913, of whom 100,000 were Jews who had survived the Holocaust, but the total number of people who left was larger because 'a few hundred thousand left without registering for official transports'. From Lviv many were sent to Breslau, in Silesia, which was German until 1945, when it became Wroclaw and was incorporated into Poland. Here too the Jews had been killed but what had been an overwhelmingly German city now became a completely Polish one as the Germans fled or were expelled. Many artistic, religious and other cultural treasures were taken from Lviv to Wroclaw, including a vast circular panoramic painting of a 1794 defeat of the Russians at the hands of the Poles, which came out of hiding to be exhibited again only in 1985.

Just as the Poles were being sent to Poland, some 483,099 Ukrainians were sent to Ukraine from the regions they inhabited in what was to remain in Poland. In the so-called Operation Vistula another 140,660 Ukrainians were ethnically cleansed from their homes and sent to settle in other parts of Poland. Those who came to Ukraine were not sent to Lviv though because most were peasants and they were needed in the countryside to replace the Polish peasants who had been sent to Poland. Whole villages on either side of the border were uprooted, but their inhabitants were often kept together and transplanted on the other side. While they were sent to villages, as Lviv industrialized they, or their children, or other Ukrainians who had always lived in the countryside, came for work to the city. This process only took off massively in the 1960s though, because Soviet laws did not allow people to move freely from the countryside.

Still, by 1950 Lviv was already well on the way to becoming the almost totally Ukrainian and Ukrainian-speaking city that it is today. By then about half of the population were Ukrainian, 27 per cent Russian and 6 per cent Jewish, though many of the latter had not been natives of Lviv before the war.

Svetlana Zymovnya is the chief statistician for the Lviv district and the story of her family is typical. Her father was born in Sanok, which is now in south-eastern Poland. Before the Second World War this was a heavily Ukrainian area. 'When he was fourteen they were sent here,' she said, 'to a village near Lviv where they lived in a house built of clay which only had one room.' There were five children in the family. But in Poland, 'they were rich and had a lot of land'. Their new circumstances left them with not enough money and there was little to eat, so her father walked to Lviv to work in a then still Polish-owned furniture factory.

With the murder of the Jews and with the Poles being sent to Poland, a lot of Lviv must have been empty after the war? No, explained Svetlana, because immediately the war ended, what had been Polish and Jewish flats and homes were filled with Soviet military men, men from the NKVD, party members and adminis-trators, and these people, who brought their families, were mostly Russians or from the Russian-speaking east of Ukraine. Conflict in the region did not end in 1944 either, as the NKVD especially had to continue fighting the UPA until well into the 1950s.

While the demographic and ethnic transformation of Lviv was dramatic, it was not at all unique. All the smaller towns of the region were transformed. In the neighbouring and historic region of Volhynia, which had been divided between Poland and the Soviet Union before the war, Poles fought Ukrainians during the war and the Jews were again killed. At the end of the conflict those Poles that remained were sent to Poland and ethnic Germans expelled too as the Soviet Union absorbed the rest of the territory. Historically, as you went further east the Polish factor diminished, but generally a similar pattern prevailed whereby Jews lived in towns and cities, as did Russians, while Ukrainians dominated the countryside. Between Russians and Ukrainians identity was also fluid. In the past, in the areas of Ukraine which had been part of the Russian empire, Ukrainian was considered by many, especially the educated, as a peasant language or dialect of Russian rather than a language in its own right. Many Ukrainians who came to town were educated and, as they began to move up the social scale, they started to speak Russian and many in this way 'became' Russian. However, and this is very important today, others still considered themselves Ukrainian, even though they and their families spoke Russian. Likewise, many but again not all Jews who spoke Russian considered themselves Russian Jews, rather than Ukrainian Jews. In Lviv they spoke Yiddish and German, but increasingly Polish after 1918.

8.

Ruthenes and Little Russians

The 1911 Baedeker's to Austria-Hungary ('with excursions to Cetinje, Belgrade and Bucharest') is a guidebook to a world that was about to vanish. For us, most notably, all those areas of modern Ukraine which were then part of the empire, that is to say the eastern part of the region of Galicia, what is now called Transcarpathia and northern Bukovina, are in the same book as Vienna, Prague and Trieste. Secondly, while we are often given the ethnic make up of places, the word 'Ukrainian' does not exist, because here Ukrainians were still known as Ruthenes, a description which broadly speaking encompassed them and some smaller ethnic minorities who still exist, including Lemkos and Rusyns. The name 'Ruthene', which gradually began to be replaced by the word 'Ukrainian' at the end of the nineteenth century, comes from the same root as Rus or Russia. On the other side of the border, in the Russian empire, the Russian authorities pursued a policy of Russification and the suppression of anything which smacked of a separate Ukrainian identity, actual or potential. In 1876, as a Ukrainian elite began to emerge, publishing in Ukrainian or 'Little Russian' was banned, as were theatre performances and lectures.

The policy in Austro-Hungary, especially in Galicia, was different as Ruthene-cum-Ukrainian identity was to a certain extent encouraged by the authorities keen to divide and rule and to balance Polish identity and aspirations. Today, when we see voting patterns in Ukraine, when we hear that oft repeated description of the west, by which is meant eastern Galicia above all, being more nationalistic and proud of its Ukrainianess, this is the historical root of the reason why. Students could study in Ukrainian, though there were constant struggles with the Poles over this, and a self-consciously Ukrainian elite began to flourish. In the latter decades of the nineteenth century a Ukrainian nationalism began to develop which envisaged eventual union with Ukrainians on the other side of the border inside the Russian empire. Some of the Ukrainian leaders were nationalists who saw themselves as Ukrainians above all but others were Russophiles who looked to Russia for their future and believed themselves a branch of the wider Russian people, not a separate nationality.

The collapse of both the Austro-Hungarian and Russian empires left everything to fight for. The Ukrainians also had an embryonic army in the west of what is now Ukraine, that is to say soldiers who had served as members of the Sich Riflemen, an Austro-Hungarian unit. Ukrainians in Lviv proclaimed an independent West Ukrainian People's Republic on 1 November 1918. In Kiev an independent state was also declared amid the chaos of the Russian Revolution and civil war. Lviv was plunged into conflict. The Poles fought the Ukrainians for the city and the region and the Poles won. In

the Lychakiv cemetery they built a triumphant war memorial to commemorate their dead, including the so-called Lwow Eaglets, or young fighters, who had died, there. The Jews, uncertain what to do, had decided to stay neutral. Once the Poles had won, pogroms broke out to punish the Jews for what was seen as their pro-Ukrainian position.

Interwar Poland was an authoritarian state. As the years wore on it was also increasingly anti-Semitic, as were many of its people, but Ukrainian nationalism was repressed too and activists jailed. The most extreme of them resorted to terrorism and assassinated Polish officials. It was this nationalism that, in the 1930s unsurprisingly and given Galicia's historical links to Vienna, turned to the German-speaking world for inspiration. Likewise, as Hitler began to look east it meant that, despite his disdain for the Slavs in general and in this case in particular the Poles, he had some ready allies. They included Ukrainian former military men who also hated the Poles, grafted his anti-Semitism on to their own, and could also see what communism had done for their compatriots in Soviet Ukraine. While in the 1920s many exiles and Ukrainian nationalists had gone (or returned) to Soviet Ukraine, lured by the promise of building a new Ukrainian state of sorts, in which, at the time Ukrainianization as opposed to Russification was the order of the day, all had changed by the 1930s. These were the years of clampdowns on anything perceived as Ukrainian nationalism, the great purges and of course the *Holodomor*. And for many Ukrainian nationalists, fusing anti-Semitism and anti-communism, the Jews could be singled out as especially guilty as 'Judeo-Bolsheviks'. This was the backdrop for the catastrophe about to befall Lviv and the wider region, and one which, now that Ukraine is at war again, reverberates anew.

9.

Nikita at the Opera

When it comes to remembering the past a few things immediately jump out at you. The first is that in reality there are three very different memories of Lviv. What Ukrainians, Jews and Poles remember isn't the same. The city means different things to them. Poles remember a great city lost to them, a cultured and important Polish city, which they had fought the Ukrainians for in 1918 and managed to keep for Poland. Ukrainians recall Polish repression and the way they declared an independent Ukrainian state here twice, in 1918 and 1941. For Jews it is a city with an ancient Jewish history, swept away by the Nazis and their Ukrainian collaborators. Although in recent years there have been conferences bringing historians together, the fact is that whatever good work they might jointly do takes a long time to percolate through to the consciousness of ordinary people.

You can see one of the first acts of the drama of the destruction of the old Lviv on YouTube. It is in *Liberation*, a 1940 film made by the Ukrainian Soviet filmmaker Alexander Dovzhenko. It gives the Soviet account of the taking of Lviv and western Ukraine, a 'colony of Polish imperialism' in 1939. The war begins, we are told, at the behest of the 'English imperialists' and then the 'artificial Polish state' ceases to exist. To patriotic music the Red Army, pursuing its 'sacred duty' to liberate the Ukrainian and Belarusian peoples, pours over the border on 17 September 1939. We see crowds in Lviv cheering their liberators. Then we see happy people voting in October to elect assemblies (some dance in the streets they are so happy about this) and stirring speeches are made when they convene. In Lviv the assembly meets in the opera house. On the right of a box

close by the stage we can see Nikita Khrushchev, the Ukrainian party boss and future Soviet leader, who was sent by Stalin to oversee this operation. After that the action moves to Moscow where western Ukraine and Belarus are graciously accepted into the USSR on 1 November 1939. Stalin acknowledges the standing ovation of the assembled delegates. Finally the show moves to parliament in Kiev, the same building as the one which houses today's Verkhovna Rada, and after that, under the watchful gaze of Khrushchev, tens of thousands parade through Kiev carrying pictures of Stalin and other communist luminaries.

As well as for performances, nowadays you can visit the opera house on a Thursday afternoon, and surprising numbers of people do. Outside, it is an exuberant neo-renaissance affair and inside, a traditional meeting of deep red velvet and gold. On the ceiling of the auditorium is a roundel featuring ten naked dancing girls, swirling long diaphanous scarves around themselves. The girls and their opera house, which opened in 1900, are a poignant reminder of those final optimistic years before the First World War when no one in Europe had any conception that they were living in an era on which the final curtain was about to fall.

A middle-aged lady stands at the front to answer questions. Curious as to whether what took place here in 1939 is remembered, I asked her if Khrushchev sat 'there' and point at a box. No, she replied immediately, he sat 'in the royal box. You can see there is a crown above it.' If you look at Dovzhenko's film, though, you can see that is not true, as he sat in the box below the royal one. Still, it is a good story, unless she was referring to another event. I asked if Stalin ever attended the opera and she said that, not only did he not, but he never even visited Lviv, bar once passing through the railway station and even then few people knew about that.

To a Westerner the episode here in the opera house, with strident speeches being made while Khrushchev the puppet-master looked on, might seem like a minor historical detail. But in the wake of what has happened in Crimea, Donetsk and Lugansk it is necessary to remind ourselves of this. On 16 March 2014, in Crimea, under the watchful eye of Russian soldiers, a referendum was organized on joining Russia. Patriotic speeches followed, and Putin then graciously accepted Crimea into the fold. A similar referendum was held on 11 May in those parts of Donetsk and Lugansk controlled by pro-Russian rebels. In other words, obscure to us in the West, but in the Kremlin simply standard operating procedures, there in the text-books to be looked at again, dusted off and tweaked for modern times.

10.

Stalin's Chicken

When the Soviets marched into Lviv in 1939, an act that Soviet history commemorated as the 'Golden September', some Jews welcomed them, as did some Ukrainians, especially the poorer among them. For the Jews, Poland had been anti-Semitic and the Soviets were clearly better than the Nazis. Ukrainians thought they were now to be united with their brothers on the other side of the border. Over the ensuing period tens of thousands more Jews began to flood into the city and region fleeing from German-occupied Poland. The next twenty-two months were to be a bitter experience for all. Polish officers were sent to prison camps. Jews dominated commerce, so as the new regime confiscated businesses and closed down private enterprises, many Jews numbered among the biggest losers. Peasants in the countryside soon found themselves being forced into hated collective farms. But, with the Polish administration gone, some Jews and Ukrainians benefited as they got new jobs which had been mostly the preserve of Poles until then. With regard to Ukrainians, says Mihailo Romaniuk, a Lviv historian, within a year they were sorely disappointed by Soviet rule. Soviet propaganda had had an effect, which was why some welcomed the Red Army, despite the fact that something was known about the *Holodomor* and the purges, but 'when they raised blue and yellow [Ukrainian] flags, the Red Army soldiers tore them off them and stamped on them'. Many western Ukrainians believed that, even though it was Soviet, there was a Ukrainian state, which they were now joining, 'but they lacked information'. Anyone remotely politically suspect was arrested and sent east and that applied to Ukrainians, Jews and Poles. Romaniuk says that if

Ukrainians greeted the Red Army in 1939 with flowers, in 1944 when they came back they 'greeted them with weapons'.

What historians say is one thing, but luckily to this day there remain people here who well remember the war. It is their memory, what they remember and what they do not, that has helped shape the way people in the west of Ukraine (as anywhere else of course) see their past and interpret their present.

One is Mihailo Gasyuk, aged ninety-one. He is a bit hard of hearing but otherwise as bright as a button. He lives in the little town of Horodok which is forty minutes' drive due west of Lviv, on the road leading to the Polish border. The roads are poor here, many villages have replaced or supplemented their Soviet war memorials with ones to the UPA, the nationalist Ukrainian Insurgent Army that carried on fighting the Soviets when they returned until the mid-1950s. Mihailo was a member and loves to talk about it. A spread of sandwiches and drinks has been laid on for visitors.

When he was a boy Mihailo lived in a village very close to Horodok. Here, he recalled, there were 'Ukrainians, Poles, Germans, Jews . . . everyone'. At school he studied in Ukrainian but he never went to secondary school, which was taught in Polish, because that was 'only for rich people'. Polish boys threw stones at the

Ukrainian boys and they fought. Between Jews, Poles and Ukrainians in Horodok it seems there was not much love lost.

When the Soviets arrived in 1939 people were not 'glad' because they were Soviets, he said, but because they 'got rid of the Poles'. They were suspicious and Mihailo remembers an incident when Communist Party officials came to lecture the locals on collectivization and on how well people would live. 'One villager stood up and said that he had a tractor that had got stuck in the mud and it had been impossible to get it out, so he tied a goat to it and the goat pulled it out. Then the communist officials began to shout that he was lying and he said: "You have been lying for two hours."'

After collectivization, when people were forced to give up their land, horses and cows, they were even gladder when the Germans arrived, but no one knew much about them or what to expect from them. The Germans quickly started appointing Ukrainians to positions of power and everywhere 'Ukrainians were in charge'. They began recruiting a police force too. Mihailo tried this but did not like it and anyway he wanted to see the world so he volunteered to go and work in Germany. Later on Ukrainians were sent as slave labourers to Germany, rather than going there as volunteers. In 1943, when he returned he 'met guys from the UPA', which was the armed wing of the Organization of Ukrainian Nationalists (OUN), its political party. It was split however and its two wings were in conflict, but the one led by Stepan Bandera was to win. Bandera's men had proclaimed independence in 1941 when the Nazis entered Lviv, but they were quickly rounded up and imprisoned by the Germans for whom an independent Ukraine was not part of their plans. In his first actions Mihailo fought not the Germans but Soviet Partisans. In 1945 he was wounded fighting NKVD troops, was arrested and sentenced to death but survived as his sentence was commuted to twenty years in prison. Stalin died in 1953 and after Khrushchev's denunciation of him three years later, Mihailo was released. It was hard to find a job at home though so he worked in Crimea and then Debaltseve, in the east, as a miner. All he had wanted was 'a free Ukraine and to fight all its enemies'. When he came home after being in prison, he remarked matter-of-factly that everything had changed. There were no more Jews and the Poles had gone too. It was good that the Poles had left, he said, because now there was no more animosity and they were neighbours, that is to say in Poland, rather than literally next door.

When I asked what had happened to the Jews, Mihailo said he was not there when the Germans 'took care of them'. But his granddaughter Oxana Stasiv, who is thirty-four and sat at the table helping when he could not hear and laughing that she had heard all these stories a hundred times before, said that there was a monument nearby where they were buried. According to village lore, after the Jews had been shot, the earth that covered the pit they were thrown into moved, because they were not all dead. Today, this Soviet-era monument is unkempt and overgrown. In Soviet times ideology dictated that the fate of Jews could not be separated from that of others so, as with other monuments from that era, it does not state that the victims buried were Jewish, but rather that here lay more than 2,000 'Soviet people' who had been killed by the 'German-Fascist invaders'. A modern metal plaque in Hebrew, English and Russian, affixed it is said by the children of Nathan and Ida Mandel, recalls that the victims were Jewish. Some old and broken Jewish tombstones have been laid up against the monument.

After the war survivors of the Holocaust would compile *Yizkor*, books of remembrance of their communities. This extract, the testimony of one Pitciha Hochberg, comes from the *Sefer Grayding* or *Book of Griding*, which was published in Tel Aviv in 1981. Grayding and Griding are two transliterations of the Yiddish name for Horodok, which is also known by its Russian name of Gorodok or its Polish one of Grodek Jagiellonski. First Hochberg describes how the Germans arrived in June 1939 but then pulled back as the town had been allotted to the Soviets under the Molotov–Ribbentrop pact. At this time, says Hochberg, there were about 800 Jewish families in and around town. When the Germans returned at the end of June 1941, 'they allowed local criminals to murder Jews and take away their possessions. Peasants started arriving from throughout the district, in order to murder and steal. Jews were killed and thrown in the lake.' However, she writes, a local Ukrainian priest called Rozdolsky appeared like an 'angel' and attempted to stop the mob. 'He forbade murdering and stealing from Jews,' and told the crowd: 'In that fashion we cannot establish Ukraine.' It did not make any difference: locals helped the Gestapo hunt down Jews who were hiding. The Nazis demolished the cemetery, used the headstones to pave the road and blew up the synagogues. A ghetto was established, as elsewhere, and the Germans used the local Jews as a workforce.

> In August of 1942, half the Jewish population of Griding was taken away. The Gestapo, aided by the Ukrainian militia, closed off the streets and started taking the elderly, sick, and children out of their houses. They put them in cars, and took them away. Previously, during the same summer, all men and women above fifty years of age were taken out of the town. They were forced to lie face down. Then the German commander ordered to shoot all of them. Hundreds of Jews were killed. One woman was not hit. After everyone left, she escaped back to the town, and told of what had happened. She was later caught and murdered.

Those who remained were killed in two bouts, in November 1942 and finally on 3 February 1943. The same story was repeated in thousands of places across Ukraine. Curiously, in those parts of Ukraine which had been Soviet before the war and suffered from the famine, there was less Ukrainian collaboration with regard to the murder of the Jews, despite propaganda about 'Judeo-Bolshevism' and the fact that historically these regions had been more prone to pogroms than areas in the west. During the civil war for example, which did not affect Galicia as it was at the time part of Poland, all sides, from the tsarist Whites, to the anarchists of Nestor Makhno, to the Red Army and soldiers loyal to the Ukrainian People's Republic led by Symon Petliura, committed pogroms.

In the church of Saint Lazarus in Lviv, I met Olha Voloshyna, who was pottering about arranging the flowers. She was eighty-nine years old. The church was originally built in the 1630s and had been part of a fortified hospital and a home and refuge for the poor and elderly up to the Second World War. Used for a variety of purposes after the war the building had become a church once more when the Soviet Union collapsed. Like Mihailo, Olha was happy to talk about the past and what she remembered. She sat in a pew and pulled her coat over her shoulders to keep warm.

When Olha was growing up her father died and she went to live with a well-off lady who looked after her in exchange for her help about the house. Before the war, the lady would send food parcels to young Ukrainian activists who had been imprisoned by the Poles, as many were in Bereza Kartuska jail. (The site is now in Belarus.) 'They were young people, boys, who fought for Ukrainian independence.' She sent them *salo* (salted pork fat), garlic, cheese and dried bread.

In 1939 Olha had been living in the little town of Stryi, which is 70 kilometres south of Lviv. After the Soviets came, she said, life had been terrible. 'They took everything from us, but not immediately. They arrested everyone they just didn't like the look of. Then they started to organize the *kolkhoz* and took houses from people.' Just as the Germans attacked, those prisoners were killed by the Soviets, who threw their bodies into a nearby lake. Some were not dead when they disposed of them. When they were shooting they turned on the engines of all their cars and trucks to mask the sound. By one estimate the number of those killed was 1,101. So, she recalls, 'yes, people were very happy when the Germans arrived, and when the Germans had to leave those who could, fled abroad'. When they came, 'the Germans were very kind and shared food and chocolate with us . . . I have only positive memories of the Germans.' In this way history refracts: the same period is remembered differently by different people.

When I asked Olha if she could recall what happened to the Jews she replied that she remembered looking through the window with the lady she lived with and seeing a column of them being marched down the street on their way 'somewhere'. People 'said they were killed. People were worried.' In the marching column the lady spotted the local paediatrician and cried: 'What will happen with the children? Who will look after them when they are sick?' The day after the Germans left Stryi, in 1944, she saw the dead body of a Jew and a child on the street. She said forcefully:

> Many hid Jews. Some took Jewish children and brought them up. To do this was a big risk and there were cases where people were denounced, but just a few. The Germans were pitiless and killed [Ukrainians] for this. I know a family in Stryi who looked after a Jewish girl. The mother had been rounded up to send to a labour camp. She was with the girl, who was three or four, and somehow, from the vehicle she managed to push her out. The Ukrainian family found her crying in their garden and they took her in. She was very beautiful and had lovely, curly hair. At the end of the war, the mother, who had survived, remembered where she had left the girl and came to find her. The girl was hanging on to her second mother because she did not remember her real one. It was such a tragedy. The second mother was devastated, but let her go.

As the war ground on the UPA, encouraged by the Germans, fought the Poles first in neighbouring Volhynia in 1943 and then in Galicia. Some 300,000 Poles fled and 100,000 were killed. Up to 20,000 Ukrainians died in this war-within-the-war. 'It was such a bloody page,' said Olha. Just after the war she remembers a woman coming to the house. 'She had a baby in her arms and a small boy by her side.' Olha went to fetch the lady in whose house she lived. The woman on the street told them she was from Volyhnia and the wife of a priest and that she had escaped when Ukrainians, including her husband, had been forced into the church by Poles and burned alive. 'Yes there was hate. How can we love people we suffered from? But we don't remember evil done to us , this is the way we are.'

In 1949, Roman, her sixteen-year-old brother, who had joined the UPA, was caught in their home village near Stryi. He was arrested and interrogated in a nearby house.

> They treated him terribly and my mum heard all of his screaming. They tortured him and tried to force him to tell them about the insurgents. On the third day there was no more screaming to be heard. He was then thrown, half dead, into a car and driven to Stryi. In Stryi the car stopped on the square, right near the house where my sister Maria lived. She heard shouts of pain, looked through the window and recognized our brother and began to shout 'Roman! Roman!'

The neighbours quickly moved her away from the window realizing the danger she was in. Olha does not know where he was buried. She and two sisters joined the UPA, carrying messages and equipment and doing intelligence work. About the troops who were deployed to fight the UPA in what was a major counter-insurgency operation, she said that they were mainly Russians 'but there were also traitors among the villagers who helped them. We called the Russians "Moscali".' The word is still very much a derogatory term for Russians. Her sisters were caught and sent to the Gulag in Karaganda in distant Kazakhstan, returning after the death of Stalin, when, she recalls, many from there and Siberia also returned.

After the war Olha made a career for herself as a teacher of deaf and dumb children. She was religious but after the war the local Greek Catholic Church, which had nurtured western Ukrainian nationalism, was banned by the Soviets. Priests were arrested and sent to the Gulag and its churches were handed over to the Russian Orthodox Church. Many priests who remained continued to serve their flocks, though in private. 'We had an underground priest.' When you wanted to say confession or fix a baptism or any other such event, you would go to his house and ask him to come and visit on such and such a day. When he arrived at the block where you lived, someone would keep a watch out for 'tails' to check if anyone was following him. In 1989, as part of Mikhail Gorbachev's *perestroika* the Church was legalized again.

Olha is a woman of strong views. The young people who went to the Maidan in 2014 and were the backbone of the revolution were the new generation that she had been waiting for. She thought nothing could be expected from generations who had known Soviet rule because, she said, she could see in herself how deep Soviet 'slav-ishness' had 'entered our souls'. Sometimes 'I can spot Soviet thoughts in my head.' To explain herself and her idea of how oppressed and craven Ukraine had been, especially that part which had been Soviet since the revolution and civil war, she told an anec-dote about Stalin. One day he gathered all his top men. 'He took a chicken and it ran around. He caught it and began to pluck it until it was naked. Then it did not run around but leaned in on his leg, and he said: "Now you can do whatever you want with him." ' When the *Holodomor* started, 'Stalin plucked all the feathers from Ukraine and those that remained alive were ready to do anything to stay alive.'

I asked her about the war and people in the east. 'I don't blame those people so much,' she said in a thoughtful tone. 'They were brought up as animals. Their goal is just to eat and dress and they never saw God. They never had a thought of helping anyone and would be ready to sell their own mother for bread or a few coins.'

The UPA was a brutal organization, infused with anti-Semitism and hatred of Poles, though of course there were also instances of people saved by the UPA or those connected to it. The UPA wanted to create a Ukrainian state for Ukrainians and was a product of its time. Ironically, what its partisans had started, i.e. fighting Poles, who responded where they could with equal brutality, was a job finished by Stalin when he sent the Poles to Poland and brought Ukrainians to Ukraine. In the minds of many ordinary people in the west of Ukraine and indeed elsewhere, what is remembered is that the UPA wanted an independent state, nobly fought the com-munists when they returned in 1944 and defended Ukrainian villages from the Poles. The Nazis recruited police and militia forces and guards for Nazi death camps and egged on local anti-Semitism. Today, the evil is forgotten and the noble is played up. A prominent monument in the Lychakiv cemetery in Lviv commemorates the fallen of the Galicia Division which, seven weeks before it surrendered to the Allies in 1945, was renamed the Ukrainian National Army. Although some other nationalities served within its ranks, the Galicia Division was an overwhelmingly Ukrainian unit of the Waffen SS. After the war thousands of its men ended up in Britain, Canada and elsewhere. Some were volunteers, some were mobilized and some of those who fought alongside the Nazis were men who, like tens of thousands of Russians, joined them to escape their POW camps, where men were starving to death. Failing to untangle this poisonous legacy has proved to be a Ukrainian Achilles heel.

When Ukrainians waved the red and black flag of the UPA on the Maidan, what it represented was seldom explored by Western journalists. But for the Kremlin it proved a godsend – 'proof' that Ukrainians are fascists and Nazis. Andreas Umland, a German academic who teaches in Kiev and is an expert on the far-right in the post-Soviet space, says most Ukrainians regard it simply as a flag of freedom. They don't know that the red and black stand for the concept of *Blut und Boden* – 'blood and soil' – adopted by the Nazis. Granny Olha and Grandpa Mihailo have their memories, their prejudices and their understanding of what happened according to their own experiences, but younger Ukrainians have only the selective filterings of a confused post-Soviet history, which also varies across the country. In the east, one set of memories is propagated and in the west another, and in between there are regional variations. But there is a history war and one full of bitterness and prejudice. As Mihailo Romaniuk, the Lviv historian and admirer of the UPA, explained:

. . . in the east of Ukraine they continue the Soviet historical tradition and in the west and centre we began to study the documents on issues which were forbidden before, for example the UPA, the Greek Catholic Church and the *Holodomor*. People in the east literally don't read. They don't look for information, and don't look for sources. So they don't know the other version of history . . . they don't recognize the *Holodomor* but parts of their family could have died in that famine!

Looking out of his window we could see a strange memorial to the Soviet past. At the end of the Soviet period a big new building was built for the local party. Now it is used by the local tax authority. In front of it a vast round redbrick edifice was constructed with an imposing helipad on top. Party officials had envisioned themselves coolly zipping in and out as they ran Lviv and the rest of the country. The building was never finished.

II.

The History Prison

The bitterness of history in Lviv is nowhere better tasted than at the Lonskoho Street jail. On one side of the slightly run down, classic late Habsburg building is Stepan Bandera street, which eventually leads to the huge memorial to him just outside the city centre. Built in 1889–90, this was first an Austro-Hungarian gendarmerie barracks. Between the wars it became a Polish prison, then a Soviet one, then a Nazi one, then a Soviet one again. When Ukraine became independent it passed into the hands of its intelligence services, the SBU. Part of the building is now an ordinary police station but the jail, empty since 1996, has been turned into a museum.

A casual visitor who did not read all the explanations in great detail would learn that this was a jail where the three totalitarian regimes – the Poles, the Nazis and the Soviets – imprisoned heroic Ukrainian nationalists. In the explanatory notes the Polish state is almost, but not quite, equated with the Nazis and the USSR. Most of the cells have been left as they were. Chicken wire remains in the stairwell, installed to stop prisoners throwing themselves over the bannisters and committing suicide. One cell has been reconstructed to show what a Soviet inspector's office would look like. In another, arty portrait photos have been hung of elderly UPA veterans with captions in which they reminisce about things that happened to them. Another cell is set aside for Soviet memorabilia, with an emphasis on its barbed wire frontiers, and yet another commemorates the Lviv heroes of the 2014 Maidan revolution.

From the prison building you can go outside into its large courtyard which, we can tell from photos, remains eerily as it was in 1941. It is a large space overlooked by middle-class blocks of flats in

61

the surrounding streets and bounded on one side by the prison wall, punctured with its small windows. The central and most important part of the museum is devoted to what happened in the building and the courtyard between 22 and 28 June 1941. Lonskoho, also spelled Lontskoho and known as Lonski in Russian or Lackiego in Polish, was one of three prisons in the city. As the Nazis and several hundred Ukrainian nationalists in the German Nachtigall Batallion approached, the Soviets evacuated a few prisoners and released a few more, but in an orgy of blood they went on to murder thousands across Galicia – as many as 100,000 in all of the areas they retreated from. A brief Ukrainian uprising halted the killings in Lviv but the NKVD returned to finish the job before fleeing. According to the museum's figures 1,681 were murdered in Lonskoho and up to 3,391 in total in the three Lviv prisons, though numbers vary quite dramatically, even in explanations given at the museum.

When the Soviets had arrived in Lviv in 1939 they concentrated on arresting Poles, intellectuals and anyone connected to the Polish military or security services. Large numbers of Jews, regarded as 'class enemies', were also arrested. By 1941 many of those prisoners had been despatched eastwards to the Gulag. No one knows the exact numbers but, according to the museum's calculations, about half the dead of the June massacre in Lonskoho were Ukrainian, a quarter Polish and the rest Jews and others. For the Nazis the massacres were a godsend. For twenty-four hours no one was in charge, but as the Germans arrived they secured the buildings. Then Jews were rounded up to exhume corpses from the fresh mass graves and also to bring out bodies from the cells. The Jews were responsible, said the Nazis, because many of them had worked for the NKVD. An explanatory note acknowledges that Jews were used in this way, as it does that Poles and Jews were killed here too. But two things are clear. This is above all a shrine to the UPA and Ukrainian nationalists; everyone else, while not completely unacknowledged, is more or less forgotten. What is totally missing however is a full account of what happened when the Jews were brought here after the NKVD had gone.

Edmund Kessler was a Lviv Jewish lawyer who, with his wife, was hidden by Poles during the war and wrote an account of this period, including these few days at the end of June and beginning of July. 'The Ukrainian mob,' he wrote, 'encouraged by the behaviour of the Germans is . . . prodded by rumours spread about the bestial tortures Jews supposedly inflicted on arrested political prisoners.' Pogroms and murders began.

Beaten, whipped, and tortured, the inhabitants are dragged into the streets. Hiding in the cellar or attic does not help. Gangs of Ukrainian children inspect the nooks and crannies of houses and apartments and point out hidden Jews. The violence and fury of the attackers grow. No one is spared . . . Tattered masses of tortured Jews arrayed in military formation under the supervision of German soldiers, police and Ukrainian militia are led to the prisons in sight of crowds.

At Lonskoho 'the wall is lined by German guards and on both sides of the gate stand rows of Ukrainians wearing the uniforms of Soviet militiamen'. Quite possibly these were former Soviet policemen quickly adapting to the new reality. The crowd threw rocks at the Jews who then retrieved the corpses. Several were shot.

The Ukrainian servants of the Germans dishonor these corpses, kick them, and spit on them, but not before searching them thoroughly for anything of any value. Despite the duration of the executions, the public's enthusiasm does not wane. The onlookers encourage them with shouts to become even more brutal. What ensues is competition of hitting the victims and kicking the corpses. Their crescendo of curses and shots silence the death rattle of the dying on this devilish day of slaughter.

The pogrom of those days is recorded in many photos and films. Several show women stripped naked or in their underclothes being abused or chased by locals. These pictures are now being used as part of Russian propaganda, to demonstrate that 'the fascists are back'. Some 4,000 are believed to have died then, killed by both the Germans and Ukrainian thugs.

At the end of July another pogrom was organized which was given the name of the 'Petliura Days', for Symon Petliura, the exiled head of the Ukrainian People's Republic. Another 1,000 or so died in this massacre. In 1926 Petliura was assassinated in Paris by a Jewish anarchist in revenge for pogroms carried out by Petliura's forces during the civil war. Many Jews, but not all, regarded the assassin as an avenging angel and hero. Others argued that Petliura was not anti-Semitic and had tried to stop the pogroms committed by his men who were out of control. The Paris trial of the assassin Sholom Schwartzbard (1886–1938) was a *cause célèbre*, not least because he was acquitted although he confessed to the murder. The affair did much to deepen the gulf between Jews and Ukrainians and fuel the belief in 'Judeo-Bolshevism', because Ukrainians claimed he was a Soviet agent. In 1967, Schwartzbard's remains were reinterred in Israel.

The pogrom, in the wake of the NKVD massacre, is not the only part of the history of Lonskoho that is not commemorated. For example, members of the Polish resistance against the Nazis are also forgotten. Ruslan Zabilyi, the young historian and director of the museum, who walked me around, showing me everything from the Polish-era drinking fountain to the Soviet padded cells, is defensive about charges that he has created a shrine to the UPA. Those who have attacked him, he argued, sometimes want to blacken the name of Ukraine or are pro-Russian. He said 'it is partially true' that the whole story is not here, but accusations against him are unjust. 'We try to speak about everybody but we lack information and this is exactly what I am doing – looking for information.' With regard to Polish prisoners, 'all the files were taken to Moscow and I doubt we will ever see them'.

One of Zabilyi's critics is Tarik Cyril Amar, a historian at Columbia University, who has argued that the modern 'glorification of

Ukraine's, especially western Ukraine's and Lviv's, Second World War ethnic nationalists' means the

> suppression of the experiences of Lviv's two other major war-time ethnic groups of Poles and Jews, in particular where remembering them would disturb the glorification of Ukrainian nationalism or implicate ethnic Ukrainians in morally reprehensible behaviour, such as collaboration with the German occupiers, participation in the Shoah or the ethnic cleansing of Poles. The essence of this defensive striving for retrospective innocence has been summarized concisely by a former aide of Roman Shukhevych [one of the UPA leaders]: 'Our Ukrainian nationalism is pure (*chystyi*) and self-sacrificing (*zhertovnyi*).'

What is significant, though, is that while this was definitely the trend in the 1990s and especially between 2005 and 2010 during the presidency of Viktor Yushchenko, the position changed when Viktor Yanukovych became president in 2010. He began putting the brakes on this interpretation of history because – being Russian-oriented and from the east – none of this sat well with his constituents or worldview. Yushchenko's awards of posthumous honours to Shukhevych and Bandera were revoked and the place of the *Holodomor* in Ukrainian history and outlook was downgraded, which is to say it was not denied but placed in the context of a famine that stretched well beyond the borders of modern-day Ukraine.

A signal that the policy had changed was Ruslan's arrest by the SBU in September 2010, which under Yushchenko had opened its archives to him. He was interrogated for fourteen and a half hours and a case against him was instituted, he told me, 'for collecting information that was a state secret with the aim of passing it on to third parties. So, I was accused of spying.' The case was closed in 2012 for 'lack of a crime'. According to him, colleagues were threatened and scared. The fact that a historian investigating Soviet crimes first had the archives opened to him and, when the policy changed, was arrested, only goes to show just how sensitive these issues are to this day. Indeed, now the pendulum has swung again. In May 2015 President Poroshenko signed into law two acts passed in April by the Verkhovna Rada. One banned communist and Nazi propaganda, meaning it would be illegal to deny 'including in the media, the criminal character of the communist totalitarian regime of 1917–91 in Ukraine'. The second criminalized denying the legitimacy of 'the struggle for the independence of Ukraine in the twentieth century' including the role of the OUN and UPA.

Before signing the law some seventy scholars of Ukraine, mostly but not only in the West, signed an open letter to Poroshenko asking him to veto the acts. They had been passed with little or no debate. 'The potential consequences of both these laws are disturbing,' they argued:

Not only would it be a crime to question the legitimacy of an organization [UPA] that slaughtered tens of thousands of Poles in one of the most heinous acts of ethnic cleansing in the history of Ukraine, but also it would exempt from criticism the OUN, one of the most extreme political groups in western Ukraine between the wars, and one which collaborated with Nazi Germany at the outset of the Soviet invasion in 1941. It also took part in anti-Jewish pogroms in Ukraine and, in the case of the Melnyk faction, remained allied with the occupation regime throughout the war.

The scholars went on to argue that over the past fifteen years Vladimir Putin's Russia had invested 'enormous resources in the politicization of history', and it would be 'ruinous if Ukraine went down the same road'. The 1.5 million Ukrainians who died fighting the Nazis in the Red Army 'are entitled to respect, as are those who fought the Red Army and NKVD'. If Poroshenko signed the laws it would be 'a gift to those who wish to turn Ukraine against itself'.

They will alienate many Ukrainians who now find themselves under de facto occupation. They will divide and dishearten Ukraine's friends. In short they will damage Ukraine's national security, and for this reason above all, we urge you to reject them.

As soon as the laws were passed, pro-Russians were able to say that this was yet further proof that Ukraine was now run by neo-Nazis who had come to power as a result of an American and European sponsored coup. Headlines appeared in Western publications usually sympathetic to Ukraine reporting for example, in the words of Leonid Bershidsky, a *Bloomberg View* columnist, that it was 'goodbye Lenin, hello Nazi collaborators in Ukraine these days'. It was a baffling own goal by the president and the Verkhovna Rada.

12.

The Shtreimel *of Lviv*

In Lviv, the murders at the Lonskoho prison and the pogroms that followed were only the prologue. A ghetto was established to the north of the city and then a slave labour camp called Janowska in the north-east. Those Jews who did not die there were mostly sent to the Belzec death camp. Some managed to hide or were given refuge by non-Jewish friends. One of the most famous survival stories, recalled in a 2011 Polish film called *In Darkness*, tells the tale of a small group of Jews who survived in the sewers, where they were fed by Leopold Socha, a Polish sewer worker, his wife and a colleague. Ask people in Lviv about this story and you are almost certain to draw a blank. It is one that is remembered by Jews and maybe Poles, but more or less unknown to Ukrainians.

Some memorials were built in the 1990s but now more are planned; for example, one at the Janowska site and one at the rubbish-strewn and boarded-up site of the Golden Rose synagogue, built in 1582 and destroyed in 1943. Around it, in an area that was once Jewish, cafés and restaurants vie for the custom of tourists and locals alike. At the nearby Lviv Handmade Chocolate shop and café you can buy chocolate Putins, one version complete with devil's horns.

There are few Jews left in Lviv, as many of those who lived here when the USSR collapsed subsequently emigrated. The community is looked after by Rabbi Mordechai Bald, whose wife, Sara, runs the small Jewish school. Twenty years ago she told me, it had 180 children, now it has a stable sixty. On Shabbat, the Hassidic Rabbi Bald, who is American but has lived here since 1993, dons his big fur *Shtreimel* hat and walks briskly home from synagogue. He told me that now there is a not single Jew left in Lviv whose origins are in the city. Once thousands would have been walking home on a Friday night in their *Shtreimels*. Mostly he and his family have no problems, although there have been ugly incidents in the past.

In the meantime Ukraine's tortuous relations with its Jews is changing. Close to the Golden Rose synagogue site a small exhibition has opened, purporting to be about Jewish life here in general. In fact it has a specific purpose, which is to highlight the number of Ukrainians who saved Jews, foremost among them the Greek Catholic Metropolitan Archbishop Andrey Sheptytsky (1865–1944). Two things have happened. The first is that some Ukrainians have woken up to the issue that – especially now that Ukraine needs all the friends it can get – courting Jews, particularly abroad, might be a good idea. Since they might well have been brought up on tales of how 'the Ukrainians were the worst', it might be a good idea to look for positive stories to tell. Secondly, those Jews that remain have become *Ukrainian* Jews rather than, for example, thinking of themselves as Russian Jews who live in Ukraine. Ukrainians and some Ukrainian Jews are at present campaigning hard to have Metropolitan Archbishop Sheptytsky included among the Righteous among the Nations at the Yad Vashem memorial to the victims of the Holocaust in Jerusalem, where his brother Kliment has already been recognized, along with more than 2,000 other Ukrainians.

Sheptytsky is a fascinating and controversial figure. He was a staunch Ukrainian patriot and welcomed the Nazis because he thought they would be better than the Soviets and that their invasion would lead to an independent Ukrainian state. But Sheptytsky had been friendly to the Jews and was soon horrified by what began to unfold. So he ducked and weaved. He protested to Himmler about Ukrainians being used to kill Jews, and in November 1942 wrote his famous pastoral letter, 'Thou Shall Not Kill', which, although it does not mention the murder of Jews as such, is extremely clear by virtue of its time and context. Then he blessed the foundation of the SS Galicia Division, but at the same time was

harbouring some 150 Jews in monasteries and other buildings
including famously Rabbi David Kahane in his own palace in Lviv.
Rabbi Kahane later became the chaplain of the Israeli Air Force and
a staunch defender of Sheptytsky. So the issue of the Metropolitan
Archbishop is a live one in the info-war and in the battle to win
friends and influence people. As to the issue of the numbers of
people rescued, the historian Frank Golczewski writes: 'it suffices
to realize that there were too many acts to make them irrelevant,
yet too few to change the overall picture'.

13

The Scottish Book of Maths and All That

If the relationship between Jews and Ukrainians has slowly been changing, the same is true of the relationship with Poles. Today Poland is Ukraine's staunchest defender, but getting to this position – above and beyond one of a simple calculation of 'my enemy's enemy is my friend' (the main foe being Russia of course) – has been hard. Today the Polish consulate in Lviv is a huge and imposing modern stone and glass building in a residential part of town. One of its main tasks is issuing visas and it issues an absolutely enormous number of them. According to Marcin Zieniewicz, the deputy consul, in 2013 they issued 335,000 and in 2014 they were on course to issue 338,000. Today, tens of thousands of Ukrainians go to work in Poland. Some are unskilled and going to do jobs, in construction for example, that Poles now do in places like London, which are easy and legal for them to get as EU citizens. But people with skills are going to Poland too. Ukrainian English teachers are in high demand, says Marcin, because so many Polish English teachers have also gone to Britain. The same is true of medical staff. Lviv is even close enough to the Polish border town of Przemysl, from which so many Polish doctors, nurses and medical technicians have left, that they can replace them by commuting from Lviv.

When it comes to discussing modern history though, Marcin, who is both erudite and emotional, describes how historians have been meeting for years, and while relations are better, 'we would like it to happen faster, but we try to understand the situation and hope they will hear us and our pain connected to this'. Then he warms to his theme: Polish football began in Lviv. Then modern

law, novelists and filmmakers came from here and in fact, he says, Poles 'cannot imagine' their 'culture and science' without Lviv. He mentions what is called the *Scottish Book*. In this thick notebook, which was later published, prominent Lviv mathematicians wrote down problems, which they discussed in the Scottish Café after the weekly meetings of the Lviv branch of the Polish Mathematical Society between 1935 and 1941. 'Almost everything began in Lviv,' says Marcin, 'and this is why it was very difficult to cope with this city being part of the Soviet Union.' For Poles the problem is that, especially in the 1990s, Ukrainians tried to incorporate Lviv's Polish history as theirs. So, a foreigner visiting the city might, for example, think the mathematicians were Ukrainians.

Being in Lviv as a foreigner you might not notice that Lviv was part of Polish culture. For us this is painful but we also see a tendency that is more open than in the beginning of the 1990s. Before, if you mentioned Polish history, they said 'You are our enemy.' Now there are many common projects, which began in the 1990s, when we started to discover each other from zero.

With regards to the Lonskoho prison, where the inter-war Polish authorities had kept Ukrainian nationalists, this has been the source of much friction. Inter-war Poland 'was not a paradise for Ukrainians', he says, but to equate the Poles, Soviets and Nazis is 'unacceptable'.

Marcin says that on some historical issues like this on which Ukrainians and Poles see things so differently, 'it is difficult to remain calm' but doing so is 'our mission here and it is not easy. We do everything from our side politely. We speak with our Ukrainian partners and we don't want them to think we are trying to take Lviv back for Poland. That is a joke!' Only not quite. According to Radek Sikorski, the foreign minister of Poland in the government of Donald Tusk, between 2007 and 2014, Putin suggested to Tusk in 2008 that they partition Ukraine. 'He went on to say Ukraine is an artificial country and that Lwow is a Polish city and why don't we just sort it out together.' At the time it might have seemed like a lurid joke, but now the question arises as to whether Putin was testing the water to see what the Poles might say. 'We made it very, very clear to them – we wanted nothing to do with this,' said Sikorski. When this interview was published in 2014, a Kremlin spokesman claimed it was 'a fairy tale'. But maps of how extreme Russian nationalists see the future, with Russia taking all of the east and the south, leaving a small Ukrainian rump state around Kiev, do indeed give the west back to Poland. Perhaps we will see the Russian info-war move to inciting Poles to return to Lviv one day.

14.

Tourists and the Tower of Death

Andriy Sadovyi, a suave, blond 46-year-old, has been mayor of Lviv since 2006. Since the general election of October 2014 he has also been leader of the third largest party in parliament, which is Samo-pomich or 'Self-Reliance'. But he has decided to remain in Lviv. The city has a lot to show for itself, he says, and much more can and will be done to recall its Jewish and Polish past, not least because 'we want to see guests from all over the world in Lviv'. Sadovyi has worked hard to put his city on the tourist map and he has been very successful in doing so. Twenty years ago Prague reopened to the world, fifteen years ago it was Cracow, 'and now it's Lviv's turn'. Pushed as to whether remembering the Jewish and Polish past is also important and healthy for Ukraine, he answers simply: 'Yes.'

In the future, and even if we leave aside the desire to attract money-spending tourists, Lviv will most likely better reflect its past. But unless Poles and Jews had asked for this, nothing would have happened. It is an irony, for example, that some visitors to the city might stay in the luxury Citadel Inn hotel. It is inside a large, imposing, round redbrick fortification that was part of a major Austrian military development built in the 1850s. The area overlooks the historic city centre with its church spires and domes. You can read all about this in the history section of the hotel's website. What you can't read is *anything* about the fact that between 1941 and 1944 this was the centre of the Nazi POW camp Stalag 328. Roughly 280,000 prisoners, the vast majority of them from the Red Army, passed through here and (numbers vary) up to 148,000 are said to have died. Most were starved to death by the Nazis, but others were shot or died of typhus. According to some accounts, the Nazis even brought from elsewhere prisoners already infected with typhus, so that they would infect and kill more. As prisoners arrived they were filtered, and Jews and those known to be communists were quickly earmarked for death. Some French and Belgian POWs were brought here as were Italians, who were fighting alongside the Nazis until the country capitulated in 1943. No one it seems really worries much about remembering what happened here. The Nazis, keen to have the Ukrainians as allies, let out many Soviet Ukrainian soldiers. As for Russia, since the overwhelming majority of the prisoners were Russians, it is not, it seems, interested either. In the Soviet period, says Ruslan Zabilyi, the director of the nearby Lonskoho prison museum, the fact that there were so many POWs was something shameful and had to be hidden. Soviet soldiers who had been encircled by the Germans were 'not supposed to have surrendered and such information would destroy the myth of the invincible Soviet army'. During Stalin's lifetime they were even officially called traitors. It is not surprising that some – how many is unknown – then joined the army of Soviet General Andrey Vlasov, who, once captured, switched sides. Because Russia sees itself as the main, if not sole heir to the story of what in the former Soviet Union is called the Great Fatherland War, a story of Russians fighting alongside Nazis, and not against them, is certainly not a subject to be remembered.

Meanwhile, on the website of the Citadel Inn we can read that it incarnates 'a revival of royal hospitality' and the 'majestic traditions' of Austro-Hungarian 'authentic imperial luxury'. In the last few years, whenever there has been building work around here, or trenches have been dug for pipes and cables, the workmen have found human remains. During the war, what is now the hotel was known as the 'Tower of Death'.

III. FRAYING EDGE

15

The Bessarabian Ticket

You need a ticket to go to Ukrainian Bessarabia. You leave Odessa, cross the bridge over the Dniester river and ten minutes' drive down the road arrive at a Ukrainian border post. There they give you a slip of paper with some stamps on it. The border guard writes down on the slip how many people are in your car and the time, and tells you to drive on and not to stop. For the next 7.7 kilometres you are in Moldova, or sort of. You don't pass a Moldovan border post unless you turn off at a junction, and a few minutes later you arrive at another Ukrainian one.

'Why did you stop?' demanded the policeman.

'To buy apples.'

'You are not allowed to do that.'

'How did you know we had stopped?'

'Because I can see how long it took you to get here.'

This is the way the Soviets drew the border. Now the road is under Ukrainian jurisdiction but the woman who sells apples from bright red buckets on the side of the road is in Moldova. If you stepped off the road to buy them, you entered Moldova illegally.

16.
Winds of Change

Even most Ukrainians don't know much about Bessarabia. It is not a part of their country that looms large in their history or imagination. Politically, geographically and ethnically it is something of an anomaly. It is a kind of footnote, albeit home to more than half a million people. Sometimes they refer to it as an 'appendix'. And they mean that in a literal sense. Many don't even seem to know why it is really part of Ukraine. It hangs off the bottom of its body politic and, as Ukraine went to war, some of its people, and those in Moscow planning the destruction of Ukraine, wondered if a quick surgical operation would suffice to extract it from the country.

Look at modern histories and accounts of Ukraine and Bessarabia barely rates a mention. Maybe this is because historically there were not so many Ukrainians or Russians here, but I suspect that it is because it doesn't fit into the big narratives people want to create or believe about the country. Unlike many elsewhere, especially in the west of Ukraine, most of its people did not yearn for generations to be part of a united and independent Ukrainian state but, as conflict engulfed parts of the east in 2014, they realized they did not want to die to be part of Russia either.

Bessarabia is isolated and often forgotten, but in many crucial ways its stories and those of its people are just the same as those in the rest of the country. After nearly a quarter of a century of independence almost everyone in Ukraine, unless they are very rich or a politician, or quite often both, feels angry and resentful at someone. This is the story of the modern Ukraine, only in Bessarabia it is often more so. In that sense, understanding Bessarabia means understanding why you need a ticket to get here, and understanding that means understanding something about Ukraine.

To understand what 'Ukraine' and 'Ukrainian' mean, we need to understand how names are used in different ways in different contexts. Here the issue is: what is Bessarabia? Today the appendix curls out west of Odessa. From the rest of the country there are only two roads in. One crosses a rickety bridge over the Dniester, which also serves as a railway bridge. To the north of this is a vast *liman* or lagoon-cum-estuary where the river flows out to the Black Sea. At the top of the *liman* is the second road. Here you cross the bridge over the Dniester at the town of Mayaki and you get to the border point where they give you the ticket. To the west, Bessarabia is bounded by the Danube and to the north by Moldova.

Bessarabia has nothing to do with Arabs as its name might lead one to conclude. Its name derives from that of the Basarabs, the medieval Moldovan princes who once held sway here. Historically, the region that is now Ukrainian, most of which also has the alternative name of Budjak, was the core of Bessarabia. Once the

Russians took it from the Ottomans and consolidated their control with the Treaty of Bucharest in 1812 it became a part of what they called New Russia or Novorossiya. The Russians then used the name Bessarabia to describe both this southern part, what is now Moldova, and some lands to its north, which are also now in Ukraine. Today, says Anton Kisse, an ethnic Bulgarian politician and local bigshot, it is hardly surprising that people are worried. After all, war and change come here every generation or two.

In my notebook I started to write down the dates of who had ruled this land during the last 200 years during an interview with Alexander Prigarin, an ethnographer and specialist on the region at Odessa University. After a few lines he became exasperated and took my book to write himself.

1812–1856 Russia
1856–1878 Moldova
1878–1918 Russia
1918–1940 Romania
1940–1941 USSR
1941–1944 Romania
1944–   USSR

It seems odd that he ended his list like this and not like this:

1944–1991 USSR
1991–   Ukraine

And perhaps not to complicate things he left out:

1917–1918 Moldovan Democratic Republic

. . . which only lasted a few weeks.

And this is the simplified version! In detail it is an even more tangled web as some districts remained Russian after 1856 and Moldova united with Wallachia in 1859 to form Romania. But the result of this history is the ticket. In 1939 Stalin and Hitler drew their infamous line from the Baltic to the Black Sea in the Molotov–Ribbentrop Pact. The Soviet Union had never recognized Romanian control over all of the old Russian province of Bessarabia after the First World War. So now, in the new circumstances, they explained in the wake of the pact that they were just reasserting control over what was rightfully theirs, a forerunner of what would happen in Crimea in 2014, although there Russia had previously recognized Ukraine's territorial integrity. After the Soviets took control of this southern part, with its higher proportion of Slavs, it was amputated from the rest of the region and given to Ukraine and a sliver of territory to the east of the Dniester river given to the new Moldovan Soviet republic. But, as it was all in the Soviet Union, it did not really matter if the road from Odessa passed through Moldova and that Moldova itself, already stripped of the Bessarabian Black Sea coast, had no access to the sea even via the Danube. In 1999 the Moldovans and Ukrainians made a deal though. Ukraine got to control the road which runs through the village of Palanca, where women sell apples by the side of the road, and in exchange Ukraine gave Moldova a 430-metre strip of territory which adjusted the map and allowed the Moldovans to build themselves a port on the Danube at Giurgiulesti, which otherwise was cut off from the river by a virtual stone's throw. From afar, all this seems like obscure detail – but to those who live with the vicissitudes of Soviet cartography coping with the results is everyday life. These are small places but Ukraine is now faced with a war based on maps and history. Why did much of the Russian-speaking east, south and Crimea end up Ukrainian ask those who reject its sovereignty – not Russian?

In much of Ukraine, small villages tend to straggle and run into one another. Here things are a bit different. Like almost all of the rest of the country the land is flat but, oddly since it is bounded by rivers, water has always been a problem here. With the imposition of Russian rule from 1812 the Russians expelled most of the local Muslim Tatars who roamed the steppe here with their characteristic Karakul sheep, which can thrive in areas with little water since they can store fat in their tails. (If Karakul means nothing to you, think Astrakhan hat or coat.) Now the Russians had to repopulate the place: Bulgarians came along with Cossacks from the east, Christian Albanians, Gagauz (who are Christian but speak a variation of Turkish), Russian and Ukrainian peasants, Russian Old Believers and thousands of Germans who trekked from Prussia, what is now Poland and elsewhere. For their loyalty they were given land and were free peasants, unlike serfs in the rest of the empire. For this, they and their descendants were eternally grateful. Today two communities who leavened the Balkan-like makeup of this region are gone: the Jews, who mostly died in the Holocaust when Romania briefly retook the region, and the Bessarabian Germans.

The end of the Bessarabian German story constitutes a fascinating detail ignored by all mainstream history books of the region, not least because of the bad light it casts on the Soviets in those years which helped create Ukraine within the borders it has today. When Stalin's troops occupied Bessarabia in 1940, part of the deal with Hitler was that its Germans would be sent 'home to the Reich'. Notices were pinned up in German areas informing people of this. Some 400 German members of a 'commission', SS men according to Edmund Stevens, an American journalist who witnessed the Bessarabian Germans arriving across the new Romanian border, were then sent in to persuade people to leave and itemize their property. They would be given exactly the same when they arrived at their destination, they were told, which for many was to be the property taken from Poles in occupied Poland. Once they crossed the border the SS separated able-bodied men from their families because they were to be inducted into the German army, which would soon attack the Soviet Union. Stevens wrote that these men were particularly valuable to the Nazis because 'they knew every inch of the frontier zone, and most of them spoke Russian in addition to German and Romanian'. He witnessed them cross into Romania in covered wagons like those their ancestors would have taken to get here and wrote that they shouted 'Heil Hitler!' as they left the USSR. Those who sooner or later obtained land and farms taken from Poles would lose everything at the end of the war as they fled before the advancing Red Army. Meanwhile, at the same time as the Germans were leaving the region, Jews were fleeing from anti-Semitism in Romania into Bessarabia, the Soviets were shooting and deporting political undesirables and the more prosperous peasants and many Romanians (or Moldovans) were crossing out of the USSR into Romania.

Today, determining exactly who lives in Bessarabia is a problem, because there has been no census in Ukraine since 2001 and anyway, in such a mixed area identities are even more fluid than in some other parts of the country. If someone has an Albanian, a Moldovan, a Bulgarian and a Gagauz for grandparents but speaks Russian, which is the *lingua franca* here, then being Ukrainian is not so obvious. Also, as in other regions of Ukraine there was immigration from other parts of the country and the rest of the USSR during Soviet times, and since the collapse of the country, a general decline in the population. The young are leaving to work elsewhere and the population is becoming older. In 1930 according to ethnographer Prigarin there were 900,000 people here. In 2012 there were estimated to be 577,574.

According to the 2001 census 40 per cent declared themselves Ukrainian, 21 per cent Bulgarian, 20 per cent Russian, 13 per cent Moldovan with the rest split between other small groups. According to the politician Kisse, this is wrong. Only 7 per cent are really Ukrainian, he says, because many people declare themselves as such even though they may not be. When it comes to what people regard themselves as, and what language they speak, statistics in Bessarabia do not lend themselves to the same sort of interpretation as they might elsewhere. Speaking Russian as your mother tongue does not indicate here, as it does not elsewhere in Ukraine, that you regard yourself as Russian. This is something many in Russia either don't understand, or don't want to understand.

Kisse is a controversial man. When I met him in his office in Odessa the 57-year-old had a Ukrainian flag behind him and was dressed in a Ukrainian Olympic team tracksuit. His detractors say he is an opportunist and survivor and indeed he has come far. One of his first jobs was as a tractor driver. Now they say, if it had looked as though Odessa and the south were not going to stay part of Ukraine, like Crimea, he would have adjusted to suit the time. That is what he has done, being one of Bessarabia's deputies in the Verkhovna Rada. Before the Maidan revolution he was a member of Viktor Yanukovych's then ruling Party of Regions. Now he is creating a local party of his own called Our Land, which is suitably ambiguous as it could mean Ukraine, or Bessarabia or just a village.

Like him or loathe him, what he says about many of his constituents whom he concedes are often 'pro-Russian' is true not just for Bessarabia but for much of Ukraine as well. 'The best period was in Soviet times.' In the 1960s and 70s especially, he explained, sports centres were built, palaces of culture, which act as local community centres, went up, roads were built, people got gas and piped water for the first time and irrigation channels were dug. Money was channelled into culture and local, national folk troupes. 'Bulgarians performed all over the Soviet Union,' he said. 'Through culture the Soviets reached the hearts of the people.' But there was a catch. Education was in Russian, which came with its own culture and the gradual political effect of Russification. So, many of those whose ancestors came in the nineteenth century retained vague, positive images of Russia, because it was thanks to Russia that their ancestors had come to put down roots here; positive memories of the USSR outlasted negative ones and language helped make a link between Russia and the Soviet Union. 'This is what remains in people's memory.'

And now Kisse told me, since Ukraine had been independent 'we can't talk about the development of Bessarabia'. Privatization and the dividing up of former collective farms and declining social security provisions had made people more and more worse off he said. You can argue that this is not in fact true and that most people are better off in many ways than they were before, but as always in politics, it is perception that counts, not reality. Many people are still pro-Russian, said Kisse, but now they are far more inclined to keep quiet about this than they would have been before. Now 'the vast majority are for Ukrainian unity'. Surely that was a contradiction, I asked. Yes, he agreed, it was. On 2 May 2014 some forty-two anti-Maidan, pro-Russian activists died in a fire in Odessa after running street battles with pro-Ukrainians in which some five others died. Then the declaration of rebel republics in the east did not result in the regions being snapped off cleanly like Crimea and people becoming instantly better off, but in war. In those circumstances, the wind began to change.

17.

Bones of Contention

In the centre of Tatarbunary, a couple of hours' drive south-west of
Odessa, there is a classic Soviet-era memorial. One man holds a flag
aloft, one crouches with a rifle and one brandishes a pitchfork. It
commemorates the Tatarbunary Uprising of September 1924, when
a group of locals, with covert Soviet help, organization and arms,
rose up against Romanian rule. The leader went under the *nom de
guerre* of Nenin. Once he and his men had seized the town, he summoned the locals and, standing on a table taken from the town hall,
proclaimed the founding of a Moldovan People's Republic. Red flags
were raised. Tatarbunary was a good place to start the revolt
because much of the population was Ukrainian or Russian and
resented the government's policies of Romanianization. The region
had been under martial law since its annexation in 1918. So, when
Nenin told people that the Soviet cavalry was on the brink of entering Bessarabia, many rallied to the call. Within a few days it was all
over. At first the police summoned help from a posse of some forty
Bessarabian Germans from the nearby town of Sarata and then
Romanian troops arrived to finish off the revolt. Some 500 were
arrested, 279 put on trial and the following year eighty-five were
convicted.

The Tatarbunary Uprising was not the only one egged on by the
Soviets in Bessarabia in these inter-war years but many of their
other plans fizzled out completely. Still this history does give pause
for thought. In the West these events can seem like very obscure
historical details. But, if you are in Moscow and thinking about
how to destabilize Ukraine, all this is part of the textbook, the back
catalogue. One account of the uprising in English was published in

89

1927 by Charles Upson Clark, an American academic who knew Romania and Bessarabia well. He wrote that the region was:

> . . . honey combed with revolutionary organizations financed and directed from Soviet Russia. These exploited the post-war economic and political difficulties of the country, the mistakes of the new regime, all forms of discontent, intensified by financial stagnation and the drought; and indiscreet or corrupt Roumanian officials played into their hands.

And so, in our times, the story repeats itself. Modern Ukraine is similarly 'honeycombed' with organizations and individuals tied in one way or another to Vladimir Putin's Russia whose authorities have exploited the dire economic and political situation created by Ukraine's venal and corrupt politicians, giving those who look to Moscow a source of succour and support.

Today cars and trucks speed through Tartabunary, which lies on either side of the road between the Danube port of Izmail and Odessa. People stop here for a meal or drink at the modest hotel just out of town which, over the Christmas period, displays over the porch an illuminated model of reindeers whose heads slowly move this way and that. Horses and carts trot past the 1924 memorial. On the other side is an ordinary building on the corner of the street with a metal onion-style dome atop a mini steeple. It is the church of Father Vasily. It is an unusual place because it was not built as a church. Vasily is Gagauz and was a priest in Izmail for fifteen years and his wife was Ukrainian, from Tatarbunary. She wanted to come back and did so with their four children. 'I decided that nobody would feed or dress them or give them an education so I left my church and came here.' Then he found this building and said, 'God, if you will it, let it be a church.'

Religion in Ukraine can be complicated. The mainstream Orthodox Church is divided between the Moscow Patriarchate and the Kiev Patriarchate. There is also the Ukrainian Autocephalous Church, founded in 1921, and the Greek Catholic Church, which is

part of the wider Catholic community but draws on Orthodox rites and traditions. Most priests in this region belong to the Moscow Patriarchate.

Wanting to open his new church, Vasily went to his bishop, whom he described as an 'agent' of Moscow, and said: 'If you don't give me permission I will go to Kiev.' The bishop said, 'Calm down Gagauz – I know you people have hot blood.' Vasily replied that there was someone 'with higher rank than him' and went to Kiev to seek a blessing. But he could not get it there either. A scandal ensued, as he proceeded to open his own church unaffiliated with either patriarchate but, miracle of miracles, people in town began to arrive with icons, crucifixes and other religious artefacts, many of which they had kept hidden during the Soviet period and some of which had been saved from churches that had been destroyed. 'I did not buy anything,' he said enthusiastically. There was an old man who, when he was younger, had had the job of shovelling coal into the furnace of a heating system, he said, pointing at a fine large image of Christ with a radiating golden halo. One day stuff from a church was brought in and he was told to shove it all in the fire. He burned the first item but, realizing no one was looking, he hid three more under piles of straw. Some time later, a few years after the end of the Soviet Union, when Vasily opened his own church, the old man rescued the items from their hiding place, put them on a cart and brought them to him.

For those who go to church their priest can be an influential figure, even telling them whom to vote for. During the 2010 presidential election Vasily said 'the other priest' told his flock to vote for Yanukovych because he would be 'an Orthodox president'. The 'other priest' was clearly more influential. In this area, over 80 per cent voted for Yanukovych's Party of Regions. Now, says Vasily, 'we see that part of the population is for Russia and part for Ukraine, and that is the same for Gagauz too'.

Up the street and round the corner you come to the office of local ecologist and political activist Iryna Vykhrystyuk, who is forty-six years old. It is easy to find because it has solar panels on the roof and flies a Ukrainian flag. Iryna, blue-eyed and determined-looking, has about as deep roots as you can get around here. One branch of her family descends from Cossacks who settled in Tatarbunary in the 1790s. Some of her relatives took part in the uprising of 1924. It failed, she remarks tartly, because the help they expected to come from Odessa never arrived.

It is December and in the office of her organization, Vidrodzhennia, which means 'Renaissance', there are Christmas cards made by children, to be sent to soldiers on the front. They say things like 'Stay away from evil,' 'May God protect you' and 'We are waiting for you with victory.' Iryna has three sons, one of whom is fighting. He is a volunteer with the army, not one of the many militias that have sprung up. At first the army refused to take him because they had not mobilized him, but he and others who were in a similar situation protested and the army relented.

Now Iryna is doing what she can to support Ukraine's soldiers and before that she supported the Maidan protests against Yanukovych, but much of her activist life since 1996 has been devoted to reversing the ruinous legacies of Soviet policies on the local ecology. What is stunning though is that so long after the collapse of the USSR she and her colleagues have not succeeded. The reasons for this are vested interests and corruption, a classic tale which, replicated thousands of times in different ways across Ukraine, does much to explain how the country has been reduced to such dire straits.

Tatarbunary, which means 'Tatar Wells', sits at the top of the 210 square kilometre Sasyk *liman*, the lagoon-cum-estuary that runs out to the sea. At the mouth of the Sasyk, as with neighbouring *limans*, there is a broad sandbar, up to 500 metres wide in places. But the sandbar did not seal Sasyk off from the sea so, while small rivers ran into it, it was a saltwater lagoon and traditionally a source of fish to eat and sea salt to sell. On land the villagers grazed goats and sheep and Iryna's ancestors began to plough up the steppe and planted vineyards. In the 1960s an ambitious project was approved by the Soviet authorities. The idea was to dam Sasyk by building a massive 14 kilometre-long dyke along the sandbar, digging a 13.5 kilometre-long canal from the Danube and filling it with freshwater and thus make it the centre of a huge irrigation project. (Switch to satellite mode and you can see all this easily with Google Maps.) The aim was to eventually link the Danube with the Dnieper in order to irrigate 8.7 milllion hectares of land.

Work began and Sasyk was closed off from the sea in 1978; irrigation began in 1981. Giant pumps extracted the salty water, which was being replaced with fresh Danube water. According to Iryna, the majority of people around Sasyk were enthusiastic. 'There was not enough freshwater here.' People got their water from wells and small steppe rivers but now demand was escalating, especially due to the consumption of local *kolkhozes* or collective farms. They had, she says, good Ukrainian *chernozem*, the fertile 'black earth' that Ukraine is famous for, but not enough water. 'In Soviet times we always wanted to be ahead of America in terms of producing grain, wheat, corn, sunflowers and grain for cattle.' Before the advent of *kolkhozes* people knew how to look after their land and especially when to leave it fallow, which is particularly important when land is dry. 'Then this system was destroyed.' The *kolkhozes* used all of the land all of the time and so it lost its potential and the soil degraded. Then came the Sasyk irrigation plan. Among some of the scientists who worked on the project there had been some sceptics but, according to Ivan Rusev, a well-known local ecologist and activist, whom I also met, these were Soviet times and so they kept their heads down and did not want to fight against the prevailing trends. The project was disastrous. Instead of turning Sasyk into a freshwater lake, the result was that the earth in the newly irrigated land turned salty due to the fact that saltwater continued to enter Sasyk through springs and underground caverns.

In 1994 irrigation from the *liman* was restricted but not before almost 30,000 hectares of soil had been destroyed or their productivity badly damaged. Wells started to fill with salty water and some 3,000 people had to leave the irrigated area. The water also began to destroy the local ecosystem. There were floods and birds died. Now the *liman*, said Rusev, who trained as a biologist, is 'a soup of pathogens'. Historically Odessa was afflicted by cholera, which Rusev said 'is like plague. It just sleeps. The microbes are just waiting and cholera could come from Sasyk again.'

The next morning Iryna took me down the bumpy road on the western shore of Sasyk. We passed a defunct old Soviet brick factory, the earth pockmarked with craters where the clay was dug up. Iryna said that on paper the factory still exists as a going concern, despite the fact that money was provided to close and move it even before the end of the Soviet Union. Now she thought the director used the premises to do something for his own benefit. On the other side of the road there is a monument indicating that this was the beginning of Trajan's Wall, an earthwork system or defensive line supposedly built by the Roman emperor. It is hard to see anything here, and whether Trajan or the Romans really had anything to do with the earthwork line is hotly disputed by academics. Next we came to Borisovska, a neat village lining a road leading to a decrepit collection of old buildings, some in a state of virtual collapse, by the shore of the *liman*. This used to be one of a group of sanatoria around Sasyk and one of the best-known in the Soviet Union. Part of the building is a bakery now. We walked down the muddy track to look at the scruffy rubbish-strewn shore and returned to buy freshly baked bread.

People used to come here, said Iryna, for the healing effects of the water and mud baths. After Sasyk was closed off, the once therapeutic mud was lost as it filled with polluting heavy metals coming from the Danube. 'There was a TB sanatorium and ones for children and adults. They treated bones, heart disease and abdominal diseases and then the system was destroyed.' Now, said Iryna, locals suffer from these diseases which used to be cured here and which they were less prone to before by virtue of living close to the lake. Since the closure of Sasyk respiratory diseases and cancers have shot up around the *liman*.

A few kilometres away is the village of Glubokoye. At the edge of the village, down a muddy path is a cemetery. It is a bleak and windswept place. The gravediggers were digging and most of the modern graves are, like everywhere else in Ukraine, wreathed with bright and colourful plastic flowers. The first Cossack settlers began to bury their dead here when they arrived in the eighteenth century. Then, as now, the cemetery overlooked Sasyk, but every generation since has buried its dead further from the water and closer to the village. When Sasyk was closed, however, the water level changed. Before the closure it was 20 centimetres lower than the sea. When it was closed and the water remained too salty, the engineers raised the level to 60 centimetres above sea level causing floods and land erosion. Now land on which the cemetery is situated ends abruptly as an earthy cliff above the water and this has gradually been falling away.

Valeriy, a man in his sixties, out for a walk, pointed down to one place where the earth was crumbling into the water and where there used to be a beach. In his childhood, he said, it was always packed and it was hard to find a place to put down your towel. Villagers made lots of money renting rooms to holidaymakers. Years ago, he continued, the cemetery stretched another 150 metres out towards Sasyk. Today the last graves before the cliff are from the 1880s. A century or so of graves, including all the old Cossack ones with their characteristic Cossack cross stone tombstones, have gone, lost to the village and to history.

Gingerly we followed a slippery mud path down to the shore. Behind us there was a crashing sound as a little slice of land literally slipped away. Under the cemetery they have tried to stop the erosion by trucking in rocks but the earth is still falling away because of the wind. It is a bizarre sight. At the top of the cliff, bones and coffin planks protrude from the earth where they were buried. The wind wears away the soil and eventually the remains fall on to the shoreline below. Bits of tombstone lie in the mud along with the odd bones and pieces of skull.

It is logical to conclude that, as this great Soviet engineering experiment has failed, the simple answer is that it should be reversed. The sluices should be opened, the sea should be let back into Sasyk and nature should be allowed to reverse the effects of human interference. This is what Iryna, Ivan Rusev and others have campaigned about for years. Appeals have gone to the government, commissions have been created to examine the problem and politicians, said Iryna, 'pretend to do something'. It is a story that could be repeated ten thousand times across Ukraine. Politicians promise they will resolve a problem and 'people start believing "finally this guy will do what he has to do" and after that he forgets'. In the end real decisions are not taken here in little Tatarbunary but still, in and around town, there are too many who 'are literally parasites on this ecosystem'. They have all been fighting hard and have hitherto had the connections to prevent change. There is no more irrigation from Sasyk, but there are defunct pumping stations and they employ people. In total about a hundred work for the Ministry of Ecology, looking after the dyke, the pumps and the pipes. They are, she said, 'pumping out budget money' in the form of pay, but more than that, over the years, they have been stealing and selling off pipes and machinery, some of which is still in good condition. Still, if Sasyk was opened again they would no longer have their 'phantom jobs'. And worse: 'The other criminal thing,' pointed out Iryna dryly, is that the local authorities benefit from this system because they collect tax from these salaries and thus they are 'fed for doing nothing'.

The next reason Sasyk is not reopened is fishing. Before the closure Sasyk was a spawning ground for Black Sea fish, but there were also freshwater fish, which now are the only ones to survive, albeit in tough conditions. The water is brackish and afflicted by suffocating algal blooms. It is also contaminated with the heavy metals washed down the Danube from industry upstream and then trapped in here. The water is thus toxic and does not meet sanitary norms so, said Iryna, neither she nor others who know how bad the situation is would eat Sasyk fish. Still, people are poor and some can make a little money by fishing. But they cannot just cast off or take their boat to the middle of the *liman* as their grandfathers would have done. Now a businessman owns the fishing rights here, secured thanks to his political connections. Locals must buy expensive permits, adding to their costs such as equipment and fuel. And woe betide anyone who dares to fish without a permit. 'He has guards and they will punish you.' Or worse, she said matter-of-factly, you could risk getting killed. If the lake was opened again then people could fish freely once more, so obviously the well-connected businessman has lobbied hard to keep his fishing preserve.

What has happened at Sasyk over the years has happened in different ways everywhere in Ukraine. Imagine a big ship. If you make a very small hole in the hull it will leak, but not sink. But if you make enough holes, the ship will keel over and begin to slip below the waves. Sasyk is one hole.

18

Jumping Ship

There is another small hole at the little town of Mayaki. I stood with Ivan Rusev on the bridge over the Dniester and he pointed to a complex of luxury houses being built illegally in the national park just on the Bessarabian side of the river. Since the Maidan revolution, he said, illegal building had soared. The reason was that the new government had stopped building inspections in order to save money and on the basis of its conclusion that the system was so rotten and corrupt there was no point in sending out inspectors just so they could be bribed some more. They were indeed corrupt, said

Rusev, but now, with no inspections whatsoever, those building illegally 'are more active than ever'.

His burly colleague Anatoly Zhukov, who is from Mayaki, has been compiling files on what has been happening and sending the information to the president and the prosecutor's office but to no avail. 'Many people in this region are very corrupt,' he said, and 'they have just changed flag and changed party'. In other words, former Yanukovych loyalists have simply jumped ship and now support the new people in power. In Mayaki people were particularly angry because since the town was founded in 1521 its inhabitants had had free access to the riverbank and now those areas had been acquired by a company to build houses for 'rich and corrupt' people. Sitting in a dingy café Anatoly began to name local bigwigs, explained their connections to Yanukovych and how they profited from that relationship and how now, being connected to top people in Kiev, they had survived the transition wrought by the Maidan revolution. He singled out a top local official. 'He is totally corrupt. He was a Yanukovych man and now he has been promoted. Nothing has happened.'

Anatoly is a sceptic when it comes to Petro Poroshenko, who was elected president in May 2014. 'He worked for Yanukovych for too long and now change is happening too slowly.' But he is still a believer. 'I was on the Maidan as were two of my sons. One was beaten. He had his head smashed. For my part, it was my rights I was protecting.' Rusev said, 'With Yanukovych we had no chance. At least now we have a chance.'

Rusev was born in 1959 in a village near Sasyk. He is an ethnic Bulgarian and his family came to Bessarabia in 1821. Back in the village no one shared his views. 'Many of my relatives are waiting for Putin. It is very sad. Bulgarians remember how Russia supported Bulgaria during the Balkan Wars. They believe that with a Russian system it will be better. Most people voted for Yanukovych in my village. It is hard to explain why. They just want to work on their land but they were worked upon,' he said, using an expression popular in the post-Soviet world, 'by different political technologies.

They believe Putin will solve all their problems and they don't believe the Ukrainian authorities.'

A few months later, in May 2015, something unexpectedly did change in the Odessa region. Poroshenko appointed Mikheil Saakashvili, the former president of Georgia, to be its governor. A clear enemy of Russia and a man who did much to transform his own country – it remained to be seen if he could change his new domain.

19.

'A patriot of this land'

There are more than a hundred villages and districts in Ukraine unimaginatively named Zhovtnevoe. It means October and was one of a selection of names celebrating the October Revolution and other Soviet themes doled out to places across the Soviet Union. Zhovtnevoe in Bessarabia looks pretty much the same as any village-cum-small town in Ukraine but it has one peculiarity. It is the *Albanian* village of Ukraine. In the 2001 census 3,308 people in Ukraine described themselves as Albanian and today about half of the country's Albanians live here. Many of the rest of the villagers are Bulgarian. The village was founded in 1811 and the ancestors of many of these Albanians came some 200 years ago from Bulgaria, where their ancestors may have already lived since the sixteenth century. The Albanians are all Orthodox. (Most but not all Albanians are Muslim.) When this part of Bessarabia fell under Romanian rule in 1856 some families moved to three more villages close to the Sea of Azov, which flows into the Black Sea, where their descendants remain. Albanians also lived in Odessa, but Zhovtnevoe, whose original name was Karakurt, which means 'black wolf' and is still in wide use today, remained a sort of Ukrainian Albanian capital village.

Elena Zhecheva, who had been mayor since 2006 was in the little town hall. She is forty-six years old and has two daughters in their twenties. She sat in the dark because for two hours a day the electricity was off, as it was across the region since there was not enough coal for power stations because much of it came from the now war-afflicted east. In her office cabinet she has small Albanian and Ukrainian flags and various souvenirs people have brought back from Albania, Kosovo, or Macedonia, including a ceramic tile portrait of Mother Teresa of Calcutta, herself an Albanian born in Skopje. There are some 2,500 villagers according to Elena, of whom 60 per cent would say they are Albanian, even if they don't all speak the language. With every passing year and with intermarriage, she said, it was increasingly hard to tell who is what.

> In my family I am Albanian from my mother's side and Bulgarian from my father. My grandfather spoke Bulgarian to my sister and Albanian to me. My husband knows Russian, Albanian, Bulgarian, Gagauz and Ukrainian but he is Albanian. However, when we argue we argue in Russian. In school the children are taught in Russian and study Ukrainian but it is not in daily use. That is not because of some attitude to Ukraine but it is simply not used.

Albanians here are desperate for contact with Albania and Kosovo. The Albanian government says it will help, but for years nothing has happened. Because they speak an old-fashioned Albanian the modern language is hard, though not impossible, to understand. Behind Elena is the crest of the village with three coloured stripes. Red is for the village's Albanians, green for Bulgarians and blue for Gagauz.

As the gloom gathered the talk moved on to the life of the village in general, and while it may on the one hand be something of an ethnographic peculiarity, on the other it is little different from Ukraine's hundred or so other Zhovtnevoes. Because of the power cut it was getting cold and Elena pulled her coat close over her. What she said was stark: 'I have bitterness in my soul.' She campaigned to be mayor with the goal of changing things for the better, but with every passing year it became harder and harder. 'I don't want to just exist in this position if I cannot do anything.' Corruption is the problem, she said, here and everywhere in Ukraine. It blocked her and others from being able to do anything to make life better for the village. 'I look at my village and the hardworking people here. Ukraine is not such a poor country and we could do well.' The main road is in bad condition and smaller roads are in an even worse state. To the west Bessarabia is bounded by the Danube, but there is no bridge or ferry over it to Romania. The only way out is to cross through Moldova. If the road was good, if Ukraine's European integration strategy bears fruit, making exports easier, if trucks did not have to waste time at customs to cross a tiny strip of Moldova to access the European Union's markets, little Zhovtnevoe might have a chance to flourish. Now it has few jobs but lots of farmland and 24,000 pigs and, said Elena, 'no one will invest here'. This is a depressed region with no industry. 'Maybe some see future prosperity, but I don't.' Would it not be better if there was a good road out directly to Romania, in which case it would take maybe ninety minutes to get there? She just laughed. She wanted a good road to Odessa first.

In Soviet times the *kolkhoz* employed 1,000 people. Now only a few hundred work in agriculture. Young people leave. There are eleven shops and one café. Others work in the town hall, the school, the kindergarten and so on. The village is full of pensioners and some stay-at-home mothers, said Elena. 'Others go to Odessa and rent an apartment and try to find a life there.' That the village ages and that kids, especially those who get an education, want to leave is nothing specific to Zhovtnevoe or to Ukraine. In these dangerous times people wonder whom to believe and whom to follow if forced to make a choice. But whom to believe? 'My opinion is that people just can't understand what is going on,' she said. They watch Ukrainian and Russian television and try to figure out who is telling the truth. 'Many people don't express their view openly. What they really want is work and to earn money for essential things and to at least live their simple lives. It sounds mercantile. Money is evil, but we cannot live without it.' Now what was happening in Ukraine was a fight for power by two big groups and many here thought it was 'not our fight'.

That night I was sent to stay in the house of Granny Stefanida Stamat. Just opposite her house was a little shop were I stocked up on supplies and the woman behind the counter totted up the bill with an abacus. Stefanida's house, with its compound and field at the back, is big. She has plenty of rooms, though most of them are unused because she is alone now. She has more land elsewhere, which she got when the *kolkhoz* was broken up. She is seventy and too old to farm it, as indeed are most of her neighbours, so like millions of others in Ukraine she has rented it to a company, which farms it together with the land of her neighbours and then, depending on what she wants, gives her a small amount for the produce it sells and a proportion of what is grown. Last year she took half of the produce to see her and her chickens through the year and 3,600 hryvnias, which in December 2014 was less than €200. Her monthly pension was 1,100 hryvnias or some €60 and much of that went on gas to keep her warm in winter. (A few months later the fall of the hryvnia slashed a third off the value of these figures.) She has two grown-up children who have moved away, thirty-two chickens, fifteen geese 'but I killed them' and twenty-five ducks. In summer she has plenty of fruit that she grows. Like every single pensioner in Ukraine she is angry about her tiny pension, but those who live in the city don't have the extra resources she has, which makes them far, far angrier. 'I want cheese and sausage,' she said firmly. She needs cash to buy these, as she does to pay for gas. Indignantly she declared: 'I was working for forty-four years!'

Some people, she told me, mentioning in particular Bulgarians in Bolgrad, the nearby town, thought that if Russia ruled here again life would be better but Stefanida did not believe it. 'I have lived for twenty-three years in Ukraine and Ukraine pays our pensions and all the produce we buy is Ukrainian.' A neighbour had commented on the small Ukrainian flag in her kitchen. 'I said "yes – *Slava Ukraini!*" ' Glory to Ukraine! Stefanida is unsentimental. When I left the next day I asked her if any of her neighbours were sent to the Gulag when Soviet forces returned in 1944. 'Yes,' she said, 'there was a man over there who was sent away.' He was apparently richer than most in the village. He never came back and his wife never remarried. I made some remark about life being tough in Soviet times and especially while Stalin was still alive. 'There was a woman who stole one and half kilos of grain from the *kolkhoz*,' she said, recalling that she was sent to jail. I misunderstood her gist. I thought she was citing this as an example of an unjust system and tough times. No. The point was that *then* you got jailed for any tiny infraction of the law but now people 'steal millions and nothing happens to them'.

The next day I was taken to see the school. Elena, the mayor, had asked the cheerful Galina Petrova, aged fifty-one, who works with her in the town hall, to take me over. There are 244 children in it. When Galina studied here in the 1970s there were 400. She introduced me to Natalya Kircheva, who is the deputy head and aged forty-four. When she studied here in the 1980s there were 300. We looked at pictures on the walls of students in years past, on school trips and having fun, and Galina and Natalya pointed out photos of themselves as happy teenagers.

The school has a small museum of village history and folk costumes. Today was the last day of school before the Christmas

holidays and small children were swirling around in the corridors in fancy dress with their parents. The history teacher is Igor Push-kov, who came to talk to me. Originally, he said, the village was one of Nogai Tatars, who are related to Crimean Tatars and were expelled from the region when Russian imperial rule was imposed. Then the Bulgarians came to settle and only later, in the 1830s, did the Albanians arrive. When he went out of the room Natalya took me aside and said that Albanians believe they came here in 1811 and because Igor 'is Bulgarian he is saying the Bulgarians arrived first'. Natalya is Albanian and would love to go to Albania for language tuition because, unlike the Bulgarians who have a trained Bulgar-ian teacher in school, the Albanians do not. The tour of the school over I thought that it was time to leave, but I was mistaken. A side room had been set aside with sandwiches and chocolates. Every-where in Ukraine ordinary people want to tell you what they think, in large part probably because they believe their own leaders don't listen or care about them. 'No one comes here. No one is inter-ested,' said Natalya.

Talk quickly turned to the war. Natalya was very vocal. 'It is politicians fighting it out, not a people's war. I would support a gov-ernment which would support peace on our land, even if it was not Ukrainian. We need stability.' She has two sons. One is a student and would fight if he was called up, the other is hiding because he does not want to be mobilized. 'We are divided.' She described her-self as 'a patriot of *this* land, not of Ukraine, but of my bit of land, of Bessarabia. If my son died in this war and afterwards Ukraine was powerful, why would I need it? It is not a price I am willing to pay. If we can't reach a solution peacefully then leave everything as it is.' People here, and not just here, feel isolated and forgotten. Ukraine has done little or nothing for them they think, while some have become rich and Ukraine is a rich country with enough for every-one. Here, where locals are not even ethnic Ukrainians, there was much less willingness to pay the ultimate sacrifice for the country. Natalya's son was at university in Odessa and like everything else in Ukraine it is permeated with corruption and she had to find the cash to help him get through. So now she thinks, 'Why defend this country? We are not waiting for Russia, we are waiting for changes for the better,' and this post-Maidan government 'won't bring them. I understand that I need to think globally but now I am thinking like a mother.' Galina chipped in: 'A mother who has lost her child has lost the most precious thing and life is not worth living then.'

Galina's own son is a seaman. In Soviet times many young men from this region, from Odessa and the coast, went to work for the Soviet merchant fleet. When the USSR collapsed, that vanished. Ships were purloined in one way or another and a few people made a lot of money selling them. Now men work for foreign companies and the pay is good. He works all over the world but says he is ashamed of Ukraine 'because people laugh at us and say that we are manipulated by people who have power'. Natalya added, 'so that Russia and the US can resolve their political issues on our territory'.

Galina said that people here were waiting for change but they had not seen it and because of their experiences in the past there was no trust that government was willing or able to introduce reforms to benefit the population. In Soviet times there was a big military airbase nearby and a paratroop division. If war had broken out between NATO and the USSR, their job would have been to secure free access to the Black Sea. Troops from here went to Hungary in 1956, Czechoslovakia in 1968 and Afghanistan in the 1980s. With the base and the soldiers came a military hospital. 'We had great doctors but they have all been removed from here. So, what was that reform? It left us fewer doctors and beds and no specialists.' And free healthcare, which is what Ukrainians are supposed to benefit from, is mostly free on paper only.

Leaving the school I asked them in the corridor if they had heard of a plan to establish a Bessarabian People's Republic, rumours of which had been circulating on the internet. A stern-looking teacher overheard me and admonished me. 'You should not even speak of such things! Even to talk about things like that risks smashing Ukraine, which is like a glass, into pieces and I don't want anyone to talk about it.' Her name was Yevdokiya Gelmintli, she was

grey-haired, grandmotherly and seventy years old. Ukraine is like a family with a broom, she said. 'The broom is strong, but if everyone has one twig each, then anyone can break you. Even rumours of such things would help those who want to smash Ukraine apart. The south of Ukraine is rich in resources and "black earth" and we want a better life but not to separate from Ukraine.'

As I left Zhovtnevoe something strange by the side of the road caught my eye. On a brick base, which might once have held a sign indicating that this was the collective farm, was a large pink cartoon pig sporting a yellow hat with a flower in it. It was the entrance to the pig farm.

20.

Conchita Wurst and the Old Idiots

Bolgrad on a dark December afternoon is a gloomy place. Maybe in summer it is nice. The first thing I saw when I arrived was a funeral progressing slowly through the streets. The coffin lay on the back of a truck and behind it came a brass band followed by the mourners. In front walked a man carrying two oranges on spikes, a local funeral tradition.

Bolgrad lies about four hours' drive from Odessa and is close to the Moldovan border. President Petro Poroshenko was born here in 1965, but the town is best known as the Bulgarian capital of Bessarabia and 60.8 per cent of the people who live in the town and the wider region are Bulgarians, according to the 2001 census. In the centre of town is a large memorial commemorating the Bessarabian Bulgarians who died fighting for the liberation of Bulgaria during the Russo-Turkish war of 1877–8. Far from being a historic monument it was in fact unveiled only in October 2012 by none other than Bessarabia's great political survivor Anton Kisse. This is his home turf.

I wanted to get to the bottom of the mysterious story of the Bessarabian People's Republic. The internet rumours suggested that it might play the same proxy role as the Donetsk and Lugansk People's Republics if Russia decided that it wanted to take the conflict further and snap Bessarabia off from the rest of Ukraine. If this project were ever to materialize, the rumours went, Russians and former Soviet Afghan war veterans could be used to proclaim the republic and mobilize pro-Russian Bulgarians. Maps of the Russian nationalist Novorossiya project show all of the south, including Bessarabia, being stripped from Ukraine. One reason why the region could be vulnerable is that there are many Russians here, especially former military men, who were originally not from Bessarabia but stayed behind after the fall of the Soviet Union and the closure of the huge military facilities that used to be here.

In this region there had been some credible stories of drones flying overhead. They might come from Transnistria, the breakaway slither of Moldova, which serves as a smuggling hub and is under Russian control and where there is a contingent of Russian troops. The drones might be trying to see what the Ukrainians are up to in the old Soviet airbase where some limited military activity has resumed. Elsewhere in Bessarabia, closer to the coast, it was assumed that the drones were flying off ships from the Russian Black Sea Fleet, based in Sebastopol in Russian-annexed Crimea. On paper, the idea of a Bessarabian People's Republic makes sense in that with determination and a small number of well-trained men it would be technically easy to isolate the region from the rest of the country, as there are only two bridges in across the Dniester, which could be blown up. In reality, such events might well simply splinter Bessarabia into several rival centres of regional and ethnic power.

To find out more, I met up with Galina Ivanova, the head of the Bulgarian cultural centre. She definitely did not want to talk politics. She showed me their small museum, containing exhibits of Bulgarian ethnographic interest, embroidery and so on and pictures and panels on various themes. One commemorates locals who fought in the Red Army during the Second World War, and includes a Soviet flag. On the other side are panels and information on the 'Communist Inquisition', the Gulag and the *Holodomor*. Those who glorify and honour the Soviet past in Ukraine usually ignore or deny the dark pages of Soviet history; likewise, those on the other side of the historical barricades in Ukraine glorify those who fought the Soviets and often collaborated with the Nazis. This exhibition is a little unusual then but actually reflects what many ordinary and unideological people think: it is possible to honour

those who fought the Nazis and fascism without denying the evils wrought by communism in Ukraine.

After a little coaxing Galina said that the people I needed to talk to about the Bessarabian People's Republic were the men of a small group called the Bulgarian Friendship Society. Phone calls were made and contacts established. Pushed a bit, she let slip that this small group of men have for years fantasized about some form of special status or republic for Bessarabia and then blurted out: 'Old idiots!'

One of them is Stepan Stojanov, who is sixty-one and works in the market. During our discussion in the little Bulgarian library in Galina's building he seemed rather level-headed. The group has been around for some thirty years, he said, so it existed in the last years of the Soviet Union and its purpose was to raise questions about Bulgarian language and culture and to establish links with Bulgaria. Now the group was no longer active. It was split by the Maidan revolution and the war and that reflected the split in town.

Because he worked in the market he said he could pick up exactly what people were saying and thinking. 'I would say that at the moment 60 or 70 per cent have anti-Ukrainian outlooks.' Then he corrected himself. 'About 20 per cent are pro-Ukrainian and 30 per cent anti-Ukrainian and all the others don't care. The rest are saying they will support whoever gives them a better life.' When the conflict began in spring 2014 there was a pro-Russian wave. 'People said "when the Russians come, they will give us gas, double our pensions and make our life better". Now we have war in Donbass though, and this pro-Russian outlook has decreased.' Stepan said he had always wanted autonomy for Bessarabia, or at least for Bulgarians, but 'me and many others think that this is not the time' because its supporters would be used by Russian intelligence and special services against Ukraine. 'They want to create chaos here and many understood that.' In conversation with him and another member of the group who had joined us, a name began to pop up repeatedly. It was that of Igor Babych, a Russian general who served his career here, retired here and is well known about town. If there was to be a separatist movement, then maybe he could lead it? My attempt to find Babych proved unsuccessful, but Anton Kisse had a few things to say about him when we met.

'I can tell you,' Kisse said, that 'we are talking' to the general 'and he is not a threat'. He has not been arrested. He is close to the Odessa police chief who has been to Bolgrad to 'drink tea with him'. Babych, he explained, had been happily swilling beer and grilling *shashlik* on his barbecue in his retirement when his name was talked about as a possible leader of a pro-Russian movement, 'and maybe the Russian special services came to him for that', and he loved it simply for the attention and status it gave him.

According to Anton Yarotsky, a young aide to Kisse and a person who likes to use the expression 'political technologies', the whole Bessarabian People's Republic story was used by pro-Ukrainian politicians to blacken enemies like Kisse whom they accused falsely of supporting it. But because Kisse was a shrewd political operator, he was able to use the story to his own benefit. By keeping silent on the issue, pro-Russians believed the story of the pro-Ukrainians that he supported it and thus they supported him, when in fact he did not. Actually, he said, Kisse and his friends are investing €5 million in a ferry across the Danube to Romania, and so they certainly didn't want any instability here to disrupt their plans. Yes, Kisse confirmed, when I asked him about the ferry plan. 'What am I not involved in in Bessarabia?' he asked with a smile on his face. The ferry is a small piece of a project, including upgrading roads, which has been talked about for fifteen years. The real problem, he said, had been in getting the go-ahead for a new customs and immigration terminal. Permission had now been granted. As far as he was concerned, Bessarabia 'was stable, is stable and will continue to be stable'. When I asked him if he was not frightened that conflict could spread here, he just said: 'Who is not frightened?'

Before leaving Bolgrad I ran into a man in his twenties called Eduard. He told me he was the head of the municipal water department and approached me with a tone of menace. Salaries had remained the same, he said, but the price of everything had gone up. His arguments were rambling and confused. Ukraine had gas (some, but in fact nowhere enough) so why should people pay the same price as in countries where they don't? 'We would like to be part of Ukraine, but not part of Europe. Europe does not accept us. They don't accept our products and what can we talk about if we are only doing business with Russia? Why is Poland on strike and 25,000 people have left the Czech Republic because of homosexuality in one week?' The Russian and pro-Russian media have been assiduous in their bigoted propaganda against the European Union and over gay marriage and in their attempts – clearly resonating with some – to contrast Putin, who rides horses bare-chested, and manly Russia, with Gay Europe symbolized by the person of Conchita Wurst, the bearded Austrian drag queen and 2014 Eurovision Song Contest winner.

21

The Deep Hole

Izmail is one of the biggest towns of Bessarabia. On the Danube it was always an important port. You can stand on the riverbank and look across the river to Romania. First I went to see Kira, an Albanian from Zhovtnevoe, a pensioner who lives in a tower block of a Soviet-era estate. Her daughter lives in London and married an Albanian from Albania so she and her husband had been to visit. She liked it but disapproved of what she regarded as its hidebound traditions. Turning the conversation to Izmail I asked her what the atmosphere was like. Many Russians had come here in the Soviet period, she said, and, although they had lived here almost all of their lives, they 'are always criticizing the government. It is very unpleasant.' She thought the town was divided fifty-fifty between pro-Russians and pro-Ukrainians, but maybe that was changing in the wake of what had happened in the east. Many were now 'afraid of Russia' and 'especially its bandits and mercenaries'. Since there is no bridge or ferry to Romania, since Izmail hangs on the very edge of Ukraine and is hard to get to and since Ukrainian citizens need visas to travel to the EU, I asked her what it felt like living here. She replied: 'Everyone says we are living in a deep hole here.'

On the riverbank an old man was fishing. A big barge went past, travelling upriver. Just downriver we could see the port cranes and behind us was an old mosque, now a museum. In Soviet times, he said, the river was much busier. I asked if he would like the Russians to come back. Yes, he certainly would. Another old man listening to the conversation said that if Putin was in charge here that did not mean, as many thought, that pensions would suddenly shoot up and the glory days of the Soviet Union would be restored

to Izmail. The response of the fisherman was spluttering invective.
The other old man was a 'fucking fascist, Nazi, *Banderovsti*' – a reference to the western Ukrainian leader from the Second World
War. The second man retreated. Listening in were two girls who
waited for their chance to speak. They were students and had just
come from the nearby church. One wanted to get her shy friend to
practise her English. Wasn't it frustrating, I asked, to be able to see
the EU 'just over there' but not be able to go there? They looked a
bit baffled and said that if they wanted to have fun they could go to
Odessa or go on holiday somewhere else in Ukraine.

The mosque was surrounded by Second World War era artillery.
On the inside you can see a vast panoramic painting of the capture
of Izmail from the Turks in 1790 by Russia's General Alexander Suvorov, and hear a recorded narration of the event. If you listen in
Russian you get sound effects of cannons too. When Suvorov took
the town most of the population were Tatars and Turks. One of the
officers in Suvorov's army was a young Baltic German called

Balthasar von Campenhausen. He wrote later that the town was 'extremely beautiful'. There were seventeen mosques, 'the most magnificent of which was built by the merchants who trade to the interior of Asia' and he added that 'the palace of the Pacha, and the khan or inn, which the Asiatic merchants frequent, were extensive buildings'. He described the fortress built by a German architect and noted that the Armenians and Greeks 'have a church and monastery here'. Then, rather laconically: 'The useless obstinacy of the Pacha, who attempted to defend the fortress, even after all his ammunition was consumed, forced us in the year 1789, under Suwarrov, to take it by storm, and on occasion this beautiful city was reduced to ashes.' It was not just the city which was reduced. Thousands of people, including women and children, were massacred as the Russians sacked Izmail – not just soldiers.

After the First World War, when Izmail was under Romanian rule, the town had a population of 37,000, of whom 11,000 were Jews, 8,000 Romanian (in Soviet times they became Moldovans), 6,000 Germans and the rest a sprinkling of Russians, Ukrainians, Bulgarians and so on. The effects of the Second World War coupled with post-war urbanization which brought ethnic Russians and others from across the Soviet Union here, plus Ukrainians, Bessarabian Bulgarians and Albanians, who had hitherto lived as peasants in the countryside, utterly changed the city. In 2001 Russians comprised 42.7 per cent of the population, Ukrainians 38 per cent and Bulgarians 10 per cent. That explains the divisions in Izmail just as the same legacy explains why people in different places in Ukraine think and react as they do today, though conclusions derived from ethnic data alone cannot be drawn simply, as they can in other conflicts.

22.

Kilometre Zero

The road from Izmail to Vilkovo is pockmarked with craters.
There has been no war here but the word 'potholes' simply does
not do them justice. Later I learned two things. A politician in
Odessa, which is the capital of the whole oblast or region of which
Bessarabia is a large part, told me two things about the road. When
I asked him why it was so bad his first reaction was that it did not
actually matter because, as it was not a big main road, 'only locals
use it'. Then he told me that it had in fact been repaired a couple
of years ago. The problem was, of course, corruption. Roads are
notorious the world over for providing an easy opportunity to
skim off extra profit. You are contracted to lay tarmac with a certain thickness, which you say you do, but you do not, pocketing
the cash for the materials not bought or sharing it with whoever secured you the contract. The problem for those who use the
road is that the surface quickly deteriorates as it is not thick
enough – just as it has here. Then a tender can go out to resurface
it once again and more money can be shared between those in on
the deal.

Vilkovo is known as a town of Old Believers, descendants of
people who refused to accept the reforms of the Russian Orthodox
Church in the seventeenth century and who scattered to the fur-
thest, most isolated corners of the empire and beyond to avoid
persecution. Today they make up some 70 per cent of Vilkovo's
population. They settled here along with Don Cossacks also in
flight, in the marshy delta of the Danube, and in this region and in
Romania they are called Lipovans. The town, founded in 1746, is
crisscrossed with canals and some have dubbed it optimistically the

Ukrainian Venice. Along some of the canals people teeter on narrow boardwalks and tiny rickety wooden bridges as they go about their business. Houses have little jetties in front, to which their owners' boats are tied. In the centre of town is a Soviet-era fisherman monument and the main, turquoise-painted Old Believer church. From Vilkovo this branch of the Danube, known as the Kilia branch, forks out into several smaller ones, which then flow out into the sea. This is how Vilkovo got its name – it derives from the word for 'fork'.

Misha Zhmud, aged fifty-seven, is a local councillor, scientist and entrepreneur. He has built a small village of holiday houses on the river, called Pelican City, from where you can set out to explore the Danube, its birds and the Ukrainian portion of the delta, the greater part of which is in Romania. As dusk fell we sat in his little office and I scribbled by candlelight because the power was off again. Twenty years ago, he said, some 14,000 lived in Vilkovo and there was work for 7,500. Now there are only 2,000 jobs and 7,500 people. 'The population is disappearing,' said Misha. In terms of work Vilkovo had gone back sixty years and 'if we don't create 300 or 400 jobs here then Vilkovo will turn into a village very quickly'. A lot of local men, who have a tradition of seafaring here, have got good jobs as sailors on foreign ships and send money home. They can earn €5,000 to €7,000 a month when they are abroad, which is huge for Ukraine, but even this influx of cash for some lucky families is not enough to stem the exodus of those who remain.

There were some big employers here in Soviet times. One was a fish-canning factory employing 1,300, which has gone, and the others were in fishing, the port and a shipyard. From here ships could sail up and down the Danube but corruption and neglect led to the collapse of the industry. The *coups de grâce* were the Yugoslav wars. First, sanctions on Serbia led to a drop in business and finally, during the 1999 Kosovo war when NATO bombed Serbia, bridges were downed into the river, halting traffic. By the time it was cleared there was no more business, at least for Ukraine.

Today, far more traffic flows up and the down the main Romanian Sulina branch of the Danube, which, says Misha pointedly, 'is in the EU', while here, once navigable parts have silted up. Tourism has created some 300 jobs but many of these are seasonal and, as it is so hard to get to Vilkovo, it has not flourished as it should. The war is hundreds of kilometres away but foreigners see that Vilkovo is in Ukraine and numbers have fallen off dramatically. Meanwhile, as the hryvnia's value has slumped costs have soared. Misha also produces and exports honey and reed used for thatch. The problem is that the Chinese are among his greatest competitors in both fields and the Chinese have launched dirty disinformation campaigns to discredit Ukrainian honey. He is happy that after the Maidan revolution Ukraine finally signed a trade deal with the EU but complained that its honey quota was far too small. One consequence of that he lamented would be the continuation of a problem they already had before the deal, i.e. honey smuggling. This meant that Ukrainian honey ended up packaged and sold as German honey. 'And it is the same with reeds.' On a positive note, that day he had a meeting with partners from EU countries about using reed as a biomass energy source.

The result of the drama of the last twenty-three years and the sheer difficulty of surviving here have left at least some of the older generations in Vilkovo 'sympathetic' to Russia, 'as they want a strong government', Misha said. Ever since independence Ukrainian governments had been simply incapable and none had done anything for Vilkovo. But of those who look to Russia, while they know their own difficult situation, the problem is that there are 'two Russias'. They see St Petersburg and Moscow which are one but do not see the other, the rest of the country where 'their standard of living is even worse than here'. Sympathy for Russia seems a vague and not very passionate force, however. In Misha's view most people here are apolitical; if called up to serve in the Ukrainian army they would do so, but equally 'they would serve the other side the same'.

Misha always supported pro-European parties but now, although he and his friends were the local partisans of the Maidan revolution, he cannot understand what President Poroshenko and Prime Minister Arseniy Yatseniuk are doing. They can't even open legal cases for corruption against Yanukovych and his cronies. 'This sleepy regime needs to be woken up!'

The next day Misha's son Alexei, who is thirty-two, took me on a speedboat down to the sea. It was cold, clear and bright. He thought that politically people here were divided along generational lines. 'Now we have children who are pro-Ukrainian and parents who are pro-Russian.' But the younger generation are disappearing because of the lack of work. Of his school class of thirty students only five remained in Vilkovo.

We saw reedbeds, stacks of cut and bundled reed ready to go and the odd fisherman. We passed a derelict Soviet communications-cum-watchtower. As we went by an island Alexei said seventy families used to live there but now there were only ten. There is no

electricity and people scrape along by fishing, growing their own vegetables and selling food to holidaymakers. I asked Alexei if, since this place is so isolated, there was much smuggling here, but he said there was not, because on the Romanian side of the river there were hardly any people as 'it is even worse than here'. Some of the old houses on the riverbank and islands have been bought by people from Odessa as holiday homes and some new ones have been built, but said Alexei they don't do them up nicely because they don't want to draw attention to them. This is either because of thieves or because the law is such a mess of contradictions that most of them exist in a legal limbo and, until the rules have been reformed and clarified, people cannot legalize their properties here.

As we came closer to the coast birds skimmed and whirled. The coastline is always changing here. Sediment and sand constantly form new low islands and sandbanks. Finally, we came to where this branch of the river flows out to the sea. A monument has been erected on the beach and become slightly lopsided. It is black, made of steel and says 'Okm'. It means 'kilometre zero'. It is supposed to refer to the end of the river, but might as well refer to the end, or the beginning, of Ukraine.

IV. EASTERN APPROACHES

23.

The Coal Launderers

Vladimir Vygonnyi is a wiry seventy-something. Even though there was no war on the morning we met he was wearing a khaki uniform including a military-style cap and badge. Later I found an article from 2005 which described him as wearing the same thing. Vygonnyi wanted to show me something. We drove on a churned-up road until we got to a massive gash in the landscape. It was an illegal opencast coalmine. Vygonnyi said he had been an activist of one sort or another since 1964. In 1985, when Mikhail Gorbachev assumed power in the Soviet Union, he, like many others in communist countries, tested the political water by creating

an ecological action group. He has been fighting ever since and Zuivka, an hour's drive due east of Donetsk, is about as hard a place to be an ecologist and activist as any in Europe.

At first many thought him an eccentric but, in 2001, he spearheaded a successful campaign to stop the construction of two factories, which would have spewed high levels of pollution over the area. Now the issue is, or at least was before the war, *kopanki*, or small illegal mines. In difficult times, he explained, locals had always taken to a bit of DIY cottage mining to make ends meet or simply to heat their homes. With coal so close to the surface it is not hard to do. But the last fifteen years or so have seen a complete transformation of this into a multimillion-dollar criminal industry. In 2012 Ukraine produced 61.1 million tonnes of thermal coal, which is the type usually used in power plants. But examinations of the amount of coal moved by Ukraine's railways showed that much more than that was being shifted. Estimates varied but between 5.8 and 7 million tonnes of coal were believed to have been mined and sold illegally. Almost all of that was in Donetsk and Lugansk, and Zuivka was one of the most important centres of the business.

On the day we visited there was heavy machinery in the pit but there were no miners. Still, in this and other illegal mines, explained Vygonnyi, miners got salaries which were far smaller than even in state-owned mines and 'there are no social guarantees if you are injured or killed. They just dump bodies somewhere. Five were found like that last year in this region alone.' Once the land here is dug for coal it means, of course, that it is lost for agriculture. Like elsewhere in Ukraine, locals received land when the collective farms were broken up. As the law stands, they cannot sell it but only pass it on to their heirs or rent it. Everywhere else people rent their land to agro-industry companies who thus consolidate large areas for commercial farming. Here, with coal just under the surface, mining companies had moved in. Ordinary people might want to use their land to raise cattle or grow something, but with so much money to be made in illegal mining this is becoming more difficult in places like Zuivka. 'People are afraid,' said Vygonnyi. If they refused a demand to use their land for mining: 'They would be threatened or killed. Only in Zuivka they want to take 10,000 hectares.' So far they had taken only 1,000 but he pointed out 'there are thousands of villages like this'.

Nikolai Ponomarenko, the mayor of Zuivka, tried to stand up for people and stop the illegal mines. Allegedly he refused the illegal miners' bribes. Then, said Vygonni, 'they planted $10,000 in his car and the police arrested him. He was killed in jail, in pre-trial detention in August 2011.' Officially he died of a heart attack.

The illegal mining industry began to grow in the 1990s as fifty-two of the most unprofitable mines were shut down. Profitable mines were privatized and many of them now belong to Rinat Akhmetov, Ukraine's richest man and once most powerful oligarch. Up to now state-owned mines have continued to be heavily subsidized though. And this is where the great criminal opportunity opened up. Companies could buy, or illegally mine coal cheaply and feed this into the state mining system which gave them a handsome profit paid for by the taxpayer. A detailed study conducted by the Organized Crime and Corruption Reporting Project (OCCRP), a well-known and reputable investigative organization that concentrates on the former communist countries of Europe, calculated that some $678 million had been stolen in 2012 in this way. The government coal subsidy, it said, 'is in effect siphoned from state mines into private pockets, as the mines claim to be producing more coal than they actually do produce'. It cited the example of one mine which exceeded its planned monthly output by 20 to 30 per cent when coal extraction in 2012 rose by less than 5 per cent. It also noted a second scam, to create companies to sell mining equipment to state-owned mines. The crucial issue was who was at the heart of all this. According to Vygonnyi it was a pyramid which led all the way to the top, that is to say to local boy made good, President Yanukovych. Vygonnyi said he had been writing to the local prosecutor to do something about illegal mining but unsurprisingly nothing had happened. People said to him: 'How come you are still alive?'

The OCCRP report was more specific about who was making money and how. It followed the paper trails via the British Virgin Islands and Switzerland and proved what many locals believed but could never prove themselves – that the heart of the business was actually controlled by Oleksandr Yanukovych, the president's son, and various presidential cronies. As we walked around the deserted mine, which might have stopped work because of the highly unstable situation in the east, Vygonnyi talked about the demonstrations by anti-Maidan pro-Russians in Donetsk. The people organizing them, he said, 'are hoping for Russian support, so they will not be punished for their crimes . . . Donbass is a bandit region and for local people things have become worse and worse since the 1990s.' The local political-cum-mafia classes were not just stealing money, they were 'carrying it out in suitcases. They are stealing our land too and our air, which is very polluted with methane gas which is everywhere and destroying our ecology. People are dying early because of the ecological situation.'

In the muddy centre of the village Vygonnyi laid out a large map to explain where the mines were and showed us a monument he had built with his own hands and money to honour local miners. The centrepiece was a small pyramid in the middle of which was a kind of shrine containing a miner's hammer, helmet and lamp.

A few hours later, when we got back to Donetsk, we found that the local Berkut, the riot police, many of whom had fought the revolutionaries in Kiev, had just seized the regional police headquarters. It was 12 April 2014. The war was beginning. Within months many of the region's mines were flooded. The rebels raided them for explosives and detonators. Some miners joined the rebels but many did not. They were trapped. If Ukraine wins the war, many mines will close as subsidies come to an end and more will lose their jobs. If the rebels win, the area will remain what it had already become a year later, an economic twilight zone with virtually no economic future whatsoever.

24.

The Welsh and the Wild East

Donetsk is the epicentre of the conflict. It has always had a reputation as a rough and ready kind of place, though before the war, during the 2012 UEFA European Championship football matches for example, there would be no reason for a foreigner at least to know this. It has a superb, even beautiful modern football stadium, the home of Shakhtar Donetsk, the team owned, like so much else of value here, by Rinat Akhmetov. (Shakhtar means 'miner'. Since the beginning of the war the team has gone into exile, playing their 'home' matches in Lviv.) The town centre is pleasant and families and friends like to stroll and bike along its lake shore. In fact, said Liliia Ivaschenko, aged twenty-six, when she worked for the brewers Carlsberg, looking after its guests during the five Euro 2012 matches played in Donetsk, she really felt that her city had made it, that its difficult two decades of transition from communism were over, and that even if its politics and business verged on the thuggish, somehow Donetsk was not such a bad place to live in after all.

Before the war the city was home to some 900,000 people. But, as in Lviv, though for completely different reasons, almost nobody here can trace their ancestry back more than a couple of generations. Until 1870, there was nothing here except for the nearby village of Alexandrovskaya. This was windblown steppe and sparsely populated as a result of three centuries of Tatar slave raiding. The region was taken by Catherine the Great in the late eighteenth century and became part of her dominion of New Russia or Novorossiya. Not much happened here on the steppe until Russia lost the Crimean War in 1856 and its leaders realized they needed to modernize, industrialize and build railways to connect the expanding but disparate parts of the empire. What happened next was perhaps serendipity. Two Russian envoys despatched to London to discuss modern steel fortifications for the Kronstadt fort near St Petersburg met a Welshman called John Hughes, who ran a factory which could make them in Millwall in east London. Hughes could barely read or write but he was a smart man, which was why he was running the factory. They discussed the fact that there was coal and iron ore in the Donbas region. As Hughes came from south Wales, his background was steeped in these industries so he decided to explore the possibilities there.

By 1869 the New Russia Company was formed, investors were committed, permissions, leases and titles negotiated and the following year Hughes, plus a group of some 150 mainly Welsh specialists, set sail for the Sea of Azov. From Taganrog, now in Russia, their equipment was hauled up by ox-train to where Hughes had decided to mine and work. And so Donetsk, or Hughesovka as it was called until after the Russian Revolution, was born. The coal was good quality and Hughes concentrated on producing rails for the rapidly expanding Russian railway network. At first it was hard to find enough workers, but he made sure their conditions were better than in other places, even if not great, and Hughes's city began to grow. In 1871 it had a population of 480. By 1884 this number had grown to 5,500, by 1901 to 36,000 and by 1916 to 70,000. A 1917 census found that Russians were the largest single group in the city, followed by Jews and third were Ukrainians.

According to Roderick Heather, who wrote a biography of Hughes published in 2010: 'The industrialisation of the Donbass started by Hughes initiated a wave of migration in the latter part of the nineteenth century.' As a whole, 'Ukrainians showed much less enthusiasm for migration to the new Donbass mining settlements and factory towns with only a third of new settlers coming from the neighbouring Ukrainian regions.' There was a reason for this. Because relatively few lived on the steppe, those who did had comparatively large farms and hence there was less pressure on them to move for work in a period of rapid population growth. Thus they tended to remain in the countryside, Russians became industrial workers and Jews worked in trade and were craftsmen. So, as Heather writes, the region 'proved an attractive destination for people from the Russian provinces of Kursk, Orel, Voronezh, Tula, Smolensk, Samara and Belorussia as well as Greeks and Tatars from the Crimea, Croats from the Austro-Hungarian Empire, Serbs and Bulgarians from the Ottoman Empire, Germans, Austrians, Poles and Jews.' The result of this was the emergence in the Donbass of largely Russified towns set 'against a Ukrainian rural backdrop'. Thus, he says:

> it became increasingly rare to hear Ukrainian spoken in the towns like Hughesovka. Inevitably this ethnic melting pot led to friction and recurring clashes. The relations between Russians and Ukrainians were particularly strained in both towns and workers' settlements, leading to confrontations and frequent knife fights. The Tatars and Muslims were often the victims of violence by Slavs and almost every strike or labour protest in the Donbass ended in violent riots and large scale anti-Jewish pogroms.

Today, oddly, the large and grand redbrick house in which Hughes lived with his family is a ruin. It is surrounded by a fence of wire and hedge. A stone's throw away is the huge industrial complex which has descended from Hughes's original mines and foundry. A local man I found working as a security guard nearby as I hunted for people who knew something about the building told me that, as long as he could remember – and he was a child after the Second World War – the building had been a ruin. Before the war, he thought it had been used as offices for the directors of the complex. In 1991 descendants of the Hughes family returned to visit the town and house and were told of plans to turn it into a museum.

In 1908 the fourteen-year-old Nikita Khrushchev, who was born in the village of Kalinovka in Russia, close to the modern border with Ukraine, joined his parents who had already moved here. William Taubman, his biographer, quotes Khrushchev as writing in 1958 that it seemed to him 'that Karl Marx had actually been at the mines' and that 'he had based his laws on what he had observed of our lives'. The British and other foreigners lived in what was called the 'English colony', which had, according to Taubman, 'neat houses, treelined streets, electricity, and a central water system'. But ordinary miners and factory workers lived in settlements 'known as Shanghais and Dogsvilles'. One of them was called 'Bitch' and another 'Croak'. In 1910, says Taubman, 'residents hauled water from twenty-seven hand pumps scattered around town; the only pump house served the foreigners. Teeming barracks housed fifty to sixty men in each dormitory room.'

Cholera, typhoid and dysentery were frequent visitors to town. Using an alternative spelling for Hughesovka, Taubman notes that many of its residents 'took refuge in drink and crime':

> In 1908 the town boasted no fewer than thirty-three wine and liquor shops. From these it was a short step to mayhem. The writer Konstantin Paustovsky, who spent a year in Yuzovka, witnessed fights that spread until 'the whole street joined in. Men came out with leaded whips and knuckle dusters, noses were broken and blood flowed.' In 1912 a visiting journalist described Yuzovka this way: 'All the dregs of mining industry life gather here. Everything is dark, evil and criminal-thieves, hooligans, all such are drawn here.

The civil war and revolution saw the city change hands several times. The Donbass, like all of the wider region, was contested by the communists, the anti-revolutionary Whites, anarchists, supporters of Ukrainian independence and other groups. For a brief period German troops controlled the city. From December 1917 Red Guards and Whites clashed 'in and around Hughesovka' according to Heather, who notes why it was so hotly contested:

> At the end of the First World War, the region had been producing 87% of Russia's coal output, 76% of its pig iron, 57% of its steel, more than 90% of its coke, over 60% of its soda and mercury as well as important manufactured and agricultural goods. It was with

good reason that Vladimir Lenin, the leader of the Russian Bolshe-
viks, then described the Donbass as not merely 'an indispensable
area' but 'a region, without which the entire construction of social-
ism would just be a piece of wishful thinking.'

In 1918 the Soviet Donetsk–Krivoy Rog Republic was declared in a
bid to resist the German-supported Ukrainian People's Republic,
which was attempting to take control of the country in the wake of
the Russian imperial collapse. In 1919, says Heather, three tanks supplied to the Whites by the British were used in action near
Hughesovka. By 1921 the fighting was over, but the region afflicted
by famine. The Soviets now began the reconstruction of the city
which, after seeing its population drop during the civil war, saw it
shoot up to 174,000 by 1926. Immediately after the war the city was
renamed for Trotsky but in March 1924 it became Stalin. It is widely
assumed that Hughesovka was named for the new Soviet leader, but
in fact this is not true. The word *stal* means 'steel' and the local communist leadership thought it appropriate, and in their dedication
linked the name to that of Lenin and his steely attributes. Very soon
after this, however, it was reported in the press that the town had
been renamed for Stalin and it seemed judicious, as he consolidated
his power, to let people assume that this was indeed the case and that
the local leadership had been the first off the mark in the USSR to
honour their new leader. In 1929 the name was slightly tweaked to
become Stalino.

As the city began to recover, piped water was laid on, writes
Colin Thomas, who made a three-part documentary about the
town in 1991. Thousands of peasants in the countryside around
Stalino were taught to read and write and material conditions
began to improve for the city's workers too. But, in 1928, the secret
police claimed to have discovered a 'counter-revolutionary plot'
and, as Thomas writes, this led 'to the arrest of half of all engineers
and technical workers in the area and the consequent swift promotion for those below them in hierarchy'. The town's cathedral was
torn down by the party and collectivization began. This was

followed by the campaign against the *kulaks*, which was to see hundreds of thousands from all over the Soviet Union sent into exile or executed. The result was that, even before the *Holodomor* of 1932–3, which would hit the region badly, starvation began to set in around Stalino.

One of the few Western journalists to cover the *Holodomor* truthfully (some infamously did not) was a Welshman called Gareth Jones. His interest in the area came via Hughesovka. His mother had been a tutor there before the revolution to some of Hughes's grandchildren. In August 1930 he managed to get to Stalino. Ten days later he wrote to his parents: 'In the Donetsk Basin conditions are unbearable. Thousands are leaving. I shall never forget the night I spent in the railway station on the way to Hughesovka. One reason why I left Hughesovka so quickly was that all I could get to eat was a roll of bread – and that is all I had up to seven o'clock. Many Russians are too weak to work.' Thomas also records that in September he had an article in the *Western Mail* which was headlined: 'Starving Miners' Flight from Communism, Famous Steel Centre No Longer Prosperous'.

In October 1941 Stalino was taken by German and Italian troops. The war devastated the city and region. As the Axis forces approached, many miners and others, including Jews, fled or were evacuated, many with their companies. Thousands of those who remained behind were sent as slave labourers to the west. The Holocaust was prosecuted in this region with as much ferocity as anywhere else. In Mariupol, on the Black Sea coast, Jews were shot. In Yenakievo 555 Jews were rounded up, driven to nearby Gorlovka and thrown alive down a mine shaft. In Artyomovsk, some 3,000 Jews were herded into an alabaster mine just outside town where they died of suffocation and starvation. In Stalino itself a ghetto was established and thousands killed, many by being shot and then disposed of down a mine which was no longer working, called 4-4 Bis. Ukrainian police collaborated in this, but as elsewhere at least some Jews were saved by their neighbours, and not only Jews were murdered by the Nazis and their helpers. Gas vans were also used in Stalino.

Stalino was liberated in September 1943 and reconstruction, including the draining of flooded mines, began all over again. And then, yet again, famine hit the region in 1946–7. Men came home from the war but for years women vastly outnumbered them and so many were sent into the mines to work. Gradually, a new city was born and the layout of the centre and suburbs we have today was laid down in this period. These were years of hope, and older people have fond memories of them. I met Galina Konstantinivna, an economist and academic, who was born in 1937 and lived as a child in a village near the city. Her background was typical. Her mother was Russian but her family had originally come from Latvia and her father was from the ancient Greek community which once thrived on the Black Sea coast.

Among Galina's earliest memories are 'not having enough to eat' but being 'surrounded by love'. She recalled being loaded into a freight truck in 1941 and evacuated to Saratov, a town in Russia on the Volga river. The family came back in 1943 immediately after the Germans were expelled. She did not see white bread until years

after the war was over. As a child, she had to chip in like everyone else to help with work and so 'we managed to reconstruct the destroyed city in five or seven years'. When I asked her which were the best periods of the city's history after this, she replied that one of them was at the beginning of the 1960s when the city and region were dominated by communist boss Vladimir Degtyarov (1920–93). 'He was very authoritarian,' she recalled. If he walked through the city, renamed Donetsk in 1961, and saw some rubbish, woe betide the person responsible. Degtyarov stamped his mark on the city. After a visit to Versailles he is said to have sent Donetsk's gardeners to France to learn about landscape design, which was then to be applied on their return. In this way the town acquired the name of the 'City of a Million Roses'.

As for the second period of hope and optimism in the city, Konstantinivna said: 'You will be surprised!' It started in 1997 when Viktor Yanukovych, who came from nearby Yenakievo, became governor. 'At first I laughed when he became governor,' she said. After all he had spent time in jail for assault and robbery, 'but after two years I saw a different economy emerging. Yes, there was stealing but also development. The corruption was corrosive and we did not like it and we tried to change things, but greed trumped fairness.' Still, 'we could never have imagined that that period would be followed by this one'. It is worth noting that Ukraine as a whole began to see economic growth in 2001 after its decade of post-communist collapse.

We sat in Konstantinivna's kitchen where she had packets of food aid with stickers showing that they had been donated by Rinat Akhmetov, Ukraine's richest man, who had once backed Yanukovych. He was born in 1966, his father was a miner and his mother a shop assistant. How he became the new John Hughes is another story, but one that sits well within the Donetsk tradition of being the hard city of Ukraine's wild east. Now his Donbass Arena stadium, the home of Shakhtar Donetsk, was being used as a base to distribute his aid. In exchange perhaps for his help in feeding so many people the rebels left his property alone, despite earlier threats to nationalize it.

25.

The View from the Terricone

In writing and speaking about the war many people talk about geo-politics, about propaganda and about Vladimir Putin. That is all fine. What is less well understood abroad are some of the social and demographic aspects that underpin the conflict. Some years ago a group of European academic institutions came together to study a series of 'shrinking cities', that is to say places whose populations had been dropping dramatically over the last few decades. The Shrink Smart project included Liverpool, the Italian port of Genoa, Timisoara, famous as the birthplace of the Romanian revolution in 1989, Leipzig and Halle in the former East Germany and Donetsk and neighbouring Makiivka.

The population of Ukraine as a whole has suffered a dramatic decline since independence. In 1993 it peaked at 52.18 million but by 2013 it was estimated to have fallen back to 45.49 million. So, although it is a general phenomenon, the specifics of what has happened in Donetsk and Donbass do help explain some of the anger that the ideologists of separatism or of joining Russia were able to capitalize on when the war began. The work done on Donetsk in the Shrink Smart project, undertaken by Ukrainian researchers and published in 2010, also provides answers to one of the biggest pan-Ukrainian gripes. People in Donbass often say that they are fed up with subsidizing the rest of Ukraine, while those in the west and centre say they are fed up with their taxes subsidizing the smoke-stack, rustbelt industries of Donbass. Inevitably perhaps, the truth comes in shades of grey rather than black and white.

Donetsk, and much of the rest of Donbass, is surrounded by slag heaps from the mines. Locally they call them *terrikons*, which

might be better transliterated as 'terricones'. Some are perfect pyramids, some are hills covered in trees and shrubs and some of them rise to become strange, other-worldly plateaus. On one of Donetsk's largest, a network of garages was built in the 1970s to anchor it down. From here, the men who frequent them and who have long used them for all manner of secretive businesses such as illegal brewing or, more recently, to hide cars in concealed garages to keep them out of the clutches of armed robbers, can watch the shelling of Donetsk from one side or look down on the neighbouring city of Makiivka from the other.

The population of Donetsk peaked at 1.1 million in 1992 and dropped to 974,598 by 2009, a decline of 13.1 per cent. Makiivka's population plummeted by almost 21 per cent, though the region as a whole did even worse, losing almost a third of its inhabitants by 2007. The main reason for this was a collapse in the birth rate coupled with high death rates. While male life expectancy had been 63.87 years in 1991, by 2008 it had dropped to 60.35 years. What this meant was that the Donetsk–Makiivka conurbation's residents were among the oldest in Europe but paradoxically those with 'the shortest lifespan on average'. The region was becoming older because fewer babies were born, the young, especially the educated, were choosing to leave and the old were dying younger.

Between 2001 and 2007 all of Ukraine went through a period of economic recovery, but it was patchy. While the economies of Donetsk and Mariupol on the coast started to strengthen, Makiivka began to be left behind. According to the report:

> As late as 2007, the overall level of economic activity has not yet recovered to its 1990 level. Even after almost a decade of revival, the area remains a lower-middle income economy. Donetsk region's gross domestic product per capita stands at only €2,000. In August 2007, the average monthly wage in the Donetsk region was €230. The protracted neglect and lack of public investment into housing, heating, transport, and environmental protection infrastructure has resulted in the degradation of urban landscape (outside the city centres) and natural environment, and the overall retrogression of the urban quality of life. Combined with seriously under-financed healthcare and educational systems, the negative consequences of economic transition only exacerbate the demographic crisis faced by Greater Donetsk and the Donbass.

In Donetsk, while mining and metallurgy remained important, their share of the economy dropped. Donetsk modernized and began to create white-collar jobs (unlike Makiivka) but as the report noted new jobs 'were in market consumer or producer services, which required from applicants . . . a different skill set from the traditional coal and steel vocations. Manual industrial workers and, most prominently, the unskilled and low-skilled personnel have been the main losers of the urban economic reconstruction.' In Makiivka 6,000 steel workers lost their jobs in 2008 when the Kirov Iron and Steel Works had to close because of the drop in demand due to the world financial crisis. Meanwhile, in Donetsk new apartment blocks and houses were shooting up to accommodate the new middle class while old Soviet blocks increasingly became the homes of the elderly and the poor. Drugs, Aids and crime were big issues. Growth was driven in Donetsk by two of the biggest companies in Ukraine, one being Rinat Akhmetov's System Capital Management, and the other being the Industrial Union of Donbas, dominated by Sergei Taruta, another fabulously rich, albeit comparatively minor oligarch.

Now look at how people identify themselves. According to the 2001 census 77.8 per cent of the population in Ukraine saw themselves as Ukrainian and 17.3 per cent as Russian. For the oblast or province of Donetsk those figures were 56.9 per cent and 38.2 per cent respectively, but for the city of Donetsk it was 46.7 per cent Ukrainian and 48.2 per cent Russian. With regard to the wider Donbass however, and if you gave people the option of a regional identity, the report noted that 41 per cent identified themselves as Ukrainian, 11 per cent described themselves as being 'Soviet' and 48 per cent opted for a regional or local identity of 'Donbas', 'Donetsk', etc. Ukrainian was the mother tongue of 11.1 per cent in Donetsk and similar figures prevailed in the rest of Donbass, though the number of children being educated in Ukrainian was shooting up. But these ethnic-cum-nationality issues when reflected in percentages should not be interpreted as rigid and inflexible, in the sense of people being *either* Ukrainian or Russian or Ukrainians speaking Russian. Simply because there were more Russians here meant that there was more intermarriage too. A survey from 1991 found that almost three quarters of Russians here said they had close Ukrainian relatives and in 1992 some 47.7 per cent of children were born to parents of different backgrounds though their own parents were just as likely to be of mixed identities. Bearing all this in mind, and that this part of Ukraine, being Russian-speaking, watched more Russian TV and fell more within Russia's cultural and media sphere than Ukraine's, it is not surprising that when Putin says that Ukrainians and Russians are practically the same, here at least his words have resonance. Also, noted the Shrink Smart report, which we should remember was written well before the war:

The Donbas's absence of cultural and ethno-linguistic affinity with the Ukrainian nationalist project, combined with the depth of the economic depression suffered by the region and its large industrially oriented cities in the wake of the dissolution of the USSR on 26 December 1991, have led to a creeping sense of alienation in the region . . . Ukrainian identity politics have eventually added to unhappiness, depression and psychological stress in the Donbas, exacerbating out-migration pressures and adding to mental health problems amongst most of the urban dwellers.

As to the question of where money was going and who was subsidizing whom in Ukraine, the answers begin to become clear. Ukraine has twenty-seven regions. Before the war Kiev was the richest, Donetsk was the fifth richest. Seven regions of Ukraine contributed more to the central budget than they gained. Crimea and Lugansk were net gainers. But within Donetsk oblast some areas were much better off than others, so the picture was complicated not least because much of the mining industry was subsidized by the state, i.e. by the taxes of all Ukrainians. Nevertheless one can see how, when the time came, there was dry tinder in Donbass. Many here had been part of the Soviet working-class elite, that is to say well-paid and well-regarded miners and industrial workers. The end of the Soviet Union stripped them of status and in many cases jobs and comparatively their standards of living, including in the provision of healthcare, declined. At the same time individuals such as Akhmetov came to own the most profitable assets of the region and, while local politicians such as Yanukovych could boost local pride and help the employment of those close to his party, in reality and despite monikers such as 'pro-Russian' he and they were not. They were pro themselves.

Most of the issues that afflicted Donetsk and Donbass were not unique to them, but the low level of identification with Ukraine, the fact that the most pro-Ukrainian part of the population was the comparatively small but educated middle class, who mostly fled as the war began, meant that there remained plenty of angry people here ready to believe that this was the moment to take action to better their lives when the flags of the Donetsk and Lugansk People's Republics were raised. If they had known that supporting them would spark war and the now probable economic death of their region, history would have been very different.

In terms of population the war has been a catastrophe, especially bearing in mind that the region had lost almost a third of its inhabitants well before the conflict began. By spring 2015, from the wider Donbass region afflicted by the conflict, some 45 per cent were believed to have fled, either west into Ukrainian-controlled territory or to Russia. The educated middle class tended to flee west and, as the fighting dragged on and people began new lives elsewhere, it was clear that fewer and fewer would ever return, whatever peace eventually looked like.

26

Getting to 'Yes'

On 11 May 2014 the rebel authorities held a referendum in which people were asked: 'Do you support the act of state-self rule of the Donetsk People's Republic?' Since pro-Ukrainians boycotted it or had fled and anyway the referendum was a chaotic affair, it is quite possible that 89.7 per cent of those who voted – and no one knows for sure how many did – actually said 'yes'. In the DNR the rebels claimed a 74.87 per cent voter turnout but the Ukrainian Ministry of Interior claimed the figure was 32 per cent. Meanwhile, the Ukrainian presidential election was due to be held on 25 May and posters

for a couple of candidates had gone up in Donetsk, though the DNR authorities would prevent this from happening in the territory they controlled and it was far too dangerous for anyone to campaign here.

A week before the Ukrainian poll I went to a cigarette kiosk in Donetsk and asked the woman inside how business was. As the war was beginning, all those I had previously asked unsurprisingly said business was terrible. Well, she said, as everyone was stressed, they were smoking more and so it was pretty good in fact. But she added angrily, 'I am so tired . . . I just want peace and quiet.' While we talked a stream of people came and went buying cigarettes. Everyone agreed with her. When I asked her about the presidential elections she said that she supported Ukrainian unity but not the current government in Kiev, 'which took power by force'. One of the election posters was for the new leader of Yanukovych's old party, which used to have overwhelming support in Donetsk. About the two candidates whose posters could be seen in the city one woman, picking up her cigarettes, snapped that they were 'werewolves'. I asked a dishevelled old lady what she thought of Denis Pushilin, one of the main separatist leaders, and she said shrilly: 'What did he do? My pension has not increased!'

Two girls came by and a middle-aged female Jehovah's Witness who opined that everything that was happening was God's will. The girls, who were both seventeen, said their parents wanted to vote but did not know whom for. The Jehovah's Witness gave them some leaflets, the only ones being handed out in this election in the east, and wandered off. Then one of the girls said that her parents had voted in Donetsk's referendum. Whatever happened, said Nastia, they just wanted there to be 'no war'. The woman in the kiosk was getting hot and bothered. She excused herself and slammed shut the tiny window to preserve the cool air from her air conditioning inside.

I could have interviewed as many analysts and political scientists as I wanted but would never have got as concise a snapshot of what people in the east were thinking as that. Not only did they not feel represented by any politician but, when it came to what the DNR was about, there was utter confusion. Some had thought they were voting for independence in its referendum, but others for autonomy within Ukraine and hence they could still vote for the country's president. The reason it was so unclear in the DNR was because the term 'state-self rule' could be interpreted in different ways, and presumably this was done intentionally to lure voters who were against independence but in favour of a federal structure for Ukraine, which had been discussed over the years. (The Lugansk question was much clearer and asked about 'state independence'.)

What was also clear, if you look at the past, is that people here, as in the rest of Ukraine, are always 'for' something, because they want their future to be better than their past. In recent history too supporters of one side or another always point to a referendum in which people have voted *for* something they approved of, and then ignore the ones where they have voted for something they do not want.

On 17 March 1991 for example, Mikhail Gorbachev, the last Soviet leader, held a referendum in which people were asked whether they wanted to preserve the USSR 'as a renewed federation of equal sovereign republics'. The Baltic states, Georgia, Armenia and Moldova did not take part and a boycott was called for in western Ukraine. Still 71.48 per cent of those who voted in Ukraine did so for a renewed USSR and, although this was the lowest 'yes' figure in the Soviet Union among all those who voted, it was still overwhelming. However, in Ukraine, people were asked some separate questions as well. Did they want Ukraine to be 'part of a Union of Soviet Sovereign States on the basis of the Declaration of State Sovereignty of Ukraine?' The meaning of this was extremely opaque, at least to ordinary people. In fact this had been adopted in the Verkhovna Rada the year before and amounted to a virtual declaration of independence. It established that Ukrainian law, not Soviet law, was supreme, that the republic had the right to its own army and so on. The answer to that was 'yes' too with 81.7 per cent, and it meant that a majority had been voting 'yes' simultaneously to ideas which in reality could never be reconciled. At the same time people in the west, in Lviv, Ternopil and Ivano-Frankivsk were asked if they wanted complete independence, to which the answer was again 'yes' by 88.3 per cent.

All this voting was obviously too much for the old guard and it was clear to them that it was a factor in the dissolution of the state. But it was their own rearguard action which was to deliver the final blow to the USSR, when they launched a coup against Gorbachev in August 1991. Leonid Kravchuk, the canny Ukrainian leader, was noncommittal until it was clear that the coup would be defeated and then came out against it. Then the Verkhovna Rada voted in favour of independence by 346 to 1.

On 1 December Ukrainians were voting again. They were asked if they supported the act of independence. This time 92.26 per cent were in favour. Not a single region voted against, including traditionally pro-Russian Crimea, which voted 54 per cent in favour. The next two regions with the lowest support were Donetsk and Lugansk, which still voted 'yes' by 83.9 per cent and 83.3 per cent respectively. For many nothing was really clear. Many believed that independence would mean a new start, but at the same time everyone in the Soviet Union would somehow stay together under the umbrella of the new Commonwealth of Independent States – no one really knew, and indeed this is an important point. None of these referendums, which are often taken as such important benchmarks of popular will, was anything that anyone in the West would ever remotely accept for their own country. In no case were there years of erudite discussion, in the media above all, of the cases 'for' and 'against' as there were in Scotland in 2014 or Quebec in 1995 for example.

In Mariupol, I talked about the recent Donetsk referendum with Liubov Ivaschenko, a doctor aged sixty-one, and asked her what she had thought at the time of the 1991 independence referendum. 'I was very hopeful,' she said, 'but at the same time I felt nostalgia for Soviet times and for our capital Moscow.' This seemed to encapsulate something.

For many, those heady days of hope were to evaporate very quickly with the complete collapse of the economy. In Donetsk,

Crimea and some other places small groups agitated for a restoration of ties with Moscow and even a restoration of the USSR. So, in 1994, concurrent with the general election a new 'consultative' referendum was held in Donetsk and Lugansk. Consultative meant that it could be considered more of a glorified opinion poll rather than something with a legal status. People were asked if they wanted Russian to be a state language with equal status to Ukrainian, the language of the local administration, and whether they wanted a federal Ukraine. As usual the response was a resounding 'yes'. But then nothing happened. Small groups agitated, politicians from the east such as Yanukovych came to power, lost it and regained it and tiny groups grumbled, moaned and organized, some talking of restoring something called Novorossiya or the New Russia of Catherine the Great and some of the Donetsk Republic of 1918. Hardly anyone in the Donbass noticed these people or what they were doing on the far fringes of political life.

27.

Empire and Virility

When I first met Sergei Baryshnikov he was hurrying off to give aid to soldiers. A political scientist and a member of the DNR's then unelected parliament, at the beginning of September 2014 he was a man whose time had arrived. A few weeks later the DNR authorities appointed him to take over the university. He had worked here for some twenty years but resigned in 2012, although there were allegations that he had departed under a cloud and amid rumours of bribe-taking. As the war began he was part of the small group of pro-Russians who played a role in organizing the rebellion in

Donetsk and calling for Russian troops to intervene. As he left to hand out his aid, I asked him if there were any here and he replied enthusiastically, 'Yes, thousands!' Then, perhaps remembering that the official Russian position was that there are no regular troops in what he was calling 'the former Ukraine', he noted that all of them were 'volunteers'.

Officially the university has gone into exile in Vinnitsa in central Ukraine. Many academics and students have left and some are following courses online. But for those that remain, who either did not want to leave, could not leave or are academics not purged by Baryshnikov, he is now the boss. He is important not only because of that but because he is one of the leading ideologists of Novorossiya and the DNR. On his desk he has its flag and on the wall a portrait of Vladimir Putin. He is 'our president', he said, 'de facto, our leader'.

I wanted to discuss the origins of the DNR. In the early 1990s a welter of political organizations sprang up in the east, all trying to represent the Russian-speaking population of the Donbass and Ukraine. Most were small and now forgotten. But the one Baryshnikov mentioned was set up in 1989 and was called the Inter-Movement of Donbass. It aimed to preserve the USSR and was related to similar movements in the Baltic republics. One of its leaders was Dimitry Kornilov, a man who was fascinated by, and collected information about, the 1918 Donetsk–Krivoy Rog Republic and, according to a declaration of the DNR parliament in 2015, was the first to resurrect its flag in 1991.

At the time, said Baryshnikov, he was not so involved politically. He had just got married, just had a son and was preparing his doctorate. But he was against Gorbachev, because he said it was clear he was leading the Soviet Union to destruction. The Inter-Movement idea was to 'save a multinational sovereign state and stand against nationalistic ideas', in this case the nationalistic ideas being Ukrainian of course. Baryshnikov supported the coup against Gorbachev in August 1991. The problem with Donbass, though, was that unfortunately its people proved to be 'apolitical, passive and apathetic'. People like him who wanted to keep the USSR together and who might be prepared to do something about it were few and far between. Baryshnikov does not believe, however, that the numbers recorded of those who voted for independence in December 1991 are real.

In the ensuing few years he was involved with various organizations which militated for Russian language rights. When he was asked to teach in Ukrainian he refused. As to Yanukovych's later Party of Regions which, when in power, did pass language laws aiming to settle the issue of when Russian could and could not be used officially, he says the party was really just a disappointment. In 2012 Baryshnikov began to cooperate with a political activist called Andrei Purgin, who was one of the founders in 2005 of a tiny group called Donetsk Republic. It wanted to recreate the short-lived state, but, he said, they were only a handful of people, some of whom, like Purgin, are important today and some of whom are forgotten. The idea, he explained, was to create a federal state and then to separate from Ukraine. 'I was for joining Russia', Baryshnikov said. 'I had always been against Ukraine, politically and ideologically,' though he stopped here to say that what he did like about Ukraine was its food and its women. Now he was warming to his theme. Donbass should be part of Russia, he argued, because historically it had been part of Russia. In fact now the idea was to recreate a great and single Russia from the Far East to the Baltic states, which would have to become part of it. All of Ukraine should become part of this Russia except perhaps for Lviv and Galicia in the west, which had not been part of the Russian empire before the First World War. 'Ukraine should not exist.' The creation of the DNR, he explained, was just the 'first stage' and people like him had a 'historical mission' to complete.

> We have to destroy the idea of Ukrainian identity and its national idea. Who are Ukrainians? They are Russians who refuse to admit their Russian-ness . . . The Ukrainian idea is one which can be compared to a difficult disease, like cancer. I think we must suppress

it . . . the easiest and shortest way to do that is by war and repression. There is another way that is longer and that is psychologically and through evolutionary change, but we do not have time. The thing is, we want to do it fast and decisively, because we are under the threat of depopulation. If we prolong this process then there is a possibility that we will cease to exist as a national group and each year there are less and less Russians.

With disastrous demographics for Russians in general, in Donbass, not to mention Ukraine, it was unclear to me why destroying and subjugating Ukraine would change things. To Baryshnikov it was very clear: victory would restore Russian virility.

Russians need a triumph to give them historical inspiration. They need something to believe in for their own future and that of their grandchildren and that is the idea of greatness. My children and grandchildren must be Russians not neutral, uncertain and pro-European. There should be no multiculturalism. French must be French, Germans German and Serbs Serb and so on.

After the demise of Ukraine what would be next? Perhaps it could be Kazakhstan, whose ethnic Russian population was in 2009 a declining but considerable 23.7 per cent of the whole, much of it concentrated in areas adjacent to the Russian border. 'I believe that sooner or later the artificially divided Russian nation will be united again,' said Baryshnikov.

Everything that Baryshnikov believes is consistent with the beliefs of Alexander Dugin, the influential Russian philosopher and proponent of a Russian-dominated Eurasian empire which would not only reunite ethnic Russians but dominate the West too. Dugin has chastized Putin for being too soft on Ukraine, and is a visceral opponent of anything that smacks of Western liberalism. His philosophy has drawn elements from fascism and Stalinism and from the original proponents of Eurasianism who were White Russian exiles living in the West after the Russian Revolution. His views are often quasi-mystical and, to most Westerners and not a few Russians, deranged. But not to all. In the West he has his fans too and in the past at least was in contact with Alain de Benoist, a French philosopher and founder of the far-right New Right movement. He foresees a Europe returning to some form of pre-Christian past in which regional identities play a far more important role than today. As for Dugin though, Baryshnikov said, 'Yes we support his Eurasian project. He is our friend.'

A few minutes' walk away from Baryshnikov's office is that of Andrei Purgin. Before the war the 43-year-old had a small building materials business. Now he is the deputy prime minister of the DNR. On one wall of his office he has large photos of rearing sharks but he says he inherited these from the previous occupant of the office. He has a Soviet military flag, a portrait of Putin and, on his desk, a crystal ball in which, if you look at it from a certain angle, you can see Stalin's face. This was a gift, he laughed. 'We have nothing to do with Stalinism,' but he did not want to offend the Russian communist who gave him the crystal ball by not having it on his desk. Purgin was one of the founders of Donetsk Republic, the miniature group of political activists who from 2005 had been working to recreate the state of 1918. The group was born in the aftermath of the Orange Revolution of 2004 in whose wake Viktor Yuschenko, a man with Ukrainian nationalist credentials, became president.

The Donetsk Republic was a successor to the Inter-Movement of Donbass and also the groups which helped organize the referendum of 1994 on federalism. It had a newspaper and was close to the ideas of Dmitry Kornilov, who published a history of the 1918 republic. Dmitry died in 2002 but his work was carried on by his brother Vladimir. In 2007 criminal cases were opened against Purgin. He was accused of promoting and inciting inter-ethnic conflict. These accusations, he said with the polished skill of a man who knew the ins-and-outs of the Ukrainian legal code, are hard to prove and there was no evidence that he had been 'arming'. Yes, he conceded, they had a flag and coat of arms, a historical foundation for their claim 'and so on', and in this the DNR was unlike

Montenegro, which had become independent in 2006. 'It is no secret in Europe,' he said, that the little Balkan state had 'gained its independence though it had only had a week-long previous history of statehood', an assertion which is simply wrong. He claimed the aim of the indictments was to 'suppress' his group's ideas which 'were getting more and more popular'. In fact, hardly anyone in Donetsk had ever heard of them. After 2007, he explained, the organization developed as a kind of network, without a party structure in order to make it harder for the SBU, Ukraine's domestic intelligence service, to keep track of them.

> In different places people had different beliefs ranging from monarchists to nutballs via extreme leftist groups. The idea of regionalism and of protecting regional interests was non-ideological. It meant that people with absolutely different ideologies raised the flag of the Donetsk Republic which was the flag representing the protection of regional interests.

Small groups of young people did military training. 'We organized trips to the countryside,' Purgin said, for young people with 'patriotic inclinations'. Ukrainian sources say that these camps were facilitated, especially when held in Russia, by Russia's security services. There was a lot of cooperation with people in Lugansk and also with students and academics in Rostov and Voronezh in the neighbouring regions of Russia. Asked whether they also aimed to create an independent state, he said the question was wrong. 'When we started our activity Ukraine was still part of the "Russian World" and remained within the orbit of Russian Orthodox civilization, so the issue was only about federalization. American groups such as Freedom House, however, helped create civil society organizations in Ukraine and then the issue became pertinent.' Thus: 'It was impossible to stay in a state which aimed at deindustrialization. So, as Donbass is an industrial region, we came to the conclusion that federalism was not enough for solving the issue of protecting people.'

Freedom House is a human rights NGO that has long worked closely with USAID, which distributes US government money for human rights promotion as well as regular aid and which has been condemned as Russophobic by Russian officials. As far back as 2004 – before the founding of Donetsk Republic – it was also accused in Ukraine, Russia and the US of indirectly supporting organizations working to promote the election of Viktor Yushchenko.

For now it is too early to say to what extent or not Russia's security organizations promoted and assisted the takeover of buildings in Donetsk and elsewhere in the aftermath of the Maidan revolution. In the same way it is hard to know to what extent former Russian security officials such as Vladimir Antyufeyev and Igor Strelkov, who had prosecuted the war for the DNR from Sloviansk, were under the direct control of the Kremlin or not. Purgin said: 'We are not spontaneous revolutionaries. We are conscious revolutionaries.' In the wake of the fall of Yanukovych, 'people were literally seething all over Ukraine'. The way he put it, Ukraine's political players were playing chess, 'but then it turned out that one part of Ukraine continued playing chess but the other part took out a baseball bat'. In his mind, of course, that part is Ukraine, not the DNR.

Hunt on the internet and it's possible to find an old Donetsk Republic organization site which asks people to determine whether they are Ukrainian or Russian. This can be worked out by your answers to four questions: 'Do you talk and think in the Ukrainian language?'; 'Were your ancestors in the Wehrmacht or did your grandfather serve in the SS Galicia Division?'; 'Are you a Catholic?'; and finally, 'As a child were you brought up on the tales of Ivan Franko?' (the great Ukrainian poet). There is a map of Ukraine. It is divided and each section can be identified by its flag. Crimea is part of Russia. The east and south are the DNR, Odessa and Bessarabia are the Odessa Republic, the west is depicted with a Nazi flag and is identified as 'Galician Fascists', Transcarpathia is a separate little entity called Sub-Carpathian Rus and the remaining rump in the centre is simply Ukraine.

It is interesting that the map assigns Crimea to Russia but does not do the same for the rest of the east and south. Asked about the future, Purgin was a little ambiguous. Today, 'We don't consider ourselves as part of something separated from Russia. We consider ourselves as a part of the "Russian World". Therefore our intentions are close economic and political cooperation with the Russian Federation.' Only time will tell, he said, what form that will have, that is to say whether 'federal' or – referring to the Eurasian Union, launched by Putin in January 2015 – 'in such a form as Belarus and Kazakhstan'. The problem was that he could not see that far ahead. 'You can see that the world is going through a very serious crisis and it is unclear what the end will be.'

So, what about the other parts of the map? Again, he did not know. 'We are part of the industrial Ukraine that includes all the south-east,' and here he mentioned Kharkiv to the north, Odessa, the regions of Zaporizhia and Dnipropetrovsk and the industrial city of Krivoy Rog. 'We really hope that somehow we will be united with the rest of this industrial part . . . Moreover we hope that in the future we will somehow be able to help those people who are now left in Ukrainian-controlled territory and who are now persecuted by the Ukrainian authorities.' Clearly the most important target for the DNR is the port of Mariupol, but, 'sadly', so far it had proved impossible to take it. He pinned his hopes on Ukraine going bankrupt and it being very hard to keep Mariupol's angry and then unpaid people 'under the barrel of a large calibre machine gun . . . I think in the end the people of Mariupol themselves will decide its fate.' We were talking a few weeks after a second ceasefire agreement had been signed in Minsk in February 2015, but Purgin did not think the war was over. 'A civil war can finish only in two ways,' he opined. 'Either with the interruption of a third side or when both sides run out of people ready to fight.'

I asked a final question about Dugin and whether Purgin would regard him as a kind of ideologist of the DNR. The answer was 'No'. He knew him personally and 'I can't say I completely follow his theories but nevertheless I take my hat off to him because he is a remarkable person in the intellectual field. There aren't many people like him in the world.'

28.

Crimea: Because He Could

In Kiev, the end of the Maidan revolution was greeted with relief and by many of course with jubilation. However, while there was a respite for the people of Kiev, the end of one chapter in the Ukrainian drama was followed instantly by the beginning of a new one. Protests began in Crimea, the most pro-Russian part of Ukraine and the only one with an ethnic Russian majority, and armed men seized the autonomous region's parliament and other buildings. A referendum on union with Russia was held on 16 March 2014, though what proportion of Crimea's population, which was 58 per cent Russian, 24 per cent Ukrainian and 12 per cent Crimean Tatar, actually voted is unknown, unless you believe the 'official' figures of more than 80 per cent for Crimea and the city of Sebastopol, which is a separate jurisdiction. Those who opposed the break with Ukraine did not vote. The referendum was illegal under Ukrainian law and there was no pretence of this being a real exercise in democracy. Even if the majority of Crimeans were indeed in favour of reuniting with Russia, pro-Ukrainians were keeping a low profile and several Tatar activists were murdered or disappeared. There was no debate on the issue as, for example, there had been in Scotland for years before it voted against independence.

Within a month of the flight of Yanukovych from Kiev on the night of 21 February 2014, Vladimir Putin signed a degree making Crimea a part of Russia. In the past he had accepted that the peninsula, which had become part of Soviet Ukraine in 1954 when it made little difference to anyone, was an undisputed part of Ukraine. Now Putin compared it to overwhelmingly Albanian-inhabited Kosovo, which had broken away from Serbia and declared independence in 2008. Most Western countries recognized it but Russia did not. The comparison was spurious since Russians had not been oppressed in Crimea as Albanians had been in Serbia, and polls had showed that the majority of the population of Crimea had since independence been in favour of staying part of Ukraine. If the opportunistic seizure of Crimea had rather been characterized as revenge for NATO's seventy-eight-day bombing of Serbia during the Kosovo war in 1999, which the then enfeebled Russia had been unable to prevent, that might have been closer to the mark. It was a forceful way of saying 'Russia is back.' Like all such moves in politics, it set off a train of wholly unexpected events – though the same could be said of Yanukovych's balking at signing the EU deal the previous November.

Putin did what he did because he could. He had some 25,000 regular Russian troops there as part of Russia's Black Sea Fleet, whose presence had been secured by treaty, and he used them in a semi-covert way, only later confessing that they had been deployed. He had been rattled by protests against him during the winter of 2011–12 and this move, backed by the info-war against the 'fascist junta' of Ukraine, sent his popularity ratings shooting sky high again. Only one deputy in the 450-seat Russian Duma or parliament, Ilya Ponomaryov, voted against the annexation and he soon went into exile.

Just before this the Verkhovna Rada made a cardinal error. It voted to pass a law to downgrade the official status of the Russian language. This was immediately vetoed by Oleksandr Turchynov, the acting president, but the damage was done. It frightened many Russian speakers and gave Putin, the 'anti-Maidan' and pro-Russian constituency just what they needed in terms of 'proof' of their claims that neo-Nazi Ukrainian nationalists had taken over.

Why the Ukrainians did not use their military – some of whom defected – in Crimea to fight back is not hard to fathom. The government feared that if they gave the orders to fight this might not just prompt a crushing defeat in Crimea but trigger a full-scale invasion. In retrospect maybe that was a mistake. As Oleh Shamshur, a former ambassador to the US who then went on to represent his country in Paris, said: 'If a hooligan meets no resistance he is emboldened. We should have fought and resisted.'

More than a year later, as the May holidays approached, long lines of traffic waited to cross over into Crimea from the Ukrainian mainland, where once there was no border. Foreigners who needed a visa for Russia could not enter unless they had one. People crossing on foot were getting across relatively quickly, those in cars waited for hours and trucks were waiting for days. People blamed both sides for the delays, saying that one day the Ukrainians slowed things down and the next day it was the Russians. Lines of trenches had been dug on the Ukrainian side. Three roads lead to Crimea and all of them from Ukraine; Russia has no land connection to the peninsula. Along one, at the Kalanchak checkpoint, is the main canal supplying Crimea, and especially its agriculture. What remained at the bottom of it, now that the flow had been turned off by the Ukrainians, were just stagnant pools and sandbanks. All of Crimea's infrastructure is integrated with Ukraine's, which was one of the reasons why Khrushchev transferred the peninsula to Ukraine and not, as Russian legend would have it, because he was drunk.

UKRAINE

LUGANSK OBLAST

• Sloviansk

• Kramatorsk
Popasnaya •   • Pervomaysk

Kostyantynivka •   Lugansk •

Gorlovka •

Krasnoarmeysk •

Pervomais'sk •   • Donetsk
                    • Ilovaysk   • Savur-Mogila

DONETSK OBLAST   • Novokaterinivka

RUSSIA

Separatist-controlled
areas   Rostov-on-Don •
                                        Don R.

Mariupol •

Sea of Azov

29.

First Blood

Thinking back on it, it could have been a lyrical scene from an old art house movie. The soft breeze had scattered cherry blossom on the pile of earth that had been dug for the grave of the boy who was about to be buried. From the cemetery we could see for kilometres across the valley and the rolling green hills. Men from the village militia pointed to the horizon and said that their enemies were 'over there' somewhere. And then the funeral party came walking up the path from the village.

At their head was a man carrying a cross. Behind him, mixed in with family and friends in the procession, some men carried the lid of the coffin. Then came the pall-bearers. For the last time, the spring sun warmed the face of Aleksandr Lubenets, who looked as though he was asleep. He was twenty-one and in a few weeks, his father Vladimir told me, it would have been his birthday. 'He was very cheerful. He loved life. And then some bastard decided to end it. They shot him in the back.'

Aleksandr, and two of his mates from the village of Khrestysche, on the outskirts of Sloviansk, decided to investigate something. They were part of the local rebel militia, which had been manning the barricades there for the past few weeks. What exactly happened is unclear. Yevgeniy, the commander of Aleksandr's group, said 'he wanted to be hero'. They ran into Ukrainian soldiers or police and that was the end of it. As Aleksandr was buried, five uniformed men fired their Kalashnikovs into the air over the grave in salute.

Aleksandr died on 24 April 2014. On the same day Volodymyr Rybak, who was forty-two, was buried. A policeman turned local councillor, he remonstrated with rebels when they put up the rebel

flag in his hometown of Gorlovka. A few days later he and a man later identified as a student from Kiev were found in a river near Sloviansk. Rybak's corpse showed signs of torture. When his body had been tossed into the river it had been weighted down with a bag of sand. As mourners came to pay their respects Elena, his widow, sat by his open coffin stroking his face. Make-up had been applied to the wounds on his head.

The war had started and Aleksandr and Volodymyr were among the first to die. That is why their names are remembered, why journalists wrote about them and why they are recorded here. After that those who died became a statistic to everyone but their families and friends. Individual names and faces gave way to the torrent of numbers.

30.

Tsar v Cossacks

Since the seizure of Crimea the conflict has proceeded in fits and starts. The war in the east began on the pro-Russian side in a mood of euphoria. The oblasts of Donetsk and Lugansk would be snapped off, followed by Kharkiv and then all the other regions, including Odessa, up to the Romanian border in Bessarabia. No secret was made by the separatist side that this was their intention. The flag of Novorossiya would fly all the way from Lugansk to Izmail on the Danube, before being replaced with that of Russia. Just before the 11 May 2014 separatist referendum in Sloviansk, an A4 sheet setting out what it was all about was pasted to the walls. It explained that the Donetsk People's Republic had to become independent before it joined Russia, because the region could not be incorporated into Russia as long as it was 'still part of the territory of another country'.

As soon as Crimea was taken the campaign began in the east. Key buildings were seized, one by one, by armed men. Exactly how this operation was coordinated will be for historians to lay bare, but it was clear to almost everyone that this was not something that could be done without the involvement of the Russian security services. Putin denied this was the case but he had denied that Russian troops were involved in the takeover of Crimea and later had admitted it and they were decorated with a specially struck medal.

At first Ukrainian authority seemed to evaporate and the Ukrainian military appeared uncertain what to do and how to react. There were good reasons for this. Since independence in 1991 the armed forces had been starved of funds. Almost the entire defence budget had gone on paying (poor) salaries and there was little left over for modern weapons and training. It was not as though Ukraine did not make arms either. In the period 2009–13 it was the eighth largest arms exporter in the world, responsible for 3 per cent of global sales, though a good proportion of this went to Russia. It was simply that with money being stolen and siphoned off, the military could not afford the modern stuff, which the country's arms manufacturers exported. Some of the top ranks of the military also had an extremely close relationship with their Russian counterparts. One of the consequences of the break-up of the Soviet Union was that brothers and friends now found themselves as senior officers in armies which, all of a sudden, had become enemies. The result of all this was an army with only a few thousand combat-ready troops with very low morale. I discussed this with a senior intelligence official, who began by talking about the police, claiming they had been turned into a 'racketeering organization' for their bosses in the regions and in Kiev. Since independence, he said, Ukraine had claimed to have 'an intelligence service, counter-intelligence and an army, but it was all just a façade'. In an apposite phrase, Tetiana Sylina, a well-known Kiev journalist, summed up the reason for this: Ukrainian politicians had a 'bulimic' appetite for corruption. The security source drew parallels with African countries.

In the wake of the Maidan revolution several things happened on the Ukrainian side. In the first weeks after the flight of President Yanukovych, there was such chaos that few were really in proper control. This was why it was possible for Crimea to be taken so easily and why it was then wrongly assumed in Moscow that the east and the south would fall just as easily into their lap. But now, dozens of militias began to spring up on the Ukrainian side, the kernel being men who had fought on the Maidan. At the same time a plan to set up a National Guard was put into place. Igor Kolomoisky, one of Ukraine's richest and most powerful oligarchs, who was appointed governor of Dnipropetrovsk after the revolution, put up money to pay for some of them. The problem was that at the beginning this led to anarchy on the battlefield, which provided a window of opportunity for the anti-Maidan, pro-Russian rebels. With at least some Russian direction and help, including from leaders like Igor Strelkov in Sloviansk and some of the first DNR commanders who were from Russia, not locals, the rebels were able to take territory quickly, given that there was initially no real resistance. When I asked the security service source who was in charge of the volunteers on the Ukrainian side he said bluntly 'nobody'.

Quite apart from there being no credible force to oppose the rebels and Russia, no one had any real idea what to do. The reason for this was simple, said the intelligence source. A few years back he and his colleagues had written a paper on a possible Russian threat, which they argued could happen after the Sochi Olympics of 2014. Extraordinarily these ended on 23 February, a few hours after the flight of Yanukovych from Kiev. However, when they wrote the report it had all seemed like a far-fetched 'intellectual game'. He said, 'In my soul, I did not believe we would fight with Russia.' So, no one ever made any preparations for any such conflict in any possible variation of it. For this reason much of Ukraine's threadbare army was positioned in ways which reflected its old Cold War Soviet background, i.e. prepared, albeit barely, to fight a war on its western flanks – not its eastern ones.

I talked with Ihor Smeshko, a former intelligence chief, who in October 2014 was appointed head of the president's Intelligence Committee. Ukraine had no proper modern military intelligence-gathering capacity, logistics, command and control and so on, he said. The volunteer battalions were run on an 'amateur level' and this was leading to defeats on the battlefield; it was necessary for Ukraine to reorganize and regroup its military. Warming to his theme of the chaotic military situation, Smeshko explained that he thought what was happening made it clear that Putin did not understand Ukraine. The nature of the volunteer militias was a big problem but they were also a modern reversion to Ukrainian Cossack roots. Russia had a different tradition. Historically the heartlands of Ukraine were populated by free farmers and warriors. The Russian tradition was that of 'total rule', he said, that of 'God, Tsar and Motherland', but the Ukrainian one was that of

'God, Freedom, Family and Motherland. For centuries we did not have a tsar.' Putin's problem was to persist in believing, as he said, when Crimea was annexed: 'We are not just close neighbours, we are essentially, as I have said more than once, a single people.' In other words, he could not bring himself to see that what might have been true long ago (and many Ukrainians would disagree even with that) was no longer true now for most Ukrainians, and by starting what he had done he was making it even less true than it was before. By turning millions of hitherto friendly Ukrainians into enemies Putin might have won Crimea but the cost was losing Ukraine.

The first phase of the war lasted until July 2014. Russian military support was most likely relatively limited because a lot of help, as opposed to a small amount of targeted operational help, was not actually needed. But now Ukraine's chaotic mix of volunteer battalions and armed forces began to retake territory. The towns of Sloviansk, Kramatorsk, Kostyantynivka and Krasnoarmeysk were reclaimed and briefly it looked as though the Ukrainian advance was unstoppable. But, having whipped the Russian media and people into a frenzy about the new Nazis of Kiev, Putin could hardly let the Donetsk and Lugansk Republics collapse. Russian regular soldiers crossed the border to halt the Ukrainian advance. Russia denied its troops were fighting but captured men spoke about it, and in the wake of the murder on 27 February 2015 of Boris Nemtsov, the Russian opposition politician, a report he had been working on detailing how Russian military help was organized was released. The report also concurred with the common sense rather than conspiracy theory view that the crash on 17 July 2014 of a Malaysian airliner over rebel territory at the cost of 298 lives was almost certainly the result of it being shot down by a Russian-supplied BUK anti-aircraft missile system when the rebels and possibly Russian officers mistook it for a Ukrainian aircraft.

The turning point at this juncture in the war came at Ilovaysk, a small nondescript town forty-five minutes' drive south-east of Donetsk. In the first week of August units from three Ukrainian volunteer militias and the police attempted to take it back from rebel control. The town was heavily shelled, but the rebels were never driven out and held on to part of it. Then, with help from elsewhere such as Donetsk, though 'not Russia', claimed implausibly Commander Givi, the head of rebel forces there, a major several-pronged offensive began on 28 August to drive the Ukrainians out. By 1 September it was all over. The Nemtsov report claimed that to that date some 170 Russian regular soldiers, as opposed to volunteers, had died, and a large proportion of them died in and around Ilovaysk.

The Ukrainians collapsed when men from one volunteer battalion unilaterally pulled out, which was typical of this period of no proper command and control. The leaders of the men trapped in the town, where they had commandeered the school as their base, now thought they had done a deal to gain free passage out of town. But the 34-year-old Commander Givi, whose real name is Mikhail Tolstykh, and who worked in a rope factory before the war, said that there had been no agreement because these were militias and not men from Ukraine's regular armed forces. 'We don't know who they are,' he said, claiming their numbers had been boosted by foreigners including Czechs, Hungarians and 'niggers'. He had arrived at his HQ in a big, smart car with music blasting; in the back some of his men cradled their guns in their laps with the muzzles sticking out of the windows. They had every reason to be upbeat. They had inflicted a catastrophic defeat on the Ukrainians.

On a 26-kilometre stretch of road from the village of Novokaterinivka to Ilovaysk, I counted the remains of sixty-eight military vehicles, tanks, armoured personnel carriers, pick-ups, buses and trucks. It had been a turkey shoot. These vehicles were, of course, only the ones I could see. Those which were not destroyed were now in the hands of the rebels.

In Novokaterinivka itself, a man hung from a high power cable on to which he was flung when his armoured vehicle had been hit. If someone had written that scene into the script of a movie, it would have been cut for being unrealistic. At one ambush site two fresh graves marked with crosses made of sticks indicated that the dead had been buried by their vehicles at the side of the road. On the main street of Novokaterinivka locals posed for pictures by destroyed vehicles and cars which were jacked up with logs because undamaged wheels had been unscrewed and looted. Rebel soldiers high on the drug of victory said they were 'cleaning up', looking for remaining Ukrainians who had fled into the fields and were still there. Stranded in the middle of a field just outside the village you could see one vehicle, which had made a futile attempt to escape by veering off the road. Later the Ukrainian authorities were to report that 459 men died in Ilovaysk and another 478 were injured.

A colleague told me that nearby two Ukrainian soldiers jumped out on to the road and stopped his car. They looked about eighteen, he said, had been hiding in a field of sunflowers and were wide-eyed as though they had not slept for days. When they saw a car taped up with the letters 'TV', which are used to signify that there are journalists in it, they took their chance. They begged him and his colleagues for a lift and then for food and water. At the same time the Ukrainian media began to carry stories of stragglers limping in to safe territory. More than 500 Ukrainians were reported to have been captured here. One, who was released, called Sergey, said that the men who captured him told him they were Russian regular soldiers. 'They told us they had arrived two weeks earlier. They were very young.'

At the same time as this was happening the rebels, again almost certainly with Russian help, most likely from the other side of the border, were clearing Ukrainian forces who were still on their side of the frontier with Russia. Along the border there were empty, shelled positions. To the south, on the Sea of Azov, the situation had also changed drastically. On 27 August the border crossing to Russia was taken by the rebels after it had been shelled with a few mortars and the Ukrainians there, with far less firepower, fled. They fled the nearby town of Novoazovsk too. On 30 August a group of twenty people with their arms stretched up to heaven by the main checkpoint on the eastern outskirts of Mariupol prayed

for peace and for the protection of the city while volunteers assembled to dig trenches. It seemed more than likely that a major offensive on the city would start soon. And it made sense. Mariupol is the port for Donetsk and this part of the east and a major steel city in its own right. With it, the rebel region might have some prospect of eventual economic viability. But, quite apart from that, if Mariupol fell, Russia could begin to make the push to create a land corridor all the way to Crimea, with which it had no connection by land. It is no wonder then that President Poroshenko agreed to a ceasefire in Minsk on 5 September. But Russia too was hurting. Its economy was beginning to feel the effects of sanctions imposed by Western countries.

The ceasefire began to falter seriously however in December and collapsed completely in the new year. At the same time Ukraine's forces were slowly growing more organized. Gradually the militias were being absorbed into a proper command and control structure and Ukrainian soldiers were becoming more effective. They were also digging in around Mariupol. The rebels, however, wanted them out of two places in particular – Donetsk airport and the town of Debaltseve, through which local roads and railways run. The airport, named for the famous composer Sergei Prokofiev (1891–1953), who was born nearby, was gleaming and new, having been among those rebuilt for the 2012 Euro football championships. By the time the Ukrainians were expelled from it, on 21 January 2015, it was mostly rubble. A new ceasefire was agreed, with a starting date of 15 February, but the rebels, even with Russian military help, were unable to push the Ukrainians out until 18 February. The airport and Debaltseve were certainly defeats for the Ukrainians, but the fact that it took the rebels and the Russians months to achieve these victories demonstrated two things: first, that the Ukrainians were no longer disorganized and that their military was getting stronger by the day; and secondly, that the rebels and the Russians were reaching the limits of what they could do unless there was a lot more help from Russia. This in turn risked triggering new sanctions and probably individual Western countries moving to give Ukraine the modern lethal weaponry, for example the targeting systems, it was asking for.

With so many people leaving the rebel territories, logic dictated that more Russians, either volunteers, troops on contract (to disguise the fact that they were regulars) or just regulars would be needed simply to hold the rebel territories, let alone to expand them. In other words, the expansive fantasy of a Novorossiya all the way to Bessarabia had collapsed and was being replaced with the uncomfortable reality of a frozen conflict, similar to Transnistria, South Ossetia, Abkhazia and Nagorno-Karabakh. From Putin's point of view, it must have seemed if not exactly glorious, still a useful outcome furthering his aim of trying to prevent Ukraine from becoming an attractive country, with a stable democracy which could both serve as an example to Russians and also have a serious prospect of eventual NATO and EU accession. For the people of the rebel territories their prospect was simply one of poverty and no hope of a better future. In the centre of Donetsk life continued with superficial normality but shops, banks and offices were closed and in many places sporadic fighting continued. For everyone here, life was in limbo.

One place where fighting continued was Adminposiolok, a badly shattered rebel-held suburb of Donetsk, close to the airport. While the Ukrainians had indeed lost it, they were only a kilometre or two away. Adminposiolok was an eerie place, almost entirely empty of people. All of a sudden Ivan Tokarev, aged seventy-eight, arrived on his bike to do some cleaning in his apartment in a large residential block. Every single flat in the front of the building facing the Ukrainian lines had been destroyed or rendered uninhabitable. His was in decent shape, however, because it was at the back. He showed me a hole in the floor of one apartment in which a shell or rocket had fallen, blowing up the flat of his son below. No one lived there any more. His son had gone to Russia. Ivan and his wife, who had moved to a safer part of town, did not want to join them he said because, while it might be fine for a month or two, then everyone would start arguing, so it was 'better to die here'.

31

The Wolf's Hook Club

The Azov Battalion, based in Mariupol, the Ukrainian-controlled port on the Sea of Azov, is small. According to Major Andrey Dyachenko, its 28-year-old spokesman, when the battalion was founded in May 2014 it had some sixty men but ten months later it had 'more than a thousand'. That is a tiny proportion of the 60,000 men under arms actively fighting for Ukraine out of total number of 250,000 in the armed forces, but judging by the publicity they have garnered for themselves in innumerable news reports, you might be forgiven for thinking that there were 100,000 of them.

As Russian officials and the Russian media have accused the post-Maidan revolution governments in Kiev of being neo-Nazis and fascists, the Azov Battalion is perfect camera-fodder, its members parading around with their neo-Nazi style flag and symbols. If they were not invented and paid for by a secret Russian department of misinformation, then those in charge of directing Russian propaganda must have been thanking their lucky stars that they came along all by themselves.

In terms of winning the war for global public opinion, the Azov Battalion and the charge of Ukrainian neo-Nazism, fascism and extreme nationalism all combine to make Ukraine's Achilles heel. Small elements of truth have painted, and allowed the Russian media and their Western fellow travellers to paint, an utterly distorted picture of the whole. In the general election of October 2014 Ukraine's far-right parties flopped. In electoral terms they are insignificant compared to their strength in Hungary, France or Italy for example. And yet, many Westerners do not see this. Many also do not see that much of the Russian propaganda aimed at depicting Ukraine as a kind of Third Reich reincarnated is a sort of displacement activity. It is after all Russia which is in the grip of nationalistic euphoria and whose once nascent democracy has died as people rally round its one and only unchallenged leader.

Ukraine's problem however, is that there are indeed real unpleasant elements that give its enemies the opportunity to exaggerate their significance. All European countries have the same extremists but the issue of their existence is not a neuralgic political one because they are not fighting wars. Also, when it comes to the Azov Battalion for example, its political antecedents mean that it has friends in high places and because it is a volunteer unit, its members are highly motivated and it garners support because it is successful. This in turn means that it receives more publicity than its numbers justify.

In its canteen we collected soup and bread. Behind us three men were talking in thickly accented English. The Azov Battalion is the one which foreigners, especially those affiliated to far-right and neo-Nazi groups from Croatia to Scandinavia, come to fight for. Just like the volunteers on the other side of the line, they are a mix of adventurers and true believers.

The Azov Battalion, or rather Patriot of Ukraine, the political movement it sprang from, was founded in 2005 according to spokesman Dyachenko. Its leader was, and is, the 36-year-old Andrey Biletsky, and it began in the north-eastern city of Kharkiv, which proved, said Dyachenko, that it was untrue 'that Ukrainian nationalism comes only from the west'. From the beginning, members of the organization had believed 'that Ukraine would have to fight for its independence . . . In 1991 Ukraine gained its independence for geopolitical reasons, without blood or fighting, but historically we know that nothing comes for free. Even though our parents did not take up arms to fight for independence now we have to do it.'

Before the war, said Dyachenko, the view of Patriot of Ukraine was that since independence not only had the country's new army been undermined, but Ukraine's youth too had been virtually emasculated by being brought up with computers and video games and not thinking about protecting the country, including taking up arms if necessary. So, he said:

> We did some military training. This was mostly in the summer because most of the youth who came were at school or university students. We would go to the Carpathians or Crimea, to the countryside, and we set up camp. We used fake guns – we did not have real guns – we dreamed of them, but we did not have them! We also encouraged young people to give up bad habits and do sports and so we had a lot of winners in sport, for example in taekwondo and boxing.

Dyachenko joined in 2011. He was studying for a doctorate in history and the subject was related to Andriy Melnyk, the leader of the wartime Organization of Ukrainian Nationalists (OUN), whose followers had, between 1941 and 1944, been involved in a bloody conflict with Stepan Bandera.

Given that Patriot of Ukraine was an eastern Ukrainian organization and existed in part in the same political and peripheral subculture as Andrei Purgin's Donetsk Republic, which was also founded in 2005 and carrying out paramilitary training, I asked if Dyachenko had known about it. 'We didn't just know about them,' he snorted, 'they were our biggest enemies!'

> We knew about their books and presentations and separatist exhibitions and sometimes we tried to disrupt their meetings. They put up their tent and handed out separatist books, so we would come and take them away and tear them up. They tried to do the same to us but we were stronger. Ninety per cent of our members were fit young men and girls, but theirs were mostly pensioners nostalgic for the Soviet Union. They could not beat us physically!

Despite their apparent physical prowess, work for hardcore Ukrainian nationalists seems to have been just as tough as it was for Donetsk Republic and other pro-Russian fringe movements in the east. 'The people of the region were not really into politics,' admitted Dyachenko. 'They seemed apolitical. It was home, work and family for them and now we have to pay for this with a destroyed Donbass and all the consequences of that.'

When Dyachenko said that Patriot of Ukraine was founded in 2005, he was only telling half the story. Its history is rather longer and more complicated and it is intimately bound up with that of the development of the far-right in Ukraine.

The story began in October 1991 when the Social-National Party of Ukraine (SNPU) was formed in Lviv. This tiny extreme nationalist organization had its roots in three even tinier parties. One was led by Oleh Tyahnybok, a medical student, and another by a young man called Andriy Parubiy. According to Anton Shekhovtsov, an academic who has followed the far-right in Ukraine, the new party wanted a national and social revolution and believed Russia to be the cause of all Ukraine's ills. For its symbol it adopted a *Wolfsangel* or 'Wolf's Hook'. In 2011 Shekhovtsov wrote:

Although its original meaning was not associated with National Socialism, the Wolfsangel – due to its employment by several SS Divisions – had become a symbol of many post-war European and neo-Nazi organisations. The SNPU modified the symbol by mirroring it (just as they seemed to mirror 'National Socialism'), so that it looked like a letter 'N' with a vertical line '|' in the middle of the letter. According to the SNPU's leaders, the symbol meant 'the Idea of the Nation'. The nation as such was – and still is – seen by the party's ideologists as a 'community of blood and spirit'.

By the time Shekhovtsov was writing, the SNPU was no more. It had been a fringe political group with no electoral success. Tyahny-bok, however, had been elected to parliament in 2002, though not on an SNPU ticket but on that of the party of Viktor Yushchenko, who would become president in the wake of the Orange Revolution of 2004. It was during this period that the SNPU, which had been establishing contacts abroad, notably with France's National Front and Austria's Freedom Party, decided that to emulate their success they should clean up their act. In 2004 it changed its name to Svoboda or 'Freedom' and dropped the Wolfsangel. It also disbanded its paramilitary 'guard unit', formed by Parubiy in 1996, which was called Patriot of Ukraine. They and their predecessor organization loved nothing more than parading in black uniforms by torchlight. According to Shekhovtsov, the SNPU also 'recruited skinheads and football hooligans'. When Svoboda dissolved it, he says in a footnote to his 2011 examination of the far-right, the Kharkiv branch of Patriot of Ukraine 'refused to disband and renewed its membership in 2005'. And, if it had not been for the war, it would have remained a footnote.

Meanwhile, in the west of Ukraine, the new Svoboda began to make advances in local elections and finally, in the October 2012 general election, it made its big national breakthrough, becoming the fourth largest party in parliament. It gained 10.44 per cent of the vote and won thirty-seven seats out of 450. It had not been a smooth and easy progression, though. In 2004 for example, just after the founding of Svoboda, Tyahnybok made a speech which was to dog him for years in his quest for respectability. Eulogizing a commander of the UPA, the wartime insurgents, and using insulting epithets for Russians and Jews, he said:

> The enemy came and took their [UPA's] Ukraine. But they [UPA fighters] were not afraid; likewise we must not be afraid. They took their automatic guns on their necks and went into the woods. They got them ready and fought against the Moskali, Germans, Zhydy, and other scum, who wanted to take away our Ukrainian state! And therefore our task – for every one of you: the young, the old, the grey-headed and the youthful – we must defend our native land!

Rising to his theme, Tyahnybok then told the crowd that they were the people the *moskal's'ko-zhydivska'ka* mafia who ruled Ukraine feared the most. A case for inciting racial hatred against him was opened but then was dropped for lack of evidence, but he was expelled from Yuschenko's parliamentary group. Tyahnybok and the party continued to stoke xenophobia and hatred especially towards anything Russian. After its breakthrough in 2012 the party briefly became a significant voice, but many of its voters then were not particularly nationalist as opposed to just fed up with everyone else. Tyahnybok emerged as one of three prominent leaders of the Maidan revolution, and in the October 2014 general election his vote collapsed. The party failed to pass the 5 per cent threshold to enter parliament and Svoboda evaporated as a political force. Tyahnybok had lost his touch. In the party's western heartlands, elected local councillors had by now gained a reputation for being as corrupt as everyone else had been.

Meanwhile, the trajectory of Patriot of Ukraine, which was led by Biletsky, a former history student in Kharkiv, was utterly different. It subsisted on the margins of politics. In 2012 though, it suddenly came to international attention. In the run-up to the UEFA 2012 championship, football fans in places such as Kharkiv came under a Western spotlight. Chris Rogers, a reporter for Britain's BBC *Panorama* programme did an investigation into the racist chanting of Ukrainian football fans and witnessed some 2,000 Metalist Kharkiv fans making Nazi salutes and shouting '*Sieg Heil!*' He then met a man called Vadym who took him to a fans' bar which Rogers described as a 'shrine to far-right extremism' decorated with swastikas, 'white power' symbols and where there also seemed to be 'an unhealthy obsession with Nazi Germany'. Vadym denied they were Nazis however. Then we learn that he is a recruiter for Patriot of Ukraine and see a video allegedly of the group rounding up what we are told are illegal immigrants, who look Vietnamese, whom human rights groups noted in 2010 were among Patriot's targets. Then Vadym says: 'One race, one nation, one fatherland.' Patriot had to be ready, he explained, for civil war. 'Of course nobody wants to have some war . . . but we must be prepared for everything.' Next Rogers was taken with what he described as football hooligans to see them being trained in knife-fighting techniques in a wood. He tells us that he has seen videos showing hundreds turning up for such events but now there are only a handful. We watch them fighting with wooden knives. Then one masked recruit says: 'We are learning to shoot and we are learning tactical combat, and well military preparation and we can take all this fight training on to the streets. I can also add, because my face is hidden, that these skills have already been used on the streets, and not just once.'

At the time it was natural for a foreign journalist to interpret this in the context of what it might mean for black and Asian football fans. There was no reason to be interested in what else groups like this might be up to, such as a lucrative sideline in being available for hire in gangland and business turf wars, or what then would have seemed obscure battles with similar pro-Russian groups. It was for these reasons however that the authorities were taking an interest in Patriot of Ukraine, just as they were in Donetsk Republic. In fact these problems had begun to come to a head the year before the football championships came to Ukraine. In 2011 three Patriot members were arrested in a case relating to an alleged attempt to blow up a statue of Lenin. In Kharkiv, Patriot members were arrested and charged with attempted murder and there was an attempt to murder Biletsky, who was then arrested himself and held in detention though not convicted of anything. He was released by act of parliament, along with Yulia Tymoshenko, the former prime minister, on 24 February 2014, just after the flight of President Viktor Yanukovych.

Even though Biletsky had been in prison, Patriot members were extremely active. Once protests began on the Maidan against Yanukovych in November 2014, its members started to play an active role and it was one of the organizations which was to form part of the umbrella of far-right groups called Right Sector. Here they found themselves increasingly in combat with two old enemies. One was the Berkut, the riot police, with whom as nationalist football 'Ultras' they had frequently clashed, and the other was fellow eastern nationalist groups such as Oplot. The latter was not a Ukrainian nationalist organization but a Russian one based on a sports-cum-fight club in Kharkiv which operated in the same political-cum-underground business circles as Patriot of Ukraine. Just as Patriot members now flocked to the fight in Kiev, its members did so too, but as part of government-sponsored so-called *titushki* groups who were recruited to join in fights against the Maidan activists. Meanwhile, a good part of the Berkut were sent from the east because they could be trusted by Yanukovych, while those from other regions of the country could not.

As soon as Yanukovych fled and Biletsky was released from Kharkiv jail, the first thing Patriot did was to attack and seize the Oplot HQ in the city. The police did not intervene, recalled Dyachenko. Then on 15 March Oplot counter-attacked and attempted to seize the HQ of Patriot of Ukraine. 'There were about fifty people inside who were attacked by a hundred Oplot guys, who even had guns. Our guys tried to fight with Molotov cocktails and stones,' and what Dyachenko called cryptically 'the classic means of the Maidan', by which he meant clubs and shields. 'The Oplot guys were surprised to see we were ready to fight and retreated.' By this time Crimea had already been annexed by Russia and, said Dyachenko, it was evident that Ukraine now faced a war. In Crimea Russian troops had operated undercover, or rather without identifying themselves as such, and garnered the nickname of 'little green men'. 'It was clear to everyone that afterwards "green men" would appear in Kharkiv, Donetsk and Odessa and so on. So, Patriot of Ukraine announced the creation of its own "men in black" at the end of March.' They had few guns, he said, only some which had come to them after police stations had been attacked by Maidan activists in Lviv. 'Some guys took hunting rifles.'

Kharkiv was a big prize for the pro-Russian separatists and a proportion of the population sympathized with them. But Gennady Kernes, the mayor, who had close relations with both Yanukovych and Oplot, sensed that the city was not about to be lost to Ukraine. He switched sides. Patriot of Ukraine and Oplot continued to clash and, in this increasingly lawless situation with the police standing aside until they knew who would win, Patriot activists began kidnapping those they suspected of separatism and handing them over to the police, according to Dyachenko – who then released them. Patriot was increasingly part of what was becoming a war, as was Oplot, which played a key role in seizing the official buildings in Donetsk. Here, where they were led by Alexander Zakharchenko, a former mining electrician, or market cheese salesman according to other sources, they were more successful than in Kharkiv, where they and other groups were to fail.

As the police and security services were demoralized, uncertain what to do and in the east contained many sympathetic to the separatists, Patriot of Ukraine and other groups began to fill a gap. They were determined and not scared to fight. This was the beginning of the period of the so-called battalions, which were independent militias, doing the job of the army and police. Some got money from oligarchs such as Dnipropetrovsk's Igor Kolomoisky and some were in effect controlled by him. On 5 May, said Dyachenko, the interim minister of interior, Arsen Avakov, registered them as a volunteer battalion and two days later airlifted them down to

Mariupol, which pro-Russian groups were trying to seize. Avakov knew exactly whom he was dealing with. He was an economist, businessman and politician from Kharkiv and had been governor of the oblast from 2005 to 2010.

In Mariupol the 'men in black' fought the pro-Russians but complained that, unlike them, they did not have enough weapons. They assumed their new name, the Azov Battalion, as Mariupol is on the Sea of Azov, and from November 2014 they became part of Ukraine's National Guard. In August 2014 they had defended the city as the rebels, with Russian help, pushed along the coast towards it, playing an important role in halting their advance and thus gained a reputation as good fighters. The battalion acquired a building and the government began to supply it with heavy weapons and other equipment. On the other side of the line, something similar happened to Oplot. From the same humble beginnings it had become important. Its unit grew into one of the main separatist military battalions and Zakharchenko was appointed as leader of the DNR in August 2014. Biletsky meanwhile cooperated closely with the Fatherland Front, the post-Maidan party of Arseniy Yatseniuk, who became prime minister after the revolution, and which counted Avakov and Parubiy as leading members. Biletsky did not join the party however and was elected to parliament in October as an independent.

Outside the Azov canteen I wanted to take a picture of its flag but there was no wind so it hung limply. I asked Dyachenko about the issue of its Wolfsangel-style symbol and said that in the West – let alone in Russia – this and the neo-Nazi views of some of its members were a real problem for Ukraine. Dyachenko gave me the party line, albeit saying in an aside to Liliia, who was translating for me: 'That is what they told me to say.' The main goal of Russian propaganda was to show them as neo-Nazis because Russian propaganda 'can't say that Ukrainian people are fighting against Russian occupation, so they make it up and say they are fighting fascists'. About the neo-Nazi views of some who had spoken to the press he said: 'I admit there are some fighters with those taboos from past years and they have radical views but we cannot turn down people who want to fight for Ukraine.' He added that the battalion did not 'screen requests' to join based on ideology. Azov propagated a 'healthy Ukrainian nationalism but, if some of our fighters have their own views we won't dictate anything to them.' And he added: '*We* are fighting against neo-Nazism and chauvinism.'

As for the infamous symbol, he said unconvincingly: 'We have been told it resembles a symbol of the Third Reich but it appeared at the beginning of the 1990s when there was no internet.' As to the question of the harm it did Ukraine, he replied:

> We have to fight and throw out the occupiers, not look good for Russian propaganda. According to Russian propaganda we should throw out our blue and yellow [Ukrainian] flag. Twenty Azov fighters gave their lives for that symbol and we are not going to change it because of Russian propaganda! We are here to stop Bolshevism advancing towards Europe and we are here for a free Europe.

And if and when the Azov Battalion succeed – what then? Dyachenko's answer sounded rather humdrum and traditionally conservative more than anything. He talked of Polish economic shock therapy and large families, and grumbled that 'gay marriage is obviously negative. We stand for the traditional family.' He also spoke of his admiration for Alain de Benoist, the French far-right philosopher, whom I was beginning to realize had fans on both sides of the line.

It is undeniable that, on the Ukrainian side of the war, some politicians and some organizations have their roots in the far-right. It is a fact that is used against the country in the info-war and the negative effect of this in the West is something which many Ukrainians don't understand. Certain individuals whose political roots go back to the far-right have become important in the post-Maidan era but voters have eschewed extremism more than those in many other European countries. The reason why some individuals and organizations like Azov have been able to flourish is because they are made up of or led by highly motivated figures with a background in groups who were not afraid of violence and especially were not afraid to resort to it during the Maidan period. It is also worth noting that since independence these individuals and groups had warned that Russia was a threat. Because of their unpalatable political background, their general xenophobia and their devotion to neo-Nazi style symbolism this part of their message was lost in the cacophony. However, there is another issue which historians will debate: to what extent did they contribute to a self-fulfilling prophecy? The lionizing of Stepan Bandera and the flying of his red and black flag, especially during the Maidan revolution, did much to alarm and even embitter those in Ukraine whose fathers and grandfathers had fought in the Red Army against his movement. It gave valuable political ammunition to Ukraine's enemies and they use it to good effect. The main blame for the Ukrainian war must lie with Vladimir Putin – but such things did not help Ukraine.

At the entrance to the battalion's canteen a table was completely covered in colourful children's drawings and letters. All over Ukraine classes of children are churning them out and they are arriving in bulk to decorate concrete block checkpoints and frontline positions. The one I picked up read:

Dear Friend

Hello. I am sending a big hello to you from the south of our state, from Odessa. Be brave, stay brave and know we are supporting you and we believe in you. Victory will be ours.
   Pupil of Year 7.

Dymitro Mandichenko
Odessa

32.

From Amazonia to New Russia

I went looking for the Serbs. I wanted to write about Balkan fighters who, now their own wars were over, were fighting in foreign ones. Serbs have been fighting for the rebels and Croats for the Ukrainians. Divided only by the fact of being Orthodox Serbs and Catholic Croats, they seemed to agree about most things. These fighters hate the European Union, NATO and America and think they are fighting a good Christian fight. They are often connected to small extreme nationalist groups. Sometimes they send one another greetings. To their Serb 'friends' a couple of Croats said 'Hope to see you soon!' via YouTube. They were off to Mariupol to join the Azov Battalion.

The Serbs were lying low though. One group had kidnapped a couple from another group with whom they were in conflict. They taped material around the head of one and a blindfold on the other, who was wearing a shirt emblazoned with a Serbian flag and the motto: 'Serbian Honour'. Then they triumphantly posted the picture on Facebook. A source in Donetsk suggested I call Erwan Castel, a French volunteer, who might know where they were. He told me he was in a café by the bus station.

When I arrived Castel said that the Serbs (who had kidnapped the others) had indeed just been there, but had left. Anyway they were, he indicated with a spiralling gesture of his hand, completely drunk. He was not going to give me their numbers. But Castel himself has an interesting story to tell. While few non-Russians have come to fight in Donbass – one reliable estimate in March 2015 put the total number who had passed through on each side at 300 – the reason Castel had come to Donetsk tells us much about those Westerners who admire Putin.

Castel had arrived only a few days earlier but, he told me, he had been meaning to come for a long time. Unfortunately his father had recently died and he had had obligations to discharge before he could travel. And he had in fact, travelled a very long way. The 51-year-old had, in an earlier chapter of his life, been a French military intelligence officer, but for many years now he had lived in French Guyana, taking people on tours of the Amazon rainforest. When he had not been under the forest canopy he had been following world affairs and had begun to develop an interest in what was happening in Ukraine. He was convinced that the US and the European Union had orchestrated a *coup d'état* in Kiev with the Maidan revolution in order to install NATO bases in Ukraine. Now, however, in the face of heroic resistance by the people of Donbass against an openly neo-Nazi junta in Kiev, the US and the EU in his view were in retreat and the world order was on the point of change. Today we were witnessing the violent collapse of the liberal system led by the US and the New World Order, he told me. 'As a Russian proverb says "When a monster drowns it makes the biggest waves."'

As he talked he showed me things on his computer such as the blog he had set up in 2014 called *Soutien à la rébellion du Donbass* ('Support for the Donbass Rebellion'). Its Facebook page had 9,378 members and was tagged: 'Anti-globalization movement' and 'Novorossiya'. A younger French volunteer sat in silence at the other end of the table. Castel zipped from what had happened in Kosovo in 1999 to theories about CIA-supported Western NGOs aiming to destabilize the former Soviet republics. I was introduced to the concept of 'Thalassocracies', which are 'empires of the sea' as the British empire had apparently been and which contrasted with the Russian empire, and then to the geopolitical concept of the evil US seeing the 'road to Tehran' leading through Damascus and the 'road to Moscow' leading through Kiev. He whipped open his computer again and we looked at maps of NATO in 1990 and in 2009, by which time it included all the former central and east European Warsaw Pact nations, the Baltic states, Croatia and Albania. 'Who is the aggressor?' he demanded. 'Who is on the offensive? They are at the door of Russia and Russia has no strategic depth. Riga is only 150 kilometres from St Petersburg. So, Russia is in a defensive posture. It is not a threat.' The government in Kiev 'is not Ukrainian. It is a slave of the US and all decisions are', at which point he picked up his phone and spoke into it: 'Hello Obama, what do we do?' The US, he explained, wanted the containment of Russia, to control its frontiers and see the departure of its Black Sea Fleet from Crimea. But American plans were being thwarted.

Russia, he said, had no troops in Ukraine and lies to the contrary had to be stopped. Russia only wanted no NATO on its borders and an economy open to east and west. Castel claimed hackers had discovered that 1,037 Poles and Americans had been killed fighting in Ukraine but these deaths were being hidden. He talked approvingly of Alexander Dugin and his Eurasian vision for Europe and of Alain de Benoist and his ideas about a Europe in which emerging identities such as those of Catalonia, Flanders and presumably Donbass played a new role as the old order collapsed.

Sitting in French Guyana poring over his computer night after night, Castel had clearly become obsessed with Ukraine. He collaborated with others to 'prove' that the anti-Maidan activists who had died in the infamous fire in Odessa on 2 May 2014 had been killed in a conspiracy, and not because both sides had thrown Molotov cocktails at one another and the anti-Maidan activists had been trapped inside the building. He was excited. The old world was collapsing, the oppressed were rising up against the evil empire – America – and he had come to play his small role in ushering in the age of revolution. 'I want to participate,' he said. 'It is important for the Russian and Slavic worlds to see that there are people who support them.'

For Castel, the rebel Donbass cause is a noble crusade, which he has joined with the zeal of those foreigners who once flocked to the cause of the Spanish Republic. Everything he told me and believes about Ukraine has been said by the Kremlin's propaganda machine, but anything that counters this narrative is regarded as Western propaganda serving the interests of the American military-industrial complex. What he believes is widely believed in Russia of course, because it is the party line followed by most of the media. However, millions of Westerners also share all or some of his beliefs. They are the point where the worldview of the extreme right in the West meets that of the extreme left. This is why among the foreigners fighting for the rebels in Ukraine there are modern-day fascists ranged alongside extreme leftists who believe they are participating in a new and glorious communist revolution. In this ideological confusion communist flags fly alongside ones depicting Christ. There is no inkling that maybe Putin believes in none of this and in one thing only: power.

A few weeks later Erwan posted on his blog that he had been off-line for two weeks because he had been on a reconnaissance mission. He discussed how the militias of the two would-be republics were being turned into conventional armies and were an example to the peoples of Europe who wanted to liberate themselves from American hegemony.

33.

Leaving Home

In the spring of 2015, a year after the war began, the UNHCR, the arm of the United Nations tasked with caring for refugees, estimated that 1.25 million people from Donbass were displaced within Ukraine and 822,700 had fled abroad, mostly, but not only, to Russia. This meant that from the area held by the two separatist republics in which some 4.5 million had lived before the war, more than 2 million had left. Whatever happens, many, if not most of them, will never go back, especially if the conflict drags on or freezes in such a way that the region remains what it has already become, one with little real functioning economy.

Four of those who left are from the Yemchenko family whom I first met before they fled.

On 17 April 2014 Olena Yemchenko came to the last pro-Ukrainian rally in Donetsk. She was forty-three years old, born in Taganrog in Russia, of mixed Russian and Ukrainian background and had lived in Donetsk since the age of seven. Some 2,000 turned up to the rally, which was guarded by serried ranks of black-clad riot police. I told Olena that I thought this was not an impressive turnout for such a big city but she said she was very happy that so many had come because all day rumours had been coursing through social media that the rally would be attacked by separatists, so many had been too frightened to come. At a clash between pro-Ukrainians and pro-Russians in March one pro-Ukrainian had been killed.

As we talked a giant Ukrainian flag was passed over people's heads and the crowd chanted '*Slava Ukraini !*', 'Glory to Ukraine!', and 'We will not give up Donbass!' Oleh Lyashko, the leader of a small nationalist party, said that Ukraine faced 'the choice of shame or war and I am for war'. One man held a handmade poster with a picture of a baby wearing a *vyshyvanka*, a shirt decorated with traditional Ukrainian embroidery patterns. Underneath the man had written: 'Uncle Putin, why are you so grumpy?' Behind the stage stood several lines of riot policemen. In between the police and the back of the stage was a small playground in which mothers and small children swung happily on gondola swings.

A few days later Olena came to collect me. She had a small Ukrainian flag on the dashboard of her car, which was surprising as the war was already beginning and showing public support for Ukraine in Donetsk seemed a dangerous thing to do. Olena is an artist but made her living as an interior designer. Her brother, with whom she and her husband, Artyom, aged forty-two, shared an office, ran an advertising and web design company. While we talked Artyom browsed through designer teapots online. He had four shops in town called 'Cozy Home' selling upmarket goods for the home to Donetsk's small, but until then growing middle class.

On the walls of the office were several of Olena's canvases including some of busty, headless women adorned with old election catchphrases of former president Yanukovych – 'prosperity' and 'stability'. They also featured skulls, hearts and broken hearts. She said that the women represented her view that in Ukraine only 10 to 15 per cent of people actually think while the rest 'just exist'. Then she added that maybe this was the same in the rest of the world.

Olena and Artyom had been active supporters of the small pro-Maidan movement in Donetsk. They had come to its rallies and done shifts at the protests to keep it going. Olena's particular contribution was to paint a picture at the demonstration camp while people watched her. Like in Kiev, some of the anti-Yanukovych protesters stayed after he had fled, wanting to keep going until the presidential election, which was scheduled for 25 May. It was not to be. On 1 March a small group of fifty to a hundred people recalled Olena, came to clear them out. 'They had strange flags, including Russian imperial ones.' They were well organized and several had walkie-talkies, while others had clubs studded with nails. They shouted *'Banderovtsi!'* at the Maidan protesters and 'Berkut', the name of the Ukrainian riot police, many of whom had just returned home from Kiev as heroes to anti-Maidan easterners. Olena complained to some police who were sitting in their car watching what was going on, but it rapidly became clear that they would do nothing. So, the leader of the Donetsk Maidan group made a decision. 'We had better go, or we will all be killed.'

In her office Olena had photos from exhibitions she had organized. She complained of Ukraine's endemic corruption. She and her colleagues had been awarded a grant from the Ministry of Culture in 2013 for an exhibition, but most of the money never arrived because it was stolen. She described how she got round this problem. She had a wealthy client who had prospered in the last few years. 'My task is to take his money and use it wisely,' and in this, she laughed, there was 'no dilemma'. That meant she used some of the money to live off, but the rest was to plug the hole left by the theft of money she was supposed to have got from the state to fund the exhibitions. In that way she was part of a chain laundering money, but in her case the cash went back to where it was supposed to have gone in the first place. 'For my whole life,' she said, 'people have been robbing us.'

A few days later Olena called. The window of her car with the flag had been smashed. A friend had told her that from now on the only place for Ukrainian flags to be flown in Donetsk 'was on tanks'.

A month later I asked Artyom what he had been doing. The answer was that he had been exploring the possibility of moving to Kiev or the west or emigrating. 'If I come back in a year,' I asked, 'what do you reckon the chances of you still being here are?' Without hesitation he answered: 'Fifty-fifty.' A year later they had fled to Dnipropetrovsk, another big eastern industrial city, but one which remained firmly in Ukrainian hands.

As a politically active couple, Olena and Artyom were on one of Donetsk's local election commissions. This meant they were supposed to help organize and supervise the 25 May presidential election in one central Donetsk district. Artyom was the secretary of his commission and, as the election approached, he began calling its members and found half were refusing to take part because it was too dangerous. The leadership of the DNR had declared that no election could take place there because it was no longer part of Ukraine. Thugs began barging into offices involved in organizing the poll and closing them down. The parties appointed new people to replace those who refused to work but this did not help because the new people also did not want to come. As the situation deteriorated, Artyom and his colleagues decided to carry on in secret and determined that, come what may, it was important to open their polling station so that it could be registered as having opened, even if only a handful of people actually dared to vote. With checkpoints surrounding the city it was impossible to drive the ballots in so just before the poll they were flown into the airport, which a few days later was to close as fighting erupted around it. As the vehicle with the ballots drove from the airport however, it was stopped by rebels and the man in charge was kidnapped and held for a few days.

Thus, the election in the city, and indeed in the rest of the rebel-held territory, could not take place.

At about the same time Olena and Artyom needed to get a new marriage certificate. They wanted to send their younger son, then aged eleven, to a summer camp in Israel and to stay with relatives there. As they had married just before the end of the Soviet Union their original marriage certificate was a Soviet one but a Ukrainian version was a required part of the paperwork. By now the office which issued the documents had been taken over by the rebels. Eventually they did manage to get the paperwork together. Meanwhile, they wondered what to do. All of their lives were in Donetsk but now they could see the power of the Ukrainian police, the security services and the legal authorities evaporating. As business dried up Artyom moved his stock into a secure warehouse and began to close his shops. His ten staff accused him of treachery but he said, 'I did not want to pay tax to the DNR and so I decided not to.' In summer they closed their office, and Olena's brother Anton left with his children for Kharkiv. The situation in the city was getting worse as certain areas, especially but not only near the airport, were being shelled. The Ukrainians in the airport tried to hit the rebels who in turn were attempting to dislodge them.

Anton sought a way to extract his valuable printing machines from the city, but tragedy struck. His father-in-law was a miner in Makiivka, the neighbouring town to Donetsk. Because of the war his mine closed and he fell into a deep depression. He was taken to hospital for an assessment and there committed suicide by jumping out of the window from a high floor. Then, when Anton was at home in Donetsk, a young man smashed his car into Anton's parked one. He came downstairs and the man apologized and said he would give him some money – it was better not to get the police involved he said – but that as he did not have it on him Anton should come with him to get it. He got in the man's car and as soon as they left another car arrived and Anton was kidnapped. He had been set up. The kidnappers were Chechens whom the family believe were *Kadyrovtsy*, which is to say armed men sent by Ramzan Kadyrov,

the Chechen leader, to fight for the rebels. It rapidly became clear
that they had been tipped off that, as Anton was trying to get his
printing presses out, he must have enough money to do so. Anton's
wife used her contacts and managed to get her husband freed after
a few days without paying a ransom. The presses were extracted
from Donetsk and sent across the frontline on the payment of a
$1,000 bribe to a DNR official. Anton had been roughed up but not
badly beaten. When he was released one of the kidnappers took his
shoes.

At the beginning of July Olena and Artyom were in Kiev. They
had gone to collect their son who had just come home from Israel.
Simon, their older son, aged nineteen, stayed with his grandparents
in Donetsk because he had a university exam to sit. At exactly this
moment Sloviansk, which had been under rebel control since April,
fell to Ukrainian forces. A column of armed rebels evacuated the
town and retreated to Donetsk. As that happened Olena and
Artyom were on the train on the way back from Kiev and Simon's
grandmother called them to warn them that the city was full of
armed men, that it was dangerous and they should not come home.
So, they got off in Dnipropetrovsk, because the grandmother had a
distant relative there whom she phoned and asked to look after
them. They arrived at his flat at two o'clock in the morning and
found he had been celebrating his birthday and there were dishes of
party food still on the table. They stayed with him a few days and
then he sent them to his *dacha* or country house, about 30 kilometres away.

Olena said she decided to treat these days as a kind of summer
holiday, but it was hard there because, until Anton brought them
their car from Donetsk, it was difficult to move about and even the
nearest shop was thirty minutes' walk away. Originally they also
had only the clothes they had taken to Kiev. By August it was clear
they were not going home. They began looking for a flat to rent in
Dnipropetrovsk. Simon applied to transfer to the city's university
and they got their younger son into a good school. Meanwhile, all
of their family and all of their friends were pouring out of Donetsk

and going to Kiev. After the fall of Sloviansk Russia sent troops to stem the Ukrainian advance, which they did, but Olena and Artyom met people who were amazed they had decided to stay in Dnipro-petrovsk. Artyom recalled: 'Everyone was waiting for Russian troops here. It did not mean they wanted that, but they expected it. They said: "Why did you come here? They will come here too." '

Olena managed to get some of her paintings out of Donetsk but said she did not regret the rest. 'They are from a different stage of my life, when I had different goals.'

In the meantime their home in Donetsk is empty. They asked a neighbour to keep an eye on it but then she left. They were living on savings but Artyom had up to $100,000 worth of Cozy Home stock stuck in the warehouse in Donetsk. Life was in limbo. They have family in Germany and there was a possibility that they could go there so Olena and Artyom were spending much of their time studying German. They said that being part of a small, liberal and opposition-minded circle in Donetsk they were already increasingly unhappy before the war but now, said Artyom, one thing was for sure: 'We will never go back to Donetsk.'

Whatever happens, the fate of the city and the region without such creative people, without modern-minded pro-Europeans and entrepreneurs will be all the poorer. Some even say that in this way Donetsk is reverting to type. It is becoming again what it originally was: a small, rough and ready and violent place.

34.

Surviving Sloviansk

The little town of Sloviansk was under rebel control from 12 April to 5 July 2014. In that period it became their bastion and effective control was wielded by Igor Girkin, who used the *nom de guerre* Strelkov, or 'shooter'. By his own admission he was a former Russian intelligence agent. To what extent he was an active asset of Russia's security services was, and is, much debated. Given his statements though, it was clear that he was a true believer in the cause of recreating an imperial Russia. By contrast, and by her own admission, Viktoria Demidchenko, who was twenty-seven when he took over, didn't much care who ran the town, but just wanted a better life. Between pro-Ukrainians who had either fled or were keeping very quiet, vocal pro-Russians or those opposed to the post-Maidan government but not necessarily anti-Ukrainian, Viktoria was typical of many, especially in that first part of the war, when loyalties were ambiguous and had not crystallized into hate.

She lives on the ground floor of a classic run-down five-storey block on the edge of town that people had begun moving into in 1971. When I first met her she served strawberry tea. In the corridor she has wallpaper depicting a New York street scene with yellow cabs. Just below the kitchen window are flowerbeds, carefully maintained by the inhabitants of the block and in front of them is a place for children to play. During the period the rebels were here, if the mothers heard any fighting they popped their heads out of the windows and yelled at their kids to come in.

Viktoria's fridge is decorated with magnets of places she or friends and family have been, which are mostly in Ukraine, though in 2008 Viktoria went for six weeks to Germany to pick

strawberries near Cologne with a group from her college organized by one of her teachers. She was paid €5 an hour, earned €1,500 and bought a laptop. She has a husband and a daughter, aged two and half. Before having her child, Viktoria could not get a proper job. She had studied at the nearby teacher training college but the problem was that you had to pay a bribe to get a teacher's job and she did not have that money. When the fighting began, the furniture factory where her husband worked shut, and he was not getting paid. As elsewhere in Ukraine before the war, the problem was less one of unemployment and rather one of low pay. She explained to me in minute detail exactly how much she had to pay for gas, for electricity, for water and for her contribution to the apartment block charges. The sums were tiny but the reality was that she and her husband now had less than €15 left.

As we drank the strawberry tea Viktoria asked me what life was like in Britain. Did we, for example, have to bribe someone to get a job? Did we have to pay a bribe to get into university? The conversation moved on to Rinat Akhmetov. I said that I often passed One Hyde Park, the luxury London block where he had bought two flats and where his wife and children lived. The *Guardian* reported that according to Land Registry documents in April 2011 he had paid £136.4 million for the properties and was expected to spend another £60 million to get his 2,300 square metres the way he wanted them. Viktoria's flat was about 30 square metres. As to the future of Sloviansk, she said: 'It does not matter if I live in Russia or Ukraine. All I want is a good salary. Now I can't even afford a new pair of shoes. I don't want to be anxious about money for bread.' What concerned her most right now, apart from the risk of fighting, was that she had heard that the meagre state maternity leave pay she got was about to end (which it duly did) because Ukraine was bankrupt.

Another time, when some of her friends came over, we went for a walk in the nearby allotments, which many in the flats had, and in which some neighbours were tending their vegetables. Viktoria's parents-in-law had an allotment here. We looked at where some sort of missile had a made hole clean through the trunk of a tree by the fire station. By the line of old car tyres with which the rebels had blocked the road, there was a big flowerbed with two life-size, painted plaster models of children. One was a girl in a yellow dress with a blue collar and belt, that is to say in the Ukrainian national colours, who was watering the plants with a red watering can. The other was a blond boy in a red shirt reading a book, who, according to Viktoria and local lore, was supposed to be young Lenin. Between them was a giant red toadstool with white spots. A few paces away was a building the local rebels were using as their HQ.

At their barricade here, close to the entrance to the allotments, the men had made themselves a comfortable shelter with a table and chairs. A few of them had guns, but many did not. On the table was a vase of flowers. As we sat there a couple came by walking their dachshund, who was called Rich. They had come to drop off some picnic plates and serviettes. These were added to the other supplies, including cigarettes, biscuits and salads that the residents of the blocks of flats on the other side of the tree-lined street had brought them. Suddenly a car drove up and three local men got out with musical instruments. They were touring the barricades. They began to sing. A line from one song from the Second World War went: 'Under Balkan stars I will dream of my Smolensk!' A line from another, from the Afghan war, was: 'Under the stars of Jalal-abad, we cursed our damned war . . .'

Then something happened. All the men jumped up, got into their cars and roared off. Two suspicious men had been spotted on a nearby roof. Everyone seemed to believe that the town had been infiltrated by snipers (some of them women) and other evil-doers from Right Sector, one of the post-Maidan nationalist volunteer militias. Indeed many believed that the town was surrounded by Right Sector men pretending to be soldiers, an idea encouraged by the fact that, thanks to the chaotic situation then prevailing in the Ukrainian military and in the newly created National Guard, men from the latter were on checkpoints outside town, in black uniforms with no insignia, because, as one explained, they had not been made yet. Ten minutes later the men from the barricade were back. The two men had been sent from the municipality to repair something.

The local commander was called Yevgeniy. He was thirty-five years old and before the war had a small delivery-van business. He did not want to give his surname. 'What do they want?' he raged. 'We were peaceful people until they,' by which he meant Ukrainian forces, 'came here.' A friend of his, in fact the godfather of his child, he said, had been mobilized into the National Guard on the other side, 'and they tell them it's only terrorists here!' The men at the barricade nodded. This was a common theme at the bottom of the rebel pecking order. They were just ordinary folk who, appalled by the fall of Viktor Yanukovych, and convinced by the Russian media and the high profile of small groups like Right Sector on the other side that this was somehow a rerun of the Second World War and they were about to be overrun by the (new) Nazis. Yanukovych had not done anything for them and like most politicians was considered a son of a bitch, but at least, as he was from around these parts, they could consider him *their* son of a bitch. Still, opinion polls had consistently shown that the majority did not want to become part of Russia, but now as drama engulfed Ukraine many, like Viktoria, were just fed up and desperate. And so, with the close ties of language, family and business, and in places like Donetsk with its particularly marked Soviet demographic legacy, it was only logical that people might look to Russia rather than the West and an EU which is distant – in a way which it is not if you live in, say, Lviv.

Two months after Sloviansk had been retaken by Ukrainians on 5 July 2014 I returned to the town. Ukrainian soldiers now walked around just as rebel ones had before. In the main square, the statue of Lenin, under which rebel leaders had in spring made fiery if vacuous speeches denouncing the 'fascist junta' in Kiev, now sported a Ukrainian flag scarf around its neck. Just as before and during the rebel period, children rode around on ponies and life went on. Ludmila, aged fifty, who was selling pressed flower pictures in a crafts fair on the square was worried though. She supported Ukraine, had fled when the rebels controlled the town and now, she said, had her 'suitcase ready', in case they came back, which they daily declared was their aim.

I went back to find Viktoria. In early summer when fighting had intensified she and her family had fled to the safety of a nearby monastery in which many had sought shelter. They were away for some six weeks. All the men who had manned the barricade near her flat had run away and not come back. Many had gone to Russia, she said. Who wanted to risk retribution? On 8 September Amnesty International issued a briefing in which it accused the Ukrainian Aidar volunteer battalion of being 'involved in widespread abuses, including abductions, unlawful detention, ill-treatment, theft, extortion, and possible executions'. They were not in Sloviansk and there were no reports of such things happening here, but who would have waited to see?

In the lobby of the Sloviansk city administration building there were two transparent boxes for people to drop notes in. Sheets taped on the front declared: 'For Citizens' Letters'. They also gave the phone numbers of the police and the SBU, the Ukrainian intelligence service. Inside the boxes were notes people had written denouncing those who they said had helped the rebels. A policeman at the door said that 80 per cent of them were from people who had disputes with their neighbours, and wanted to get them into trouble. This reminded me of something that Charles King, an American academic and historian of the Black Sea, had written about in his history of Odessa. After the Second World War it was politically expedient for the Soviet authorities to declare the port a 'Hero City'. From 1941 to 1944 it had been occupied by the Romanians, who were allied to the Nazis. In fact, with some notable exceptions, its inhabitants had not been so heroic. Before the war it was common for people to snitch to the NKVD, the predecessor of the KGB, about their neighbours, if they had a dispute with them. After the fall of the city people passed seamlessly to denouncing their neighbours as Jews or communists. Then, with the return of Soviet power, they began accusing them of being collaborators. Presumably they were denouncing one another to the tsar's secret police before communism too. On the surface all looked calm in Sloviansk. Only a local could feel the nasty undercurrents here.

Viktoria's husband was looking for a new job. She still had no work and they still had no money. When the rebels fled, she said, the locals broke into the building that had served as their HQ and took the food they found there which 'they had stolen from the shops'. The SBU had come by to ask questions about who had been helping the rebels and who had given them food on the barricade. She and her husband had been standing outside having a smoke. They said they did not know who had helped the rebels because they had been away. Of course she did know, but 'I don't want problems,' and anyway 'they have left'. I told her about the boxes I had seen in the administration building and she explained that this was precisely why the SBU men had come calling. It was mostly old women who wrote these letters, when they had had an argument with a neighbour. In this case an old lady who did not like the woman who lived opposite her had denounced her. Had that woman in fact helped the rebels? 'We said it was not true,' but she had 'given them some borsch . . . once'. What did she think now the Ukrainians were back? 'I am just happy we are home,' but 'it makes no difference to me'.

One year after I first met her, things were looking up. Viktoria's husband had found a new job. She had also got a job in the local kindergarten, but left because she did not like it and still wanted to be a schoolteacher. Apart from that they were helping her husband's parents tend their vegetables in the allotment and while life was still tough, 'at least we have a lot of potatoes to eat though I don't know how we will manage in winter. The main thing is that there is no shooting.'

35

Towns at War

'Are they waiting for us?' It was March 2015, almost a year since the beginning of the war, and I had come to see Pervomaysk in rebel territory, right on the frontline. The first person I met was Olga Ischenko, the mayor. She was asking me because when I introduced myself I had mentioned that three days earlier I had been in Popasnaya, the Ukrainian-held town eight kilometres away. She wanted to know if people there were desperate to be liberated from the rule of Ukrainian 'fascists'. Outside the town hall is a statue of Lenin, in front of which have been stacked unexploded artillery shells and the remains of Grad and Smerch missiles fired at Pervomaysk from Popasnaya.

Before we started talking I wanted to get a few things straight. How long had she been mayor? Alarmingly Olga's eyes suddenly filled with tears. In January, she explained, her husband Evgeny Ischenko, who had been the mayor, was murdered along with three others, so she had taken over after that. 'It was necessary to take the position to prevent armed robbery and looting in town.' Her husband was a Cossack leader of men supposed to be part of the armed forces of the Lugansk People's Republic or LNR, to use its Russian acronym, the second breakaway rebel territory along with the Donetsk People's Republic.

The mayor was thirty-seven years old and had two children, one aged nine and another nine months old. She said 'nobody knows for sure' who killed her husband and she was vague about who might have looted the town had she not taken power. When her husband died, Igor Plotnitsky, the LNR leader, blamed Ukrainians but it was actually widely believed that the murder was an inside job, part of a bloody local power struggle. In December 2014, when Ukrainian missiles hit a building in town, the angry Evgeny, shouting on camera – you can find this easily on YouTube – denounced Plotnitsky for having signed what was then the first Minsk ceasefire with the Ukrainian side on 5 September. In fact this was negotiated with Russia, but for form's sake Plotnitsky had to sign for the LNR. Still, Evegny railed: 'You fucking vilely sign this agreement? We will turn all our weapons around . . . against you!' Pushing rubble away from the head of a woman whose body had been crushed under a piece of concrete, he shouted: 'Sign your fucking peace agreement on the corpse of this woman!'

Now there was a lull in the fighting, following the signing in Minsk of the second ceasefire agreement, which officially began on 15 February. This made it easier to travel about and to get to Pervomaysk from Donetsk, since the road between them led through Debaltseve, which had fallen to the rebels two days after the ceasefire began. Both towns were badly damaged.

In 2011 there were estimated to be just under 39,000 people in Pervomaysk. According to Olga, during the worst of the fighting the population dropped to 8,000 but now it had risen to 18,000. It was a figure that strained credibility. Since no one here believed that the ceasefire was much more than a lull, it seemed to me that far fewer had returned. 'We are going to take our land back,' said Olga, by which she meant at the very least the whole of Lugansk oblast, including neighbouring Popasnaya. In the future, she said, the LNR should become a republic within Russia.

In a nearby housing estate, I saw a block that had been completely burned out. Some apartments had gaping holes where they had taken direct hits. There was damage everywhere. The glass from most windows was gone, but they were either boarded up or patched with plastic sheeting. On one street, the corner of a building had come down. Oddly, bottles of shampoo remained on the shelf in what was once a bathroom, which was now part of the rubble beneath it. There were few people on the streets, even though it was quiet, spring had begun and that day the sun was being eclipsed by the moon.

A smart woman strolled by with her glossy black Labrador, trailed by four friendly strays who had joined them for their walk. Natalya Sokolik was a 41-year-old doctor. She talked about three waves of fighting, the last one ending with the February ceasefire. She reckoned that out of 200 local doctors only twenty-five were left. In her block, which had been home to up to 250 people, she thought there might be thirty or forty now, though some had trickled back recently. After the first ceasefire in September some returned 'even with kids', but this time no one had risked coming back with children in case they had to leave all over again. Yesterday, she said cheerfully, 'I got my first pay for eight months!' It was about $120. Today there were virtually no jobs here, and while there was food in the few shops that were open, basics were expensive and cash hard to get hold of.

Money was a serious issue. The rebel-held east had been excised from Ukraine's financial and banking system. Cashpoints were just dead black screens, banks were closed and those who did work *and* who managed to get paid, now received their pay in cash. A large proportion of those who had stayed in the rebel-held east were pensioners, but every week it was becoming harder and harder for them to collect their pensions. Officially you had to travel to government-controlled regions and register as a refugee there. That was beyond the means of many. It was taking up to two months even to get the Ukrainian permission necessary to travel to government territory and back. That was one reason why the other side of the frontline was increasingly being referred to as 'Ukraine', as though it had already become the foreign country that rebel leaders said they wanted it to be.

About the future, Nataliya was circumspect, choosing her words carefully. No one knows what it will hold and she could see I was being escorted by a man in uniform, who had been detailed to show me around by the mayor. 'Let's see . . .' she said, 'but according to the opinion of people here, they would not like to be part of Ukraine again after everything they have experienced.' At a small corner shop, close by a flat that had taken a direct hit, we met Larisa Kovalova, aged sixty-five, a retired physics teacher. She reminisced about good times in the past when she could afford to go on holiday in Crimea and the Caucasus. Now she said, hardly anyone remained where she lived, except for some other old people. Most of the others had gone to Russia but they had left dogs, cats and chickens and someone had to look after them.

Soon we came across a group of old ladies chatting in the sun.

They showed me the cellar under their block where they had been sheltering when there was shelling. They had been given some onions as part of a package of humanitarian aid and had planted some in the courtyard. Their spring bulbs were peeking into life. The women pointed out where two of their number had been killed as they ran for the shelter. A few minutes' drive away was a nuclear bunker from the 1960s, complete with pictures of mushroom clouds and instructions, beautifully preserved in historical aspic, about what to do in case of a nuclear attack. About forty-two people were sleeping here but when things were bad, up to 200 crammed in. Now some did not want to leave because they were still scared and some were staying because their homes had been badly damaged.

Alona Petrova, aged sixteen, sat on her bed with her boyfriend Rovshan Gladkikh, aged twenty. They met in the bunker and theirs was a wartime romance. They wanted to get married. Alona said that after the war she wanted to study and Rovshan said he wanted to become a miner like his father. This is mining country and a few miles away is the town of Stakhanov, named after the champion miner of Soviet legend, who worked here. Rovshan said his shell-shocked mother, who had survived a shelling incident, was too scared to go home. His eleven-year-old sister Sabrina watched TV. 'We want independence,' he said, when I asked him about the future. 'How can we live with them if they are killing people?'

Even when peace returns to Pervomaysk, a thick seam of bitterness has been laid down now. It was a dilapidated, rust-belt sort of place before the war and it is hard, if not impossible, to imagine it ever flourishing again. As in the former Yugoslavia, buildings can be rebuilt, as they were in the devastated eastern Croatian town of Vukovar for example, but if there is no work and no reason to return, then places like this will shrivel and die. The same goes for Popasnaya on the Ukrainian side.

When Gnome drove us there in his armoured car he insisted we put on our flak jackets for the last stretch of the road. (Gnome is his *nom de guerre* and he asked that his real name not be used.) Then he stepped hard on the accelerator and we hurtled down the last few kilometres of straight and exposed road. He kept glancing to his right, over the fields. A few days before, he said, one of his tyres had been shot out by a sniper from the rebel side.

Gnome was a paramedic and member of Hospitallers, a volunteer group, who draw their name and inspiration from the Knights Hospitaller order founded in 1099 at the time of the Crusades. They were doctors and medics who had established a system for front-line medical evacuations to slash the number of Ukrainian soldiers dying, not because their injuries could not be treated, but because they could not be transported to proper medical care quick enough.

In Popasnaya, which the rebels held and then lost in July 2014, things were as quiet as in Pervomaysk. In its hospital I met Dr Alexander Kovalchuk, who used to work there. Now he is the head of the surgical unit in Popasnaya. In 2011 it was estimated that there were 22,000 people here but now he said there might be just 5,000. About 70 per cent of the hospital medical staff had either remained or returned. Unlike in Pervomaysk, staff were being paid and the banking system was working here.

Many of those who remained in Pervomaysk voted for Russki Mir or 'Russian World', said Kovalchuk, using an expression favoured by Russian nationalists, and referring to the rebel anti-Ukrainian referendums of May 2014. Now they had 'tasted it' he said, many regretted it. Because the mobile phone system still worked he talked to friends and family there and they were 'really fed up'. But here in Popasnaya he conceded, there were people, especially 'simple people', as opposed to the middle class, who supported the rebels, though there were also pro-Ukrainians remaining in Pervomaysk. The war would 'last long', he thought, but for now 'we are not talking about taking back those territories, though we would like to reunite with our friends and relatives'.

In a ward I met Alexander, aged fifty-two. He had stomach ulcers. He said he had not left Popasnaya because he had to look after his parents who were too old to go. His flat had been damaged and he could not live in it. 'I don't know who shelled it,' he said, 'but it obviously came from Pervomaysk. We are fed up with everyone and everything. We want a united Ukraine but the rebels and the Ukrainians need to talk.' A man in the next bed, who did not want to give his name, said, 'Ukraine wants peace,' but added that he thought its leaders did not.

The centre of Popasnaya had been damaged, though not as extensively as Pervomaysk. Bundles of clothes lay on the rubble of a block whose top corner flat had been eviscerated by a missile. A man died during the attack. Oleg, aged fifty, said he was collecting what remained from the flat for his ex-wife and son, who had moved to Kharkiv. 'She phoned me and asked me to get everything that is left.' He was stuffing it all in his car. In a grocery shop Oxana, aged forty-one, said that her son, who was twenty-one, had gone to Russia. 'Thank goodness he did not join the rebels.' Half of her friends had gone to Russia, and the sympathies of those that remained were divided. 'I supported this country from the beginning,' she said, but many did not. 'To be honest,' the town was 'divided'. Many who had supported the rebels had changed their minds, none the least because 'it is very bad there in Pervomaysk'.

On the way out of town there is a big Ukrainian checkpoint and military position at the crossroads in the district of Cheryomushki. In Popasnaya they said that the Ukrainians had been firing at them from here. The rebel lines were more than a kilometre away. The crossroads is close to an area of low-rise apartment blocks, just like the ones in Popasnaya. Many were damaged and had holes in the roofs from shelling. The Ukrainians claimed the rebels and their Russian backers were trying to hit the checkpoint. I wanted to talk to someone but couldn't see anyone at all. Suddenly, in the distance I spotted a woman and ran to catch up with her. Ludmila, aged sixty-three, was walking home with a shopping bag. I asked her if anyone else was here, living in these hundreds of apartments. In her block, she said, 'there is a woman on the first floor and me'. She had seen light in two windows in other blocks recently. She had lived in the basement for two weeks when shelling was bad. The electricity and gas had been cut off, but now they had been restored, though the running water had not. She told me that she had a daughter-in-law and grandchildren who were living somewhere safe and they had asked her to come, but so far she had refused. 'I lost my husband when I was thirty-five,' she said, and a few years ago her only son had died of lung cancer, so she had thought to herself that if she was killed 'and buried between them, it would make no difference'.

Civilians were suffering, as they do in all wars, but in this one older people were suffering the most. The morale of soldiers on both sides was high and their leaders were thinking and talking of eventual victory rather than a peaceful end to the war. The rebels could not survive without Russian military support but with it the Ukrainians could not defeat them. The war was thus both one between Russia and Ukraine and at the same time contained elements of civil war in the east. Many pro-Ukrainians tried to deny this because it complicated their simple picture of Russian aggression and terrorists, but for anyone who had been on both sides of the line, it was evident. That was not to deny Russian involvement though, and, as Valentin Fedichev, a proud Ukrainian army colonel who briefed me, said, even in a nightmare 'we never thought we could be attacked by Russia'. He was an Afghan war veteran and, as he pointed out, an ethnic Russian. What Vladimir Putin had done, he said, was to commit an act of 'geopolitical treachery' against Ukraine. Everyone was waiting to see what he would do next.

36.

The War Poets

Before the war, Olena Maksymenko, a tall 29-year-old, loved to write and travel. 'I travelled a lot, in the Caucasus, Georgia, Mongolia, Baikal. I was also interested in ancient history, archaeology and mythology.' Not many Ukrainians are travel journalists and poets, but Olena was carving out a nice career and name for herself here.

But, as for many middle-class educated Ukrainians, something changed for her with the Maidan revolution. Like so many others, all she wanted for Ukraine was for it to be a normal European country, not one that continued to linger, as it had done since independence in 1991, in the grey zone between Russia and the rest of Europe, all the while crushed by a culture of economic and political corruption that left poor a country which should be rich. So, Olena's poems became political and she read them from the stage on the Maidan.

In March 2014 she went with colleagues to write about what was happening in Crimea. Close to the border she was picked up, or kidnapped, by people she described as 'just guys with guns'. They were, she said, Cossacks, Berkut and Russian soldiers. They threatened to kill her, pointed a gun at her and fired, though it was not loaded, hit her and chopped some of her hair off. 'They said I was an agent of the USA and they tried to get information from me about other journalists. Three days later I was released.'

When she came back from Crimea she discovered that one of her best friends, with whom she had spent the Maidan months, had committed suicide. By complete chance this moment in her life coincided with a writers' residency she had won, organized before the revolution, in Latvia. There, a novel about her friend and the Maidan simply poured out. She was angry. She trained to fight but she told me that only women with the right connections were being allowed to do so. 'If there is a choice between a woman with training and a man without they will choose the man.' Women like her, she complained, were being shunted into HQ paper-shuffling jobs or detailed to cook for soldiers.

We travelled together to Pervomais'ke*, close to Donetsk airport. She was attached to a group of volunteer medics based in what had been a hotel before the war. Here the doctors had set up a first aid treatment and evacuation centre for soldiers injured in the fighting. All the medics, including medical students who were doing time at the front, were enthusiastic and fired up by the cause of doing their bit to defend Ukraine. Standing behind the hotel reception desk was Oleksiy Reznikov, aged twenty-two, who had a shelf of small bottles of different coloured inks behind him and above his Kalashnikov. 'This is a war we need to fight and everyone needs to find their niche,' he told me. His was that of frontline tattooist. 'It raises morale . . . and then the fighters do a better job.' Soldiers and medics were having him tattoo them with their blood groups and nick-names, and some with patriotic Ukrainian themes and symbols.

From here, we could hear fighting, but the intensity was much reduced since the ceasefire of 15 February 2014. Bored, Olena was filing stories and collecting more which might appear in another novel. From her childhood, she told me, she had thought that it would be amazing to be a war correspondent and 'that I would go to foreign wars . . . but unfortunately war came to me'.

In Kiev I sat with a senior security official whom I know. We were talking about the various scenarios facing Ukraine in the next few months. Then he mused that, even though Ukraine had become an independent state when the Soviet Union had collapsed, it was not something that Ukrainians had fought for. Now they were fighting 'a classical war of independence . . . we have to force, or

---

* This is not the same place as Pervomaysk, described in 'Towns at War'.

persuade the Russians to consider us a separate people, entity and state'. And he added, 'but wars of independence have a second step and that is a war for borders'.

In rebel-held Donetsk, I met Anna Iureva, aged eighty-seven. Anna is a tiny, sprightly, grey haired woman. For the last eight months she and her family had lived in a dingy nuclear bomb shelter. With the ceasefire most of the people who stayed here had gone home but some, like Anna, were stuck. She and her family had fled from their damaged house a few minutes' walk away from the hotel-cum-field hospital in Pervomais'ke.

Anna said that she would like to go home but 'fighting is constant there' and anyway she did not want to return while it was still under Ukrainian control. 'They did a lot of harm to us. How many people have they killed? How many homes have they destroyed?' she asked angrily. Then she took me into a side room where her relatives and others slept in cramped bunk beds. It was incredibly hot because here her 43-year-old granddaughter, who has Down's syndrome, was sitting right in front of a fan heater. Anna showed me a tin with

oil and a wick that they used for light when the electricity went off because they had run out of candles, and which she said gave off a horrible, choking smoke. Then she gave me a sheaf of small and tidy sheets of paper on which she had transcribed her poems.

Anna told me that as a schoolgirl she had written poems, but that because she had been the youngest of eleven, her parents could not afford to give her much of an education. Now, bored and unable to sleep at night, she had begun to write again. A poem called 'Fighters' begins like this:

> *You are fighters of our country*
> *Our husbands, brothers and sons*
> *Liberators of our country*
> *You are going to fight, not for the sake of honour*
> *But for the State of Novorossiya*

Novorossiya is the name of the would-be state comprising the Donetsk and Lugansk People's republics. The poem goes on to refer to President Poroshenko and the Ukrainian government:

> *Poroshenko decided to give mines, factories and land to the West and*
> *then flee abroad*
> *And they destroyed so many towns thinking they were winning*
> *But now they are wiping away tears and snot*
> *They are wondering where to flee, and how to cover their bloody tracks*

And finally:

> *You have to pay with your own life for everything that was destroyed*
> *Oh God, bless the fighters going into battle*
> *Save them from any evil*
> *And bring them home alive*

At this point, in the spring of 2015, Ukraine's forces were not strong enough to retake what they call the 'occupied territories' and the rebels, even with Russian support, were not strong enough to take more territory from the government they called the 'fascist junta'. Before the war there was no oppression of Russians and Russian-speakers in the east, as pro-Russians claimed, not least because President Yanukovych, who came from here, and his Donetsk clan actually dominated the whole country. There was no hatred between people. But the war had changed that, some were leaving and the region was becoming ever more of a strange, decaying and increasingly empty place that echoed to endless lofty-sounding exhortations to fight the fascists. What was clear, though, was that in a year the situation had changed. The Donetsk and Lugansk People's republics had emerged as real political entities just as in the other post-Soviet breakaway regions and like the Serb areas did in the former Yugoslavia. In Croatia one, Krajina, was swept away by war in 1995 but, in Bosnia, the Republika Srpska exists today as a semi-independent quasi-state. People live side by side in Bosnia, but don't have much to do with one another. Both scenarios are possible in Ukraine's east, and Ukrainian politicians have talked about the 'Croatian model', by which they mean freeze the lines, build up your forces and reconquer when you are ready.

Whatever happened, Anna said that if her home remained under Ukrainian control eventually, 'in the worst case', she and her family would see if they could make a new home somewhere in Russia. She was not typical in being an 87-year-old bomb shelter poet, and neither was Olena, as a poet determined to put down her pen and pick up a gun. But, to return to the thoughts of the security source, the problem now was that, whatever opinion polls said before the war, whatever people thought then and given that the social structure of the rebel-held territories had changed, especially thanks to the flight above all of middle-class and younger people, it was not just those who fought for Ukraine who believed they were fighting a war of independence. Both sides did and thus both were fighting for their borders.

VI. ESCAPING THE PAST

37.

Defining Optimism

According to the press in Odessa, Andrey Stavnitser is one of the city's wealthiest men. That does not put him in Ukraine's oligarch class by any means but, as he runs a particularly successful port business, which was built from scratch, it makes what he has to say especially interesting. In October 2013 he was thirty-one years old. A month later President Yanukovych was due to sign the two key agreements which would begin the process of integrating Ukraine and its economy with the European Union. It was a time of fierce debate. Those who were against the proposal said it would harm the Ukrainian economy because those Ukrainian exporters who were dependent on the Russian market would lose out. They believed that Ukraine should instead join Russia's Customs Union with Belarus and Kazakhstan. Supporters of the EU option said that while the transition would be difficult, the pain of transition would pay dividends within a few years. And there was a third position, as I found out from Andrey. Though for his business it would be better to enter the Customs Union because then he could expect more Russian cargoes, EU standards would be great if they could curb corruption and 'as a citizen, I would vote for the EU'. In the Customs Union Russia would again dominate Ukraine and thus he said: 'I would not go there again.'

Eighteen months later the political landscape had utterly changed. The Maidan revolution had come and gone and there was war in the east. Odessa's people were divided, but the city remained firmly under Ukrainian control. Every now and then bombs exploded at Ukrainian volunteer recruitment offices, but as they went off at night they were clearly designed to intimidate rather than kill. Similar attacks plagued Kharkiv. On 2 May 2014 violent clashes had taken place between pro and anti-Maidan crowds. The result was that one pro-Ukrainian had died and some forty-seven anti-Maidan pro-Russians, including forty-two in a fire in the large Trade Unions House. After that, the climate in the city changed. Pro-Russians understood that Ukrainians would fight back and Odessa and the south would not be snatched from them without resistance as Crimea had been. Maybe, many concluded, this was a cause not worth dying for. Ukraine's security services were now on the lookout for separatist activists and so many of them had fled to Russian-occupied Crimea or the east.

Odessa, founded by Empress Catherine the Great in 1794, is famous for its colourful history and stories. But for Westerners its name more often than not triggers associations with a city that no longer exists. It might conjure up images of the booming nineteenth-century cosmopolitan port in which every language from French to Greek to Albanian was spoken, or the great city of Jewish memory in which a third of the population were Jews. It might make one think of Isaac Babel, the famous writer, born here in 1894 and executed in 1940, a victim of Stalin's purges. Or possibly the first association might be with the famous Odessa city steps, which lead down to the port and were immortalized in the 1925 Sergei Eisenstein Soviet movie, *Battleship Potemkin*. In the film, about the 1905 revolution, we see crowds fleeing tsarist troops who are firing on them, and in its most famous scene a pram with a baby careens down the steps. In reality none of this ever happened. Still Odessa has a lot of history, Odessans are proud of it, but it is history. It is good for bringing tourists here from Ukraine and from Russia. Before the war, large numbers of Westerners also poured off Black Sea cruise ships to be marched around the historic centre by fierce, matronly guides. Now I wanted to hear a story of modern Odessa and to hear what Andrey Stavnitser thought of the future.

The source of Andrey's wealth lies on a deep inlet from the Black Sea, 27 kilometres east of the city. The company and port are called TIS, or Transinvestservice. Ships sail up the inlet to either unload imports to Ukraine or, more likely, load its exports. Containers filled with fertilizers, grain, iron ore and coal leave from here. As grain pours down shoots into ships berthed at the terminal, clouds of dust rise from the holds. Along the dockside there are hills of coal and iron ore pellets. Vegetable oils and wood chips also flow out of Ukraine from here. The machinery is modern, the steel silos gleam in the sunlight and the foundations of a vast new warehousing section have been dug. Over the last twenty years some $350 million has been invested here and it shows. The company employs about 3,500 people and this is as modern and successful a business as you will find anywhere in Ukraine.

Andrey is burly and wears a sky-blue, long-sleeved T-shirt. The history of the port is 'very simple', he said. Oleksiy, his Jewish father, was born in 1943, the son of a well-known mining engineer, whose job at the time was to sabotage mines before the Nazis reached them, so during the invasion of the Soviet Union, he was always working one step ahead of them. Oleksiy could not have chosen a more different career. He became a mountaineer and was head of the mountain rescue service in the Caucasus until 1988 when he returned home to Odessa. The period that was beginning was one of huge opportunities for those who knew how to grab them and Oleksiy did. In 1989, he started opening shops selling imported goods. They were a success. In 1994 he came to this spot with Oleg Kutateladze, his lawyer and friend, to inspect a derelict port site. Just before the end of the Soviet Union the authorities had begun building a terminal here, primarily to unload phosphates from Morocco. The project fell foul of the new ecology movement which, as everywhere else in the Soviet Union, preceded the emergence of political parties. One ship came to dock but, confronted with protesters, never unloaded and sailed away. The port was mothballed and the project left as an unfinished building site.

Oleksiy and Oleg thought this would be a good place to load fertilizers for export. First they rented the land, went on to form a joint venture with the authorities and finally bought the place in

2001. The port began work in 1996 and in 1997 it handled its first million tonnes. In 2014 it handled 26 million tonnes and 720 ships. In 1998 they began building a grain terminal. During the Soviet period, most of Ukraine's grain went to the rest of the country. With independence producers began to export outside of the former Soviet Union. Oleksiy was a driven man and a workaholic. He built a house next to the port so that he could live right next door to what he loved most in the world. He took to the challenge of building a business as if climbing the hardest of mountains. He micromanaged everything, Andrey told me, and he delegated no decisions, whether they were about '$50 or $50 million'.

Born in 1982, Andrey was only a child when the Soviet Union collapsed but he was a teenager in the chaotic mid-1990s as his father was building a multimillion-dollar business. The relationship between father and son was tense and besides, in this violent period, the threat of kidnapping was real. At the age of fifteen Andrey was despatched to a boarding school in England. He hated the weather and the food and the school were not much good. The following year he was sent to an American school in Switzerland, not least because his father was worried about drugs in England. When Andrey arrived one of the first people he met was a Russian boy who said, 'Shall we go and get some weed downtown?' After this he was sent to a French business school in Moscow to do an MBA. This was another error, he said: 'Don't ever do an MBA before you have five or six years' experience.' Andrey belonged to the first generation of children of wealthy Ukrainians and Russians to be sent abroad and they learned by their mistakes.

Even though he was also studying in Moscow Andrey began working with his father. One of the most difficult things was that he wanted to see results straight away but in the port business it can be five years between an idea becoming a plan and turning into a working reality. 'I had lots of conflicts with my father, it was very difficult to get along and I quit twice.' Then, when he was twenty-five, his father got cancer. At that point, he says, 'all of my pride disappeared. Everything became very simple after that.' His father divided the shares of the business between Andrey and his older brother, who now looks after the finances, and started preparing them to take over the company. Just before Oleksiy died in 2011 Andrey was made CEO. 'No matter how hard you prove yourself,' he told me, 'you will always be the son of the founder . . . no matter what. It was very difficult and everyone was twenty years older than me.' Had he enjoyed it? 'It was fun . . .' In front of the TIS office building there is a statue of Oleksiy.

If the company had withered after Oleksiy died, the sceptics would have gloated that the former fun-loving party boy was not worthy of his father. But, in the last five years, turnover has tripled as has income. Despite the turmoil of 2014 the venture still prospered. Some Russian business was lost but new partners were found and anyway, said Andrey, much of what they do is a function of global demand for commodities. As long as Ukraine is still producing grain and iron ore and everything else the world needs, all of it will still need to be exported. His colleagues who have really suffered, he said, are those dealing in imports, especially of consumer goods. The decline of the hryvnia has slashed everyone's purchasing power. The next two or three years could see setbacks even for him though. Credit is virtually impossible to get for most businesses and this will affect production, especially in the agricultural sector. If that means less is produced it means less to export too.

In these turbulent times Andrey has made no secret of which side of the barricades he is on. At the entrance to the TIS port is a giant Transformers-style robot sculpture holding a Ukrainian flag. For its mouth it has a red digital ticker tape screen along which run the words *Slava Ukraini!* 'Glory to Ukraine!' More than a year after the beginning of the war in the east Andrey was fairly confident that the critical point of risk had passed and that Odessa was not about to fall into separatist or Russian hands. Anyone watching television can see what is happening in Donetsk and Lugansk, he said, and so can make their own realistic assumption about what would happen here if conflict were to spread. When there had been anti-Ukrainian demonstrations in the city in 2014 he had mingled

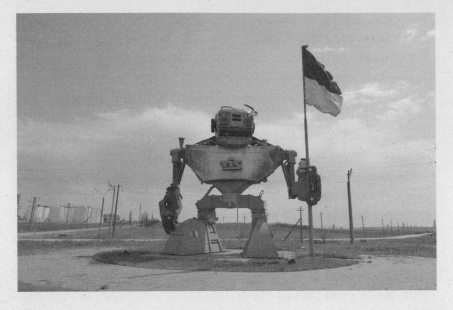

with protesters to hear what they were saying and was shocked that middle-class people were among them. 'There were doctors and teachers and government officials and their salaries are way bigger in Russia. They were just fed up with low salaries and low pensions.' At the time many thought that Odessa might fall into Russian hands like Crimea, but one key difference is that perhaps most people in Crimea wanted to become part of Russia when the opportunity arose, while the same could not be said about Odessa.

Andrey said it was hard to know what his workers thought, not least because he had decreed that politics must be left at the port gate. He estimated, 'we had people in favour of Russia, perhaps 30 per cent and maybe they still are, and then 70 per cent for Ukraine'. The difference would be if 10 per cent of the pro-Russians were actively propagating their views. When the war began and a port train driver stuck a Donetsk People's Republic flag on his loco-motive, Andrey says he was fired within two hours. More sinister was the day his security men found a man dressed like a homeless person snooping about. When they searched him they found he had a Russian military officer's identity document on him. He was handed over to the Ukrainian security services. He must have been a low-level operative and a dimwit at that for carrying ID, but it was clear what he was doing. 'This is where military ships could berth.' If Russia was going to land men and military equipment in a bid to take Odessa, the TIS port would be the ideal place to do it.

Especially at the most critical times Andrey was active in the local media. He wanted people to see that he was taking a pro-Ukrainian position at a time when many were uncertain and no one knew if, in the wake of the loss of Crimea and the beginning of the war, the rest of Ukraine might simply implode. He wanted everyone to know that 'we would be in big trouble if Russia came'. Then those close to him and colleagues in Odessa suggested he pipe down, even though they shared his views. They feared that if Ukraine lost Odessa anyone who had been prominent in support of it would lose their business and believed that whatever happened they had a responsibility to their workers and families and perhaps it was not worth risking all if it meant that the business would be destroyed. Andrey did not pipe down.

Now that the threat from Russia had receded he had another concern. The government needed to get a move on and reform the country fast. When they carry out reforms they don't explain why, he said. A year ago no one would have thought of saving water, gas or electricity because, as they were heavily subsidized, they were cheap. Now the subsidies were going and prices were rising but no one was explaining to people why this was happening and so they got angry. The revolution had also led to new people being put in charge of a system, of ministries and administrations full of people who 'need to be fired'. They were destructive elements left over from the past, he said, and sabotaged attempts to change things. New people at the top spent 80 per cent of their time fighting those who were supposed to work for them and only 15 or 20 per cent of their time on reforms. One serious problem was that Ukraine simply did not have enough individuals with the right skills to replace those he thought should be sacked. Andrey said he spent time at the Ministry of Infrastructure and it was full of people 'who are against any changes' while the new intake 'don't know anything about ports'. For this reason, and 'because it is easy to criticize and I am trying to help', TIS employees were being despatched to Kiev to give masterclasses on how ports operated. In the railway sector, energy and mining he saw the same problems.

Maidan, he lamented, had been a 'revolution of merchant bankers', by which he meant that many of the top posts in government had gone to people who worked in finance and were rich enough to take time off to take them on. Ukraine had plenty of good people with financial and banking experience, but not enough who had other types of business experience. The problem with this was that the finance types

> . . . don't like to come into conflict with anyone. By their very nature they have to be friendly and tolerant but, given the way the country is, they must be decisive and tough and it is just not in their nature, so when it comes to fighting corruption and putting people in jail they just can't do it. Some good examples: none of the former politicians are in jail. No corrupt prosecutors or judges have been arrested. How can you do reforms like this? In Odessa they changed the head of the prosecutor's office but everyone else is the same.

Judges were bribed to put people in jail and the person who paid the most wins when a commercial dispute comes to court. It is not surprising that there has been far less foreign investment in Ukraine than its size and potential suggest it should have. Many corporate agreements are done under British law, Andrey said, but whatever a British court might decide, it is of little use if its decision cannot be enforced in Ukraine. There are no multinationals in the Ukrainian port business 'because they are afraid. They say, "Why come to Ukraine when we can go to Slovenia or the Baltics?" ' Above all else, Ukraine's corrupt legal system needs fixing 'and that has not even been touched by the reforms yet'.

Before leaving and turning out from the port back on to cratered roads, I asked Andrey if he was an optimist. 'An optimist is not the first to shout "hurray,"' he quipped, 'but the last to shout "we're finished" and there is still time to shout that.' A banker who knows Andrey said that the shame was that there were far too few businessmen like him in Ukraine.

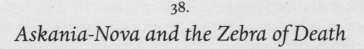

38.
Askania-Nova and the Zebra of Death

'Yes kids! We're coming!' shouted Viktor Gavrilenko happily out of the window of his green Lada Niva as we hurtled over the steppe. They stood, looking sullen and stared at him. A little bit away from the main group, one was standing beside another one lying on the ground. 'Oh my God! He's dead!' said Viktor. We jumped out to have a look. His eyes had been pecked out by crows who had streaked his body with their white excrement. If this had been an African wildlife reserve the overnight death of a zebra would have been a mundane affair. Here at Askania-Nova, less than an hour's drive from the border with Crimea, where they have lived on and off for well over a century, the murderous overnight assault, in which an alpha male had kicked a younger male to death was, said Gavrilenko, 'very rare'.

Phone calls were made and a team summoned to take away the victim for a post-mortem. After this he would be fed to the guard dogs. We moved off to see the bison nursing their young, wild donkeys from Tajikistan and rare Przewalski horses from Mongolia. Then we came to the herds of saiga antelope, with their characteristic snuffling muzzle that looks like a tiny elephant's trunk. A quarter of a century ago a million ranged across the Eurasian steppe all the way to China, but the post-Soviet world has not been kind to them. There are perhaps only 50,000 left. They have been hunted for their meat and above all for the distinctive horns of the males which are used in Chinese medicines. Now there are none left in China. Suddenly Viktor and Viktoria Smagol, his 39-year-old saiga specialist, leapt out of the car and within minutes Viktor was cradling a two-day-old foal which Viktoria put in a cardboard box that happened to be labelled 'From Ukraine'. The Chinese want them for breeding and pay $3,000 a head. Half an hour later he was in a pen with eight others. When they are four months old they will be flying to China.

There is something surreal about the zebras of the Ukrainian steppe, the camel which had just given birth in Askania-Nova's zoo, with its ostriches, immaculately kept gardens and arboretum. It is a jarring contrast to what you would expect in the crumbly and dilapidated little towns of this part of the south. But the strange thing is how, despite all the odds, this place has survived the whirlwinds of history.

Viktor is a turbocharged 59-year-old. Since 1990 he has headed up the steppe biosphere reserve and steered it through the difficult post-Soviet years. Now bad times are here again, but Askania-Nova has seen far worse. Walking round the arboretum at dusk he began to tell the tale. In 1828 this tract of land, designated as parcel '71', was bought by the Duke of Anhalt-Kothen, a small duchy in the centre of Germany. The plan was to turn the steppe here into sheep country. His retainers had experience with sheep, and the port of Odessa, just a few days' trek away, was open for business to export wool. On the designated day a long column set off from the small town of Rosslau on the river Elbe towards the planned settlement. It was to take its name from one of the duke's 800-year-old titles. In the column were fifteen men, four women, six children, two bulls, six cows, eight horses and 2,866 sheep. They travelled, according to one account, with three covered wagons which 'had been loaded with all the equipment: clothes, linen, tools, seeds – everything that had to go'. But the steppe was dry, the project badly managed and the venture was not a success. In 1856 it was sold to Friedrich Fein. He was the prosperous descendant of a man who, according to one version of his story, for accounts differ slightly, had fled to imperial Russia from his native Germany in 1763.

Fein managed to turn Askania-Nova into a successful sheep farm, and eventually there would be several hundred thousand sheep here. After his death the estate passed to his only child, a daughter, and her husband, a man called Johann Falz. By permission of Tsar Alexander ll they were allowed to create the name Falz-Fein to preserve the Fein name. It was their grandson Friedrich Falz-Fein who, in 1884, began to create a zoo, an arboretum and a reserve here and fenced off a large area of virgin steppe to preserve it. By this time the family also had a fish-canning plant and a small Black Sea port nearby from which they could export their wool. When Tsar Nicholas ll came to visit in April 1914 Friedrich had fifty-eight types of animals and 402 types of birds. The tsar is reported to have exclaimed: 'My goodness, what harmony there is here, what peace . . . What a paradise!' As he set off back to his brand-new Livadia palace in Crimea, he said he hoped to visit again in autumn, 'If we haven't got a war on our hands by then!'

The end of the war, the civil war and the revolution saw the Falz-Feins flee to Germany, sailing away from Crimea. Friedrich's mother refused to go and was shot by bandits or Red Army soldiers at her huge stately home in nearby Preobrazhenka. Fighting raged around Askania-Nova as it changed hands between Whites, backed by German troops, and Reds. With the final imposition of Soviet rule most of the animals had been killed, eaten or had escaped but perhaps a quarter survived. In 1919 the property was nationalized and in 1921 it became a state steppe reserve. An institute of animal husbandry was developed, based on the scientific work of Friedrich Falz-Fein. Just as Askania-Nova was getting back on its feet, Stalin's purges began. Between 1933 and 1937 the number of scientists and other workers here who were executed came to eighteen, with more sent to the Gulag. Oddly, as thousands of other places were given new, proper, revolutionary-sounding names Askania-Nova kept its name with all of its aristocratic connotations. In 1941 war came again and, while officially the reserve and institute continued to be run by a German, by 1943 with the return of the Red Army only 20 per cent of the animals were left. Reconstruction began again.

Now the institute started to expand and had large farms at its disposal and these required manpower. People began to arrive, or be sent to work and settle here, and the village of Askania-Nova grew into a town. At first there were just modest houses but in the Khrushchev era typical five-storey blocks were built. There were shops, a cinema, a bakery, a dairy and a meat plant. And then, said Vera Kravchenko, aged seventy-six, who milked antelopes in Askania-Nova for twenty years, 'after *perestroika* everything began to go wrong'.

Money for the institute was drying up but Viktor managed to secure the formal separation of the reserve, zoo and arboretum from it. The institute wasted away, but the reserve survived all the tribulations of the post-Soviet era. It was a popular place to visit on holidays and, according to Vera, Viktor ran, and runs, a tight ship. If you work there and get caught drunk you are out. Today Viktor is an angry man, though. Budget cuts mean that the state is paying salaries and fuel bills but for everything else the reserve and the zoo need to find the money themselves. One source of income is breeding and selling animals, such as saiga and bison, the other is ticket sales. Before the war Askania-Nova had been receiving an average of 100,000 paying visitors a year. In 2013 it had 86,216 but the annexation of Crimea and the beginning of the war saw the number collapse to 34,096 in 2014. So, said Viktor, 'I have a big bill for Putin!' He wrote to his colleagues in Moscow to protest against the takeover of Crimea and what was happening in the east, saying that scientists should not stay quiet as they had when Hitler had taken over Austria and the Sudetenland. One of the most senior men he wrote to, an old friend, did not reply but his deputy did. The response was: 'We are not free in communications.'

I was staying the night at Vera's house. She and her husband had rooms for guests and the conflict had seen their numbers tumble in line with park visitor numbers. She and her husband came, as did so many, after the Second World War. Around the house they have pictures of kittens, saints, parrots and Stalin. They have family in Crimea and Nikolai Kravchenko, who is eighty, told me they say things are great there now since the Russians have taken over. When I asked if he thought they should come here too he answered: 'Of course! They should have done it years ago.' Of Stalin he said ruefully: 'He was the leader of our lives.' The rest of the family was more circumspect. His daughter Oksana and Anatoly Ivanov, her husband, aged sixty-three, went to live in Russia in the 1990s. In the end they decided to come back when there was a crackdown on illegal immigrants. They could not get their paperwork in order without paying a $5,000 bribe, which they could not afford, even though Anatoly was making good money working for the police as a vehicle electrician. Of the family in Crimea, he said, after a period of going on about how great it was with higher pay and pensions, they had gone very quiet because prices had risen so much too. He did not want the Russians to come to Askania-Nova. In Crimea people were no longer free to say what they wanted but 'I can say whatever I like.'

Life in Askania-Nova still revolves around the reserve and the institute which together employ about 450 people. In Soviet times they employed 1,100. The collapse of employment has led to an exodus. From a peak of 10,000 inhabitants in the mid-1980s there are now only 3,500 living here and most of them are elderly. The absence of people gives the town an eerie feeling. Nikolai said that he called his street, lined with pleasant houses with vegetable gardens, 'the street of death' because so many of his neighbours have left or died. Walk down the street and it is immediately clear how many houses are empty and beginning to fall down. On the main street a new house of culture, which would have been a sort of village hall, was built at the end of the Soviet period but then sold to someone in what locals assume to be some money-laundering scheme. Now it is closed, a dilapidated eyesore just like the old cinema on the other side.

Some of those who left in the late 1980s and early 90s were Germans, or people claiming German descent who could thus go to Germany. I wondered if some of them were the descendants of the colonists who had come as part of the original settlement or with the Falz-Feins. People looked blank when I asked them about this. I went to the cemetery just outside town and met a woman and her husband. I had seen gravestones with German names and asked her about this. She told me that her father, whose grave she had come to visit, had been an ethnic German. But, she explained, he had been a Crimean German, a descendant of settlers who had arrived at the beginning of the nineteenth century. In 1941 all of the Crimean Germans, like the Crimean Tatars, were deported by Stalin before the arrival of the Nazis, and so she had been born in Kazakhstan. After the war, again like the Crimean Tatars, the Germans were prevented from returning home but they could come here, and many did to one nearby village in particular, which was about as close to Crimea as they could get.

A few hundred metres away we could see a large Ukrainian mobile radar. It was there to help keep watch on the Russians and to give early warning in case their forces move out of the Crimea and begin an invasion of the mainland.

39.
'A hundred years of crap'

A couple of times I thought Natalie Jaresko was going to cry. But she did not. It was twilight and we sat on the terrace of her house just outside Kiev. As we talked, all the emotion of trying to save Ukraine from economic oblivion bubbled to the surface. Each time, though, the Minister of Finance regained her composure. Her two daughters, aged seventeen and eleven, drifted in and out asking homework questions. The next morning her older daughter was sitting an economics exam. 'I just feel incredible pressure,' said her mother. Ukraine's very 'existence as a country' was under threat and 'we have no choice but to succeed'.

The figures were dire. In 2014 industrial production declined by 21 per cent and the hyrvnia had lost 69 per cent of its value against the dollar. The country had lost territory, resources, industries, people and markets. Between 40 and 60 per cent of economic activity is in the grey economy. In the first quarter of 2015 the economy was 17.6 per cent smaller than a year before. The war, which was costing between $5 and $7 million a day, is being fought with guns but securing the home front means saving the economy too. After twenty-three years of poor and often literally criminal management, refiring its engines, making sure that the country did not implode under the weight of its debts and generalized corruption was a responsibility which fell, out of the blue, on to Natalie's shoulders.

Natalie was born in 1965 in Chicago and her progression from diaspora girl to minister was not obvious. When, after the general election of October 2014, she was asked to take the post, she recalled thinking that if she turned down the offer,

if I had not tried to help, I would never have forgiven myself. This country has given me everything I have and my children fascinating lives. I had to give back. You need to take into account that we had a revolution, watched Crimea being stolen on live TV and then came the war. People are dying. I know people who died on the Maidan. My daughters sold their toys to help refugees! My grandparents told me stories of the war, but this is different, it is real. There are men who are going to fight and don't come back to their families . . . I thought to myself, 'If I don't do this, how can I live with myself?'

Raw emotion and finance ministers are not the most common of bedfellows, but in this case there is a straightforward biographical line that leads from a Chicago suburb to ministerial office. Natalie's father was born in 1932, in the Poltava region in Soviet Ukraine, hence was a survivor from day one: he was born just as others in the family were dying of starvation in the *Holodomor*. Her mother was born in 1940 in Germany. Natalie's grandmother, from western Ukraine, had been despatched there to work by the Nazis, even though she was pregnant. She gave birth to a daughter, who was fostered by a German family. Five years later, the girl, who did not know she had 'real' parents, was suddenly reclaimed by her mother, who arrived in a jeep with American GIs who had agreed to help her. Natalie's father's relatives fled as the Soviets returned to Ukraine and both sides of the family ended up in a displaced persons' camp in Germany. Sponsored by Ukrainians in the US they were able to restart their lives in Chicago and this is where her parents met.

Natalie's father became an electrical engineer and worked for an insurance company for his whole career. Her mother was a secretary. On the weekends Natalie and her brother and sister went to Ukrainian school and participated in the community's church activities. At home they spoke English. They were raised to have respect for their Ukrainian traditions, but not to think that they would ever go back to the country. Indeed, Natalie's father believed that, as they lived in the US, 'we needed to succeed in that environment and everything else was secondary'. He insisted she study something 'useful'. Somewhat reluctantly, because she really wanted to study political science, she settled for accounting at university, though she double-majored in political science, which her father discovered only when she graduated. For her Masters, she went to the Kennedy School of Government at Harvard and her father *really* hated this. As a Reagan Republican, he disapproved of anything that smacked of government. But Natalie was now old enough to make her own decisions. Still, her father refused to come to her graduation. Next step was the State Department and then, in 1992, as a Ukrainian-speaker who by now had some experience in economic affairs in what had just become the former Soviet Union, she was invited to set up the economics section of the brand-new American embassy in Kiev. Very excited at the prospect, she called her husband, also an American-Ukrainian. He was skiing in Colorado and was underwhelmed by the idea. She told him: 'I am going.'

He was not happy, but he followed, at least for a while. Now she points out, quite apart from carrying the troubles of Ukraine on her shoulders, she is a single mother.

When she arrived it was clear that Ukraine had already been in decline for years even before the post-Soviet economic nosedive that was now beginning. Referring to the main boulevard that leads to the Maidan in the centre of Kiev, she said there were so few cars 'you could cross Kreshchatyk with your eyes closed'. But, as the difficult period of settling in began to pass, she found herself becoming ever more excited about 'the Ukraine that could be'. It was close to the rest of Europe, rich in various resources, had an educated population, ports and so on. 'What more could you ask for?' In 1995 her time at the embassy was up. As she was a civil servant rather than a career diplomat, she faced the unappealing prospect of returning to a cubicle in an office in Washington so, when an opportunity arose to stay in Ukraine, she grabbed it. USAID, the American government's aid wing, asked her to help set up an investment fund for Ukraine, Moldova and Belarus. The idea was to invest in and encourage the growth of small and medium-sized enterprises. This, in turn led to her starting her own investment house, called Horizon Capital, which was managing assets of more than $600 million when she sold her stake to take the job of Minister of Finance.

I asked her if investing had been a frustrating and disappointing experience, given that the big story of Ukraine since independence is one of lost opportunities. We had talked of how road builders and other contractors stole vast amounts, leaving the country with third-world roads. We had talked of how few paid income tax. 'It is a vicious circle. People say, "Why should I pay tax if the government does not provide me with good schools and hospitals as it is supposed to?" and the government in turn does not have the money to provide them as they are not paying tax.' The answer was surprising. Yes, it had been frustrating but not disappointing because times had been exciting, she had had opportunities she would never have had in the US and because her business philosophy had worked. This had been to pay her taxes, 'fly under the radar', invest in things like wine, chocolate and consumer goods that she understood and steer clear of privatizations, energy and natural resources, which is what those who would become Ukraine's oligarchs were interested in. And there were good times too. From 2000 to 2008 Ukraine's GDP grew by an average of 8 per cent a year, she said. Her companies were also relatively small, thus avoiding the attention of predatory raiders and for the most part corrupt tax officials. Only once was she openly asked for a bribe to complete a deal. The man she was negotiating with said cheerily: 'Only one more signature to go!' and opened an empty briefcase in front of her. He did not get the cash but she still got the deal. 'I always looked at the glass as half full,' she said.

Though the business climate began to deteriorate during the Yanukovych period, until the moment he balked at signing the deals his government had been negotiating with the EU in November 2013, there was hope. The guidelines of the free trade agreement were, she says, seen as a 'roadmap'. Once signed, 'we'd be on the way'. When Yanukovych said he would not sign and demonstrations began, it was clear which side she was on. Discreetly she began to help the demonstrators and those camped out on the square. Her children's nanny cooked up fatty meat stews to take to the men there, explaining that they needed the fat to protect them from the cold. Because she had been in Ukraine so long, Natalie knew not only many of the foreign diplomats but the political players too. She knew Petro Poroshenko, the man who would become president, for example, because she had invested in a competitor chocolate firm to his. Pupils at her children's school would go to the Maidan when the day was done or even skip class to be there. She went with hers at the weekend and supported her office staff who took part in the protests.

Then, nine months after they were over, she was visited by headhunters taken on by the incoming Ukrainian government. They asked her for suggestions of people who should be hired and asked her if she was interested in a post in the government, to which she replied that the question was hypothetical as she had not been asked and anyway she was not a Ukrainian citizen, which ruled her out. Within days she was offered the post of Minister of Finance and was granted citizenship when she took office. When she began work one of her two assistants asked if they would be getting the usual cash bonus. It turned out that the minister was expected to bribe them not to accept bribes from others who were keen to find out the minister's schedule and other interesting bits of information. As the answer was 'no', one left, but the other remained.

Negotiating with the IMF and Ukraine's debtors was one thing, but trying to get the system under her to work was quite another. Well, 'that is twenty-three years of problems which have mounted up', I ventured to suggest. 'No,' she snapped, 'it's a hundred years of crap!' We were on to the subject of why it is so hard to reform. The Soviet-inherited system was designed, she said, so that the person at the top got to shoulder all the responsibility, so that absolutely no one lower down had to take any. Every day she is given files, which can contain literally thousands of documents, and she has to affix her signature to each file. But the civil servants are the ones who know what is in the files she is being asked to sign off on, and thus 'they are in control'. The civil servants have been taught to check if anything that comes before them has a consequence for the budget, and if it is legal, but not how to solve problems. For example, when long overdue laws concerning judicial reform came up her ministry simply advised her to tell the president to veto them, because they foresee paying judges more in order that they may be less tempted to accept bribes. She refused and told them that their job was not to just say 'no' but to 'figure how we could do it'.

Likewise, when duty was raised on beer, an uncontroversial measure, she signed on the dotted line and had been bogged down ever since trying to sort out the mess. To raise the tax, for an unknown reason the civil servants reclassified beer as a spirit like vodka, which instantly made most advertising illegal. 'I had the prime minister of Denmark on the phone,' she sighed.

A big part of the problem, she said, was that while the removal of subsidies was going to make gas and heating bills far more expensive for most people now, reforms will take years to affect people's lives for the better. It was part of her job to come up with ideas which could make things better now, before people concluded that nothing was being done.

On the plus side she believed that Ukraine had never been a more tolerant place. With irritation in her voice she recalled meeting the finance minister from an EU country – 'I won't say which one!' – who told her he wanted to talk about Ukraine's 'discrimination' against Russian-speakers. Turning to her colleague from the central bank, she asked her to tell him what the working language of the bank was. 'Russian.' In her office Russian, English and Ukrainian are used interchangeably and the prime minister employed all three languages 'in one sentence'. At last, she said, 'the definition of being a Ukrainian is being a member of this society and not being ethnically Ukrainian'. And this, having grown up as an American, is something she was very happy to see.

As she poured a final glass of wine, she said her task was actually quite simple. It was to 'steer us out of this hole'. If she could do that, then the exhilaration – and exhaustion – of this period of her life would all have been worth it. Out of the gathering gloom Lady, the spaniel, came snuffling about hoping for tidbits. Her reputation was all she had, said Natalie, and so far no one had come to her office looking for similar easy pickings. Lady got nothing.

40.

Not Dead Yet

During the parliamentary election campaign of October 2012 I met Leonid Kozhara, the urbane spokesman of Viktor Yanukovych's Party of Regions. At this point Yanukovych and his party were saying that there was no dilemma: they were on the path to Europe, away from Ukraine's traditional subservience to Russia. During our lunch Leonid tugged the sleeve of his jacket. For Russia, he said dismissively, the other former Soviet republics were just like its buttons, but *'we'*, meaning Ukraine, *'are the sleeve'*. The man who would be Yanukovych's foreign minister in the next, doomed government, went on to tell a story to explain why Ukraine did not want to join Russia, Kazakhstan and Belarus in Putin's Customs Union, which was officially due to become the Eurasian Union on 1 January 2015. Some colleagues from Kazakhstan had told him a cautionary tale. They said that in a meeting to discuss plans over a certain issue the Russians had explained what they wanted to do. When the Kazakhs began to put forward their ideas, the Russians told them they were not interested because they had just explained to them what would be done, whether they liked it or not.

In the Verkhovna Rada, I met Yurii Miroshnychenko, Yanukovych's representative to parliament, who said: 'We are fully aware of the price we will have to pay for this decision, yet we are ready to make this decision as a strategic one.' In retrospect it seems hard to imagine that a party so firmly based in the east, as the Party of Regions was, was then so determined to take the country westwards.

This chapter ended, however, when Yanukovych, after pressure from Vladimir Putin, announced he was not signing the EU deals, sparking off the Maidan revolution. As it began I met Stefan Fule, then the EU's enlargement commissioner in Brussels. A Czech, he was one of the last generation of eastern European politicians and diplomats to have studied in Moscow, so he knew the Russians very well and understood that Putin was set on recreating a circle of countries around Russia which would bend to its will. In a bustling Brussels bistro he told me that for Russia, Ukraine had always been part of a geostrategic game but that the EU had struggled to decide to what extent it should play geostrategy too, as opposed to relying solely 'on our values and principles'. The Russian tactic was, 'bullying, bullying, bullying and being brutal', but 'our mistake is only ever having been half-serious about the transformation of that part of Europe and not clearly offering them membership in the long run'.

In Odessa, just before the revolution I met Hanna Shelest, then a 33-year-old researcher at the National Institute for Strategic Studies. We talked about how many people were ambivalent about the proposed EU deals because they simply did not understand what they meant. Ukrainian media funded from Russian sources had, she said, given people the impression that if Ukraine chose Russia over the EU 'then everything will be cheaper, such as gas, and that if we go towards the EU normal marriages will not exist, only gay marriages'. Russia was presenting itself as 'the big brother who will tell us what to do' and a pro-Russian choice would mean that 'we will live happily ever after and won't have to read that complicated EU agreement'. As we ate pizza her friend Irina Yakovleva, aged twenty-nine, then a journalist, said many of her friends thought that Ukraine's own politicians had 'spoiled everything' and were 'not real leaders'. Some of those friends who leant towards Russia were not so much 'pro-Russian' but said they liked Putin 'because he is a leader . . . Even in the EU there are no big figures. They say: "I like that guy, that is why I support him."'

A year after the beginning of the war all this talk felt as though it had taken place much, much longer ago. But now a new phase was beginning. Novorossiya, whose ideologues had dreamed they

would take all of Ukraine's Black Sea coast and most of its south and south-east, remained penned into relatively small, albeit before the war economically important, areas. Mariupol on the coast had not fallen and Crimea remained without a land connection to Russia. The two Minsk ceasefires foresaw some form of autonomy and reintegration of the eastern territories into Ukraine but none of this appeared very realistic. When I met Fule he said that given the way Putin had begun fighting for Ukraine – and this was before Crimea was stripped from Ukraine and a single shot fired in the east – he seemed 'like a dog with its teeth clamped into a man's neck'. A year later it seemed rather that the dog had its teeth clamped on to Ukraine's leg. Ukraine could not shake its bleeding leg free, but the dog, unable to do more harm, still would not let go.

In this new phase the question was endurance. Ukraine needed money and foreign investment to stabilize its economy, but investment especially would not come as long as there was war. Heavy industry and mining had been badly affected by the fighting in the east but Ukraine is big and a country of enormous unrealized potential. At the western edge of Kiev, for example, is Antonov, the plane maker and designer and Ukraine's only internationally known brand and company. The war had left the firm, which employs more than 12,000 people, struggling to disentangle itself from Russia. Before the war, Russia ordered their military transport planes especially and it was there that so many of their parts were made.

In its simulators I saw Cubans training for its small airliners and, in one hangar where planes were being built, a solitary grey military transport, which would soon be handed over to the armed forces. Another one, I was told, would also soon be ready, but completion was delayed because until now the propellers had been made in Russia and now they would have to be made in Ukraine, which was possible but time-consuming to do from scratch. 'We will find business and work well even without Russia,' said Dmytro Kiva, the company's 72-year-old president, cheerfully. He is only the second man to have run it since the death of Oleg Antonov himself, who founded the firm in 1946 and died in 1984. The shock of the war and break with Russia had shaken Antonov so profoundly that its leadership had been jolted into understanding that it could no longer coast along as it always had in the past. In Soviet times Antonov had been a world-beating company, but now, still state-owned, it had squandered the years since independence. With its skilled employees hunched over modern design computers, it has a future, if it can catch up and find investment. In the hangar, no one was working bolting planes together, though. It was lunchtime and everyone was eating at the same time. Some who had finished were playing netball in the sun.

With its catastrophic drop in population from 52.18 million in 1992 to an estimated 45.49 in 2013, Ukraine cannot afford to lose any more of its educated youth. The Maidan revolution had inspired many of them, but this motivating force is fast receding into the past. In Kiev, Evgenia Chernega, a 32-year-old psychotherapist, told me how she had gone to live with a boyfriend in Canada and when the revolution started they got married. On a visit to New York, she found herself crying as she read in the *New York Times* what was happening at home. 'I felt I had to be there,' she said. She had to come back to finish her studies anyway, so four days after getting married, she flew to Kiev and offered her services as a volunteer psychotherapist to those on the Maidan who needed help. She never returned to the man she had married, who had taken Canadian citizenship and did not want to look back to Ukraine, which he had left when he was fourteen years old. Now, said Evgenia, for whom normal life had resumed, things 'felt better', but what scared her was that 'they can keep us in this situation for ten years'. There would be constant stress for men, who could be called up at any time now and in the future. She had told her new boyfriend that perhaps he should think of looking for a job abroad. If people in the east really did not want to be part of Ukraine, then 'why should our men die?'

The revolution and the war also changed the life of Ludmila Makarova, aged thirty. Before the war she had worked in publishing and for a travel company, then got a well-paid job with an international legal practice. As soon as Yanukovych decided not to sign the EU agreements, it was clear there was not going to be enough work and she lost the job before she had even started it. She researched flights to India, confident of getting a job for a Ukrainian or Russian tour operator there, looking after their holidaymakers. She was not very interested in Ukrainian politics, though she had taken part in the Orange Revolution in 2004 and had – like so many others – become disillusioned with politics in its wake. When, a week into the 2013 protests, the Berkut riot police resorted to beatings to clear away the relatively few who were sleeping overnight on the Maidan, something changed. 'I felt ashamed for my country. India could wait, but Ukraine needed me.' She volunteered at a tea and soup kitchen serving protesters on the square. Afterwards, as the war began, she learned how to become an instructor to train soldiers and civilians in first aid techniques tailored for frontline injuries. She said:

There is no point in complaining and saying that everything in Ukraine is corrupt, that the government is shitty, that the system doesn't work and then just sit around moaning. You have to do something yourself. It is still worth trying and there is no other country where I can be more useful.

Ukraine was not just in combat with Russia and the rebels it sponsored. It was in a race against time to save what could be saved and to set the country back on the right path. Almost a quarter of a century had been lost since independence. Before 2003 the first words of the national anthem, composed in 1863, were: 'Ukraine has not yet died . . .' Since the state was now independent this had been modified to 'Ukraine's glory has not yet died.' You can understand why the original still served to inspire, though.

Author's Note

Some notes of explanation: to an extraordinary extent Ukraine is a bilingual country. A large proportion of the population can either switch between Ukrainian and Russian or have a good understanding of the other language. Many also speak a mix of the two called *Surzhyk*. They don't worry overly if Lugansk is written in the Russian way with a 'g' or in the Ukrainian way, Luhansk, with an 'h', so I don't feel compelled to either. I am spelling Kiev and Odessa in the way they have always been spelled in English and don't feel the need to take what many regard as a political stance by switching to the Ukrainian Kyiv and Odesa. Likewise it really does not matter if Aleksandr becomes Alexander or Oleksandr, the Ukrainian version, and so on. In the traditional Russian spelling it is Donbass and in Ukrainian Donbas. I have used both.

I asked many people their age, not just because this is normal journalistic practice, but because it is helpful for the reader to have an idea of what generation they are. Sometimes I forgot to ask people how old they were and sometimes it was not appropriate. Sometimes I have not used people's surnames because either they did not want to give them to me or they did not want me to use them.

An alternative name for the Maidan revolution is the Euromaidan revolution. Its focal point was Maidan Nezalezhnosti, Kiev's central Independence Square. The Ukrainian parliament is called the Verkhovna Rada. After the first mention, I decided not to spell that out each time it was written about.

I applied to the press service of Russia's Ministry of Foreign Affairs with regards to a visa for visiting Crimea after the annexation of the territory. I never received an answer and the press office of the Russian embassy in London told me that they could not help as it was 'more polite' to wait for the ministry's response. An enquiry at the Russian embassy in Kiev proved equally futile.

During the 1990s I covered the Balkan wars and I am the Balkans correspondent of the *Economist*. Because of this, I often notice parallels and, drawing on my experience, mention them when I think relevant.

On 4 September 2015 Olha Voloshyna, who appears in the section called 'Stalin's Chicken', sadly passed away. She was ninety years old. On the same day, in Donetsk, Andrei Purgin, one of the founders of the Donetsk People's Republic, was purged from his official position. Some analysts believed that this was because Russia wanted to get the rebels to implement the Minsk peace agreements. In the same week the ceasefire line went quiet and the world's media began reporting that Russian troops were arriving in Syria. Viktoria Demidchenko, who appears in 'Surviving Sloviansk', got a job as a schoolteacher and did not pay a bribe to get it.

Sources

Donetsk, 17 April 2014. A pro-Ukrainian rally. The abbreviation PTN PNH, which was to become common in Ukraine, translates loosely as 'Putin – Go Fuck Yourself'.

All the contemporary interviews were done by me, with one exception. My colleague Harriet Salem interviewed and photographed Vladimir Antyufeyev, who appears in 'Dying for Ukraine' in the Introduction and gave me the transcript and pictures.

Andrey Kurkov's novels paint a graphic and entertaining picture of Ukraine over the last two decades. He also chronicled the Maidan revolution in his *Ukraine Diaries: Dispatches from Kiev* (Harvill Secker, 2014). In it he wonders where he and his wife will be after the summer. He says he would like to believe that they and their children will be at their summer house enjoying themselves and talking about the future, but then he says: 'It is funny but the future never seems to come.' Ukraine's problem has always been that while the future does of course come, it is never the good and prosperous one that it could and should be.

Introduction – Just Angry

GDP figures are from the World Bank as are many of the other economic references. The World Bank's reports can be found via its Ukraine site: worldbank.org/en/country/ukraine. Researching the book I also used the Economist Intelligence Unit's regular Ukraine reports. References to the Balkan wars come from my own experiences, reporting and writing.

1. Weaponizing History

The full text of Putin's Duma speech on 18 March 2014 can be found on the English pages of the Kremlin website, en.kremlin.ru.

2. Thumbelina in Donetsk

Timothy Snyder's figure of 3.3 million dead from the *Holodomor* can be found on p. 53 of *Bloodlands: Europe Between Hitler and Stalin* (Vintage, 2011). The book is superb and above all readable and I freely admit to drawing from it. For more on the *Holodomor*, see the chapter 'The Soviet Famines' in his book.

3. 'Our history is different!'

With reference to the Carpathians, I don't quote from it but a wonderful book is *Under the Carpathians: Home of Forgotten People* by J. B. Heisler and J. E. Mellon (The Travel Book Club, 1949). It was first published in 1946 but was based on research done just before the war. So, by the time it came out, the Carpathians as described in it no longer existed. It is full of beautiful pictures. In the same section I touch on the Orange Revolution and its legacy. Excellent basic books on the modern history of Ukraine include *The Ukrainians: Unexpected Nation* by Andrew Wilson (3rd edn, Yale University Press, 2009) and *Ukraine: Birth of a Modern Nation* by Serhy Yekelchyk (Oxford University Press, 2007). Wilson is also the author of

Ukraine Crisis: What it Means for the West (Yale University Press, 2014), which chronicles the Maidan revolution. Not referenced, and focusing on events at the turn of the millennium, J. V. Koshiw's *Abuse of Power: Corruption in the Office of the President* (Artemia Press, 2013) is an excellent primer on corruption at the heart of government.

4. 'How can this be?'
This section draws on and from Vassily Grossman's *Everything Flows* (Vintage, 2011); the quotes come from pp. 127–49.

6. Chernobyl: End and Beginning
The article I refer to by Mikhail Gorbachev can be found on the Project Syndicate website. It is called 'Turning Point at Chernobyl' and was published on 14 April 2006. There is a lot of information about the work being done there now on the European Bank for Reconstruction and Development's website under the section called 'Chernobyl Shelter Fund'.

7. Lemberg to Lviv
The Snyder quotes come from *Bloodlands*, as do the statistics. Another invaluable resource drawn on here is his *The Reconstruction of Nations: Poland, Ukraine, Lithuania, Belarus 1569–1999* (Yale University Press, 2003).

8. Ruthenes and Little Russians
The 1911 Baedeker's guide to Austria-Hungary mentioned at the beginning of the chapter has been digitized and is readily available online.

9. Nikita at the Opera
Liberation, the 1940 film by Alexander Dovzhenko, can be found on YouTube. For anyone who wants to read more about Ukrainian nationalism, the OUN and UPA, see Myroslav Shkandrij's *Ukrainian Nationalism: Politics, Ideology, and Literature, 1929–1956* (Yale University Press, 2015).

10. Stalin's Chicken
The *Sefer Grayding* can be found at jewishgen.org. It was originally published in 1981 by the Society of Grayding Emigrants in Tel Aviv. The testimony of Pitciha Hochberg is the last entry in the list of contents.

11. The History Prison
I draw on and quote from *The Wartime Diary of Edmund Kessler, Lwow, Poland 1942–1944*, edited by his daughter Renata Kessler (Academic Studies Press, 2010). The quotes come from pp. 34–9. The Introduction, by Antony Polonsky, one of the world's leading authorities on Polish-Jewish history, gives a concise history of the period, including lots of statistics on Lviv's population and its changing ethnic breakdown over time. The quotation from Tarik Cyril Amar comes from his article 'Different but the Same or the Same but Different? Public Memory of the Second World War in Post-Soviet Lviv'. He has posted it on academia.edu (with many other fascinating articles). It was originally published in the *Journal of Modern European History* in January 2011. The April 2015 open letter to President Poroshenko can be found by searching for 'Open Letter from Scholars and Experts on Ukraine Re. the So-Called "Anti-Communist Law"'. It is on krytyka.com/en.

12. The *Shtreimel* of Lviv
Rabbi David Kahane recorded his experiences in wartime Lviv and how he was saved by Archbishop Andrey Sheptytsky in his book *Lvov Ghetto Diary* (University of Massachusetts Press, 1991), which is a translation of the original Hebrew version by Jerzy Michalowicz. The quote from historian Frank Golczewski comes from his essay 'Shades of Grey: Reflections on Jewish-Ukrainian Relations in Galicia'. This is published in a wonderful collection called *The Shoah in Ukraine: History, Testimony, Memorialization* edited by Ray Brandon and Wendy Lower (Indiana University Press in association with the United States Holocaust Memorial Museum, 2010). The quote can be found on p. 146. Another book covering this subject is *Smoke in the Sand: The Jews of Lvov in the War Years 1939–1944*, by Eliyahu Yones (Gefen, 2004).

13. The Scottish Book of Maths and All That
The quote from Radek Sikorski was published on 19 October 2014 by politico.com in an article called 'Putin's Coup'. It was written by Ben Judah, my son. I may be biased, of course, but Ben's book *Fragile Empire: How Russia Fell In and Out of Love with Vladimir Putin* (Yale University Press, 2013) is the best one on the subject of Putin's Russia.

16. Winds of Change

The description of the end of the German Bessarabian story citing Edmund Stevens, including the quotes, comes from Cheryl Heckler's *An Accidental Journalist: The Adventures of Edmund Stevens 1934–1945* (University of Missouri Press, 2007). On pp. 107–8 Heckler reprints the account, citing his unpublished memoirs, pp. 82–6.

17. Bones of Contention

Some of the description of the Tatarbunary Uprising comes from Charles Upson Clark, who is also quoted here. See his book *Bessarabia: Russia and Roumania on the Black Sea* (Dodd, Mead & Company, 1927), specifically chapter XXVlll, 'The Tatar-Bunar Episode'. The book has been digitized and is easy to find online. A major piece of scholarship in English used for this section is Tanya Richardson's 'The Politics of Multiplication in a Failed Soviet Irrigation Project, Or, How Sasyk Has Been Kept from the Sea'. It was published in 2014 in *Ethnos: Journal of Anthropology*, 2014.

21. The Deep Hole

The descriptions from Balthasar von Campenhausen's account of Izmail and the siege of 1789 come from pp. 79–80 of his *Travels Through Several Provinces of the Russian Empire with an Historical Account of the Zaporog Cossacks and of Bessarabia, Moldavia, Wallachia and the Crimea* (Richard Phillips, 1808). The book can be found online.

23. The Coal Launderers

The report by the Organized Crime and Corruption Reporting Project is called 'Ukraine's Illegal Coal Mines: Dirty, Dangerous, Deadly'. It was written by Denys Kazansky and Serhiy Harmash and published on 26 May 2014.

24. The Welsh and the Wild East

Many of the details about the life of the founder of Donetsk come from Roderick Heather's *The Iron Tsar: The Life and Times of John Hughes* (Authors Essentials, 2010); the quotes are from pp. 59–60 and the population statistics from pp. 131–2. William Taubman's Pulitzer Prize-winning biography of the former Soviet leader is called *Khrushchev: The Man, His Era* (Free Press, 2005); the quotes are from pp. 31–2. The quote from Heather, which ends with Lenin's view on the importance of the Donbass, is on p. 196. Colin Thomas's 1991 three-part documentary about Donetsk comes as a DVD together with his book *Dreaming a City: From Wales to Ukraine* (Y Lolfa, 2009). His quote about the arrests of engineers in 1928 comes from p. 45 and the story about and quotes from Gareth Jones on starvation in the city from p. 49. About the wartime fate of the Jews in eastern Ukraine, see pp. 193–5 of Yitzhak Arad's *The Holocaust in the Soviet Union* (University of Nebraska Press, 2013).

25. The View from the Terricone

The report discussed and quoted is in *Urban Shrinkage in Donetsk and Makiivka, the Donetsk Conurbation, Ukraine* (SHRINK SMART @ EU FP7 Socio-economic Sciences and Humanities Research, March 2010) by Vlad Mykhnenko, Dmytro Myedvyedyev and Larysa Kuzmenko. It is packed with graphs, statistics, maps and photos. An updated report was issued in 2012 and there was also a summary from which I quote. All the documents can be found at shrinksmart.eu. For the surveys from 1991 and about children of different backgrounds, see the King's College London MA thesis of Charlie Hutchinson from October 2014 called 'Waking the Beast: Along what Lines is the Population of Ukraine's Donbas Mobilized into Supporting the pro-Russian Insurgency?'

26. Getting to 'Yes'

Results of the various referendums mentioned are widely available online, and for English speakers most easily consulted via Wikipedia. See also the Wilson and Yekelchyk history books mentioned above. For a detailed account of the end of the USSR there is Serhii Plokhy's *The Last Empire: The Final Days of the Soviet Union* (Oneworld, 2014).

30. Tsar *v* Cossacks

The statistic about Ukraine as an arms exporter comes from 'Measuring the Arms Merchants', a graphic published by economist.com on 18 March 2014. The report that Boris Nemtsov was working on when he was murdered and which is quoted here is called 'Putin. War: Based on Materials from Boris Nemtsov' and can be found at 4freerussia.org. It was published in English in May 2015. The details of the Ukrainian investigation into the Ilovaysk catastrophe are from 'Up to 459 Soldiers Killed near Ilovaisk in 2014 – Ukraine's Chief Military Prosecutor', a story published on 17 April 2015 on en.interfax.com.ua.

31. The Wolf's Hook Club

The report by Anton Shekhovtsov referenced and quoted is called 'The Creeping Resurgence of the Ukrainian Radical Right? The Case of the Freedom Party'. It was published in the journal *Europe-Asia Studies*, vol. 63, no. 2, March 2011, pp. 203–28. I have also taken from this report the speech by Oleh Tyahnybok that he cites on p. 216. The BBC *Panorama* programme 'Stadiums of Hate' was originally broadcast in May 2012. Both are freely available online.

33. Leaving Home

The statistics from UNHCR come from its operational updates, which can be found on its Ukraine site.

34. Surviving Sloviansk

The *Guardian* article mentioned was 'Rinat Akhmetov Pays Record £136.4m for Apartment at One Hyde Park'. It was by Alex Hawkes and was published on 19 April 2011. The Amnesty International briefing quoted was published on 8 September 2014. It is called 'Ukraine: Abuses and War Crimes by the Aidar Volunteer Battalion in the North Luhansk Region'. Sadly there have been plenty of other such reports about abuses on both sides and in Russian-annexed Crimea, which can be found on their site. The wonderful book by Charles King mentioned is *Odessa: Genius and Death in a City of Dreams* (W.W. Norton, 2011).

38. Askania-Nova and the Zebra of Death

Apart from what I learned there about its history, I drew on the rather romantic account *Askania-Nova: Animal Paradise in Russia, Adventure of the Falz-Fein Family* by L. Heiss (The Bodley Head, 1970). There is also much about the place in the rigorously academic but nevertheless fascinating book by Douglas R. Weiner called *Models of Nature: Ecology, Conservation, and Cultural Revolution in Soviet Russia* (University of Pittsburgh Press, 2000).

Acknowledgements

Much of the early part of the war I covered for the *Economist*, but a lot of the real groundwork for this book was done while writing for the *New York Review of Books*. Some of the stories here, particularly from the east, appeared first in the *Review* and its online blog. Many thanks to *Review* editor Bob Silvers for sending me, and to blog editor Hugh Eakin.

I was asked to write this book by Stefan McGrath. I asked him what sort of book he wanted and he answered: 'What sort of book do you want to write?' It took time to work that out. Eventually it became clear: a book that, first, I would have read myself if I had not had to write it, and one that looked at things I thought were both interesting and relevant.

What was needed, I thought, was not another straight history and not a political science-cum-analytical text. From what I could see on bookshop shelves and online, there was nothing which focused on those bits of history which it is important to understand today, as opposed to Ukrainian history in general, nor was there a book which gave a flavour of what Ukraine is really like and what its people have to say, especially outside Kiev.

A long time ago Marcus Tanner, a friend and colleague, said, after reading an article about Nagorno-Karabakh, the Armenian breakaway region of Azerbaijan, that it failed to tell him what he really wanted to know, which was: 'What does Stepanakert smell like?' Stepanakert is the capital of Nagorno-Karabakh. I don't write about smells, but the point is that often what is needed and what a book gives you the opportunity to do, is to make a place and its people easier to understand. What I wanted to do was to mix people, stories, history, politics and reportage rather than explain why this event followed that one.

Some said to me that I needed to go to Russia. But this is not a book about Russia. There are plenty of those. It is about Ukraine and the people who live in it. Thank you Stefan for asking me to write it and Josephine Greywoode for editing it. Thanks to Georgina Capel, for making it possible. Thanks to Rosie Whitehouse, my wife, for persuading me to do it and telling me to stop reading books about Ukraine at home, to leave and not come back until I had written my own. Thanks to Harriet Salem for saying 'hello' in the Dolce Vita in Mitrovica and then getting me started in the east. Thanks to Dimiter Kenarov for ideas and contacts for some of my favourite stories. Thanks to Liliia Ivaschenko for her assistance in the east.

Many thanks to the German Marshall Fund and its Black Sea Trust. It was because I was invited to participate in several of their study tours to Ukraine for journalists and policy-makers that I was first able to come here and meet people. Thank you Ivan Vejvoda, Alina Inayeh, Ana Aelenei and Dinu Toderascu. Thanks to the Institute of World Policy in Kiev for also inviting me on a trip. In Odessa, many thanks to Hanna Shelest. In Ukraine, thanks, above all, to Ludmila Makarova for doing the bulk of the translating and fixing.

Acknowledgements

On page 48 the picture which shows Khrushchev at the opera in Lviv is a screenshot from Alexander Dovzhenkho's film *Liberation*. The painting of Metropolitan Archbishop Andrey Sheptytsky on page 70 hangs in the Museum of Ethnography and Crafts in Lviv. It depicts the Metropolitan as Moses symbolically leading his people out of the land of Egypt. It is by Oleksa Novakivsky (1872–1935) and was painted between 1915 and 1919. All the other pictures are by me.

Kiev,
June 2015